The New Revolutio

56420

WILEY SERIES IN INFORMATION PROCESSING

Consulting Editor
Mrs Steve Shirley OBE, F International Limited, UK

Visual Display Terminals
A. Cakir, D. J. Hart, and T. F. M. Stewart

Managing Systems Development
J. S. Keen

Face to File Communication
Bruce Christie

APL — A Design Handbook for Commercial Systems
Adrian Smith

Office Automation
Andrew Doswell

Health Hazards of VDTs?
Edited by B. G. Pearce

The New Revolution
Barrie Sherman

The New Revolution

The Impact of Computers on Society

Barrie Sherman

Visiting Lecturer at the London Business School

JOHN WILEY AND SONS

Chichester · New York · Brisbane · Toronto · Singapore

Copyright © 1985 by John Wiley & Sons Ltd.

British Library Cataloguing in Publication Data:

Sherman, Barrie
    The new revolution: the impact of computers on society.
    (A Wiley series in information processing)
    1. Computers and civilization
    I. Title
    303.4'834   QA76.9.C66

    ISBN 0 471 90485 6

Library of Congress Cataloging in Publication Data

Sherman, Barrie.
    The new revolution
    (Wiley series in information processing)
    Includes index.
    1. Computers — Social aspects. 2. Computers — Economic
aspects. I. Title. II. Series.
    QA76.9.C66S53   1984   303.4'834   84–5200

    ISBN 0 471 90485 6

Phototypeset by Dobbie Typesetting Service, Plymouth, Devon
Printed at the Pitman Press, Bath, Avon

Contents

v

PART II   THE EFFECTS

Preface and Acknowledgements

Writing a book on computers is rather like painting the Forth Bridge — by the time it is finished it needs to be started again. The speed at which the technology is changing makes this inevitable. Unlike the painting, however, which can go on indefinitely, a book must be finished at some point in time. The author has to stop scanning the technical press, stop interrogating state of the art specialists, stop consulting the tea leaves, pluck up his (or her) courage, and start to write. It is thus more than possible that by the time this book is published, indeed this preface is written, there will be new technical breakthroughs, a new IBM computer, and probably new disasters and new scandals.

Hopefully few of these developments will be sufficiently fundamental to alter the main thesis of this book or its balance. I have attempted to anticipate and preempt most of these developments so that the underlying benefits as well as the costs remain unchanged in all dimensions.

In this endeavour I have been helped hugely by my wife Anne and my son Matthew, both of whom showed great forebearance, especially during a prolonged period of ill health. Many friends at my previous employers helped in all the ways viii

that they could — offsetting those who hindered as much as it was in their power to do. My thanks go to Maureen Truman who not only managed to read my handwriting but also deciphered my typing and to Victor Frome for his help too. However, above all I must thank an old school friend from Hackney Downs, Donald Harris, who read the manuscript thoroughly and made a myriad of helpful suggestions. That he did so in the midst of a very busy business life is quite remarkable. If there are any errors, in fact, they are entirely my responsibility not his, while some of the political and social opinions remain despite his persistent and eloquent opposition.

Barrie Sherman   London

PART I
Where, When, and What— The Practical Impacts

Chapter 1

Introduction

TODAY'S SCIENCE FICTION IS OFTEN TOMORROW'S REALITY. Aeroplanes, submarines, spacecraft, television, and telephones have all been presaged, in one notable case several centuries early, by gifted writers and thinkers. As the pace of change has quickened, so it appears that we are actually living within a science fiction film (perhaps teledisc might be more appropriate). Programmes on television continue to amaze or frighten us with yet more technological break-throughs and with clever new products and gadgets. Over the last decade, and certainly through the rest of this century, the major agent for these changes has been and will continue to be the electronic computer and its derivatives.

Change has always been a feature of human society and much of it has been caused by technologies and technical innovations. Changes in society have then themselves stimulated the next wave of technical changes. Some of the breakthroughs have been fundamental, even seminal. The wheel, gunpowder, iron production, steel manufacture, the steam engine, electricity, the internal combustion engine, flight, antibiotics, and artificial fertilizers, are only a sample of inventions that have shaped different societies at different times.

Some societies, of course, have not participated in these changes. The classic aboriginal groupings, certain tribes in Papua New Guinea or in Latin America, have stayed in the iron or even pre-iron age. Others use the more recent technologies sparingly. Radio and television, flight, even motor vehicles and modern medical techniques, are not common in many parts of Asia, Africa, Latin America, or the Indian subcontinent.

Clearly such societies have felt little or no impact as yet from computers in any direct sense, although they have been affected indirectly. International transport and telecommunications rely heavily on electronics and developing countries are part of this global pattern. Yet societies are in a very real sense only the sum of their parts and the most important part is the people. A country thus may have a sophisticated airline or communications system that affects less than 10 per cent. of the population, the rest being isolated either geographically or economically. The institutions and customs that bind people together may be unaffected by computers or related technologies despite a superficial appearance to the contrary.

No book, treatise, or speech on the subject of computers and society dare ignore this separate development nor, indeed, the lesson that people and their institutions comprise state, society, and tribe or group. It would be arrogant to assume, not only that every person in the world is at the same stage of technological development, but also that high technology is desirable in its own right. For the majority of the world's population—those living in the developing countries—computers will have a different role to play and on a different timescale. For such people the idea of appropriate technology may not include electronic computers for many years, if ever.

This book will attempt to look closely at the interrelation between computers, their derivatives and their uses, and the people in mainly industrialized societies. This is because it is only in industrialized societies that computers have been used for any length of time; only in these societies have the advantages, the disadvantages, and perhaps the neutral effects become apparent or are likely to become apparent in the near future. Indeed, within industrialized societies we have all learned to accept this machine, this tool, which even our parents, let alone our grandparents, would have had difficulty conceptualizing.

The human race in general tends to lack humility. This

may historically account for its survival when the odds seem so hostile. Nevertheless, people have believed that reasoning and deduction are what marks out their species from others in the animal kingdom. Most of the technical and technological advances before the 1960s replaced human physical labour by machines or systems. Most of them had the by-product of ultimately creating more physical labour, albeit of a slightly different type to that which was intended to be replaced. None replaced the deductive or reasoning processes so jealously guarded by those who had them. Moreover, none replaced those who in the main had (or have) the abilities of literacy and verbal communication. The entire existence and *raison d'etre* of such people is threatened by a tool which, far from helping one to dig, carry, or build, actually helps in or even replaces thought processes. Yet the computer does just that!

In this limited respect, the computer is seen as a threat. Those who have worked in education and with words and numbers have had since the renaissance a privileged position in Europe. The same is true of the priests in Rome, Latin America, and Egypt in even earlier times. These are the people who had influence, made opinion, and wrote the histories that form the basis of our knowledge of their civilizations. It is their intellectual descendants who have from time to time led the charges against the computer and other scientific and technical advances. The threat to individualism so posed is in reality a threat only to some individuals who are able to express themselves in a way in which the overwhelming majority cannot. Moreover, these people have access to the organs of communication in a way that most people have not.

That the computer can be used intentionally and unintentionally for purposes that threaten many aspects of human lives would not be denied by even the most ardent electronic supporters. This does not mean, however, that the damaged pride of a few should be a major cause for concern. There are now and will be increasingly in the future many areas in which the use of electronic computers will affect the majority of people in a society. Some of these effects could be damaging; at least as many others could be beneficial.

Within any one society it is easy to divine what is right and what is wrong, although it is less easy to state absolutely what is harmful and what is good. But right and wrong varies between different societies; almost the only universally accepted 'wrong' is murder. Religions which have most often set the parameters of the prevailing moral values differ not only between the broad groupings but also within individual theologies. Christianity can be interpreted in many ways and be used to justify what seem to be irreconcilable deeds. The same is true of Islam or Judaism in their various branches. This means that to analyse the effects of any technology in terms of good and bad is not really a practical proposition. The world cannot be subdivided into such stark effects and choices: the shades of grey predominate over the blacks and whites.

While this is true of fundamental philosophical choices, the problems of benefit and cost are no less forbidding. These tend to be coloured by both short-term political environments obviously set by the governments of the day and national characteristics acquired over centuries. Examples of these differences and the problems are not difficult to find. The Soviet Union, the United Kingdom, and the United States of America all claim to be democracies, yet few people would find many similarities between them. Some countries, for example the Federal German Republic, have as a national preoccupation the rate of inflation, which can be traced back to the hyper-inflation days of the Weimar Republic. On the other hand, the British tend to regard unemployment as a greater evil, a result of the 1920s and 1930s. The Germans have a history of tolerating, even encouraging, monopolies and cartels; the United States have fierce anti-trust laws to counteract this trend. The Soviet Union, indeed the COMECON bloc as a whole, believes that the major objective of the state should be to create employment for all even if this means an aggregate loss of efficiency. Many West European and the North American societies believe the opposite.

Carrying this a stage further, a centralized economy will use the same computer systems in a totally different way from that used in a basically decentralized economy. A state preoccupied with internal security will use systems that would be considered abhorrent in other states. The range and variations between each is virtually infinite. The tolerance and ultimate acceptance of the people also varies. In some instances those affected are unaware that they are affected; in others they are aware but can do nothing about it, even if they wanted to.

It is this last circumstance that stimulates most of the fears that computers engender — and fears there are. Nobody likes to live in circumstances beyond their control and the more such circumstances there are, the more unsettled will people become. Computers become a target not only because the machines themselves and their effects are thought to be harmful but because of the certainties. The past two decades have witnessed massive changes in attitudes which, although tolerated or even welcomed, have also undermined the stability of people. This is especially true of Britain.

Attitudes to divorce, divorcees, and marriage have become far more tolerant, as have attitudes to sex in general and to pornography. Television has given the wider public the opportunity to study politicians at close quarters and, probably as a result, much of the mystery and power of politicans has been seen to be illusory. Membership of the European Economic Community has opened up traditional insularity to new laws and ideas but without the enthusiasm or understanding of ordinary people. City centres have decayed visibly and the life within them has changed. The cinemas have given way to television and video recorders. We have been through student unrest, an entire 'drop-out' scene, a drug culture, and riots. Each of these, and there are many more on a local basis, impaired the cement that holds society together. The collapse of some established religions means that the traditional spiritual values from this quarter cannot be called into action as a counterbalance.

Such changes are minor when looked at in the context of the late eighteenth and nineteenth century upheavals in the industrial revolution. The difference, however, is that modern technology enables the communication of these changes to be made instantly, not only within one country but across countries and continents. In such circumstances casual sneezes assume the proportions of major pneumonias. Indeed, one of the symptoms of our age's malaise is the instant punditry, comment, and analysis from 'experts' rather than a considered response to the happenings of the day.

Change in society, in general terms, must be a good thing. A society which is unchanging and resists change must stagnate and ultimately wither away. This is not to say that all change is good, merely that change itself is not bad. Yet it is often viewed with the utmost suspicion and fear, perhaps because so many of us feel that we cannot cope with new and unknown circumstances. Fear bred the rumours that railway travel at over 25 miles an hour would bring on heart attacks; fear forced the early motorists to have a man with a red flag preceding them. Sometimes, as we shall see in the course of this book, the fear is justified, but most often it is not. And too often the target is the wrong one and the arguments inappropriate.

Into this dynamic, turbulent era the impact of computerization will come of age and reach maturity. The impact has already arrived, with both a whimper and a bang. Its birth was heralded by stars (of a media magnitude) so great that one would have thought that society was about to change overnight. But society did not change overnight. The reason was that the technological wizards and pundits did not, perhaps, charitably, could not, anticipate the limitations of the early mainframe computers. In size the early mainframes were enormous; in speed, given current technology, they were like tortoises — they even needed special magnetic-free constant temperature and air-conditioned premises to operate. The millenium, the new frontier, did not materialize, at least not as fast as its acolytes suggested.

The electronic computer is only a tool but one that has extremely wide uses and even wider effects and implications. It is also a rather strange tool. Almost all previous tools were intended to aid physical actions or replace physical labour. From the wheel to the jet engine, from telecommunications to the dishwasher, this has remained true. (The abacus is the possible exception.) Computers, however, have traditionally acted as an adjunct to, or replacement for, cerebral functions and this makes them doubly threatening to 'thinkers'. It has to be stressed that this is the traditional view; we are now on the threshold of hybrid tools — robots, automated machines, etc. — that are capable of 'thought processes' as well as mechanical and physical actions. The widening of the scope of computers has arrived with the massive advances in electronic and computer science over the past five years or so. Machines are cheaper, smaller, and more durable than ever before.

In the late 1950s and early 1960s the Congress of the United States made enquiries into the potential effects of automation. The early mainframe computers had just arrived on the scene and there was a degree of panic. Various scenarios were produced, most of which suggested that jobs would soon be obsolete and that 'society as we know it today will disappear'. The mistake these reports made was that they were twenty-five years too early. It has taken this length of time to develop the tools that *could* — not *must* make those scenarios come true. As yet, however, computers do not really think. They have to be fed information and then be programmed to deal with this information in the desired way: the analysis is still human based.

Misconceptions surrounding computers are legion. The first is that they think for themselves. The science fiction film *2001* which had just such a computer as the leading character reinforced this view. That the computer is always right is another misconception, which ignores the now widely known adage 'garbage in — garbage out' and also ignores the possibility that the machine itself has a fault. Yet another misconception is that the machine does things on its own. The Victoria underground line in London is computer controlled yet it has drivers and guards — partly for public presentation purposes. It was no accident that during the London Transport Underground strike of 1982 the unions kept this line running — had it not been, people would have realized that it was double-named. Computers also confer an aura of accuracy and respectability to various things that they themselves do not warrant — which is not the same as the infallibility syndrome.

Economic forecasts and models, and business models and techniques have achieved respectability because they are most often worked through on electronic machines. The results from these techniques have often been most disappointing. The vast differences in predictions or results show that the assumptions underpinning the models are the important factors rather than the techniques, methods, and equipment used. The media take little notice of these factors and continue to publish results masquerading as facts, which if they had been worked out on the back of an envelope would not be considered legitimate, unworthy even of dissemination, though the odds are on such calculations being at least as accurate.

There are thus in the view of industrialized societies two distinct attitudes to computers. One is a fear or apprehension and the other an attribution of powers they do not possess. These are, incidentally, two of the prerequisites for a deity and there are indeed other similarities. Both should be temporary phenomena as both are based on a high level of electronic illiteracy. Only a tiny percentage of the total population works with or even understands these machines. Neither the schools nor the universities and colleges, even in the industrialized countries, taught electronics as a serious mainstream subject before 1981 or 1982. This is now changing. There is an awareness in Britain, France, Japan, the United States, Scandinavia, Germany, Italy, indeed the industrialized nations, that the future will be dominated by and will depend on computers. As a result schoolchildren can play with them, learn to program them, and overcome the apprehensions their parents have about them. Television and other computerized games are helping younger people to become accustomed to electronics and to keyboards. In countries such as Britain where typing is seen to be a female-only pursuit this will be most important, as we shall see in Chapter 4 of this book.

Technology centres, computer centres, and high street and home computer shops are now beginning to bring home to ordinary people the fact that computers are with us. Before these developments the machines themselves were most often well hidden from view in offices or university departments. Indeed, up until the last two years it is probable that more than 90 per cent. of the British population had never seen, let along used, a computer. They may have seen bits of computers at airline check-in desks or at cash dispensing points in banks, but that was all. Now younger people are coping with the technology with the same nonchalance with which previous generations of the young coped with telephones whilst their elders and betters were afraid of them.

One significant barrier remains to be overcome. This is the appalling language problem — not computer language, but jargon. Jargon is one of the curses of small groups of people — be they in medicine, the law, electronics, trade unions, or politics. Whilst an 'in crowd' can legitimately claim that some form of shorthand between themselves speeds up processes and decisions, its effects are far more wide-reaching than this and, one could cynically claim, deliberately so. Jargon not only gives a group an identity, it also imparts a self-justification. It debars outsiders from the mysteries of the group in a way similar to that of the ancient priests and alchemists. It has to be at the very least antisocial and at the worst socially dangerous. When the mystery actually needs to be publicly demystified, the jargon acts as the strongest of conservation barriers. If computers are to become as easily accepted as other tools then the special codes and shorthand will have to be either made available to all or dropped in their entirety. Small or personal computer users' manuals illustrate the scale of the problem. For example, the handbook of a well-known small home computer contains the following statement (near to the start of that booklet):

Four bytes contain a binary representation of that precision. It gives us the capability of specifying about 9 digits precision of a decimal number.

Most people would have no clue whatsoever about what this means. Bits, bytes, hardware, software, cursors, modems, all are words that mean little to ordinary people but are the everyday currency of computer folk. Whilst some young people will pick them up easily, most will not, and adults will remain baffled, worried, and excluded from the techniques. Thus matters which should be well within the compass of most people are alien to them because of a quasi-language problem.

Science fiction as a genre often relies heavily on stimulating irrational fears and what can be more 'scarey' than the unknown? Computers being misunderstood or not understood at all have become the shadows in a progressively science fiction present. The operations room at Cape Canaveral and space flight itself, machines capable of speaking and listening, robots, and teleconferencing are all the stuff of dreams of the 1960s translated into mundane reality of the 1980s. Yet the pace of change is such that even computer and electronics professionals find it difficult to remain *au fait* with all the latest gadgets and systems.

This is a potent, heady, and disturbing mixture: social change and reform combined with technical change at an ever-increasing pace both overshadowed by the mysterious and ubiquitous computer. Clearly there are potential benefits to the people of the world wherever they live and whatever they do. Clearly there are potential costs which will differ in quality and magnitude depending upon the prevailing ethics in different societies. Equally clearly, as attitudes change, so institutions should change too.

The institutional framework of most countries, their political and legal systems, statutory and voluntary bodies, and family concepts, were laid down a long time ago, often measured in centuries. New institutions arise to meet new needs, although most of these are peripheral to the major organs of the state and many deal directly and indirectly with the machinery of government. In Britain such bodies are called 'Quasi Autonomous Non-Governmental Organizations' (QUANGOs) and include a whole host of advisory as well as administrative bodies. They were formed to meet specific gaps in government coverage; typical are bodies such as the Housing Corporation filling the gap between public and private housing or the Design Centre acting as a centre of excellence in its field. Whilst QUANGOs have become a perjorative word in current political circumstances they do meet needs, and furthermore can be set up quickly in response to a perceived problem. The main institutions have remained substantially unaltered over time. The basis of parliamentary democracy has remained unchanged despite a progressive widening of adult suffrage, whilst the mechanisms of Parliament itself have remained static since Bagheot wrote his analytical comments upon them. Small changes like the introduction of Crown Courts have affected the legal system but the basis of common and statute laws remains sacrosanct. Now, however, problems are beginning to arise with both of these systems and more especially in the public perception and appreciation of them. Although some individual legal judgements have caused concern in some quarters, the combination of delay and costs involved in both civil and criminal law is causing major disquiet. Radio coverage of Parliament has removed the last vestige of the awe, pomp, and majesty that early writers detected and which gave its high status. Both the legal and parliamentary systems will be affected by computers and, moreover, both could incorporate computer systems into their day-to-day working.

The main strain on both, however, is coming from television, which deals both in information and images and the imagery has not been helpful in either cases. Complaints about the legal system are made in our living rooms by people who, by anyone's standards, are normal and ordinary rather than stroppy or even 'criminal looking'. Politicians themselves are subjected to keen, well-briefed interviewers and can be seen shifting, squirming, prevaricating, or fudging from time to time; their superhuman aura is dispelled. These pressures will only increase as the spread of television widens and cable and satellite transmission becomes standard procedure, and if local or community television takes off this will affect local politicians too.

When institutions are envisaged and then put into operation they are intended to deal both with the problems of the day and also, if designed by wise and gifted statesmen, for a very considerable time after that. The American constitution is a classic example. Yet the changes in social mores since the founding fathers deliberated has resulted in some odd cases reaching the Supreme Court and in some instances some equally strange decisions. The more flexible the institution the better; it can cope with change so that inappropriate bodies or laws are not subjected to the indignity of dealing with matters clearly inappropriate to them. Quickly changing circumstances require equally quick responses, unless the judgement is that they are merely passing fads and that therefore no changes are needed. Tragedy can follow slow responses. The riots in the United States and in Britain followed the neglect of problems which, if institutional conditions had been right, would have been broached and defused, if not solved. Indeed, the riots in Paris in 1968 were caused by ignoring the changing circumstances in the universities and the manifest impossibility of changing the conditions within them by existing institutional means.

Throughout history one can pinpoint wars, national liberation movements, and civil disturbances which occurred because the existing framework no longer corresponded to the demands made upon it. Some of these are worth deeper consideration. The industrial revolution transformed Britain and then other European nations from basically merchant/ agrarian societies into industrial societies. It also spawned the growth of large towns and cities, altering existing ones out of all recognition. The disciplines upon the new workforce both at work and in their leisure time were completely new and the living conditions and social contacts both alien and different. The organization of the state, however, changed but slowly and could not cope with these new circumstances— which is not surprising, given that it was not designed to do so. In Britain the Chartists grew out of this turmoil and the country literally teetered on the brink of a political and social revolution. In Europe, 1848, the Year of Revolutions, is now indelibly written into history. Whilst it may be too sweeping to attribute these happenings in their entirety to the changes caused by technology, there is no doubt that they had important effects.

If there is an appropriate lesson to be learned from this it is based on a single technology—the steam engine. Computers and their derivative—microprocessors—will spearhead the second industrial revolution. In their way the changes that will ensue should be as marked and could be as divisive as those that took place in the nineteenth century. Work, leisure, and their relationship to each other, where people live and how they live, will all change. In the industrialized world the problems of people are less about survival than about standards and qualities of living and yet they have assumed that vital and fundamental importance to those involved. The worries involved in standards have proved to be as pernicious as those involved with survival. The spread and refinement of advertising now means that expectations are higher than ever before. If these remain unfulfilled, even if only a substantial minority of people is involved, then social problems are bound to arise. It is almost inconceivable to roll back this tide of people wanting more things, let alone freeze the momentum. High expectations are the cornerstone of most political systems—the Chinese tried to avoid this route using the 'cultural revolution', but even they had to abandon the experiment.

These expectations are also at least as much political as consumer oriented. In both respects the impact of technologies today will have a greater effect than those in the nineteenth century when people actually expected very little. Health and life expectancy were poor, consumer goods basic, and few people actually anticipated control over their own lives or over the environment. The limited suffrage combined with low literacy and unrepresentative legislators cast most of the population as political victims. Yet even with these disadvantages the people in the first industrial revolution felt sufficiently upset and aggrieved to overturn or create the climate for major changes in their societies. With more to lose, the people in the twentieth century could create havoc on at least the same scale.

All of this becomes relevant in terms of the mechanisms that society has chosen to regulate itself, and how appropriate they are to the new circumstances! The inherent conservatism of all societies represents a block to changes. It is quite clear that at the top most nations resist change for understandable, if not always condonable, reasons. The people who have risen to eminent positions have done so through the use of the existing institutions and power structures. To challenge their validity would be tantamount to challenging their own positions and few people have a perspective wide enough to enable them to do so. Combined with this is the more traditional and widespread approach which suggests that what was good enough for your father is good enough for you and your children. The existing mechanisms, whether in the law, politics, education, business, or trade union sectors, will come under strain if they do not solve the new problems. The answer cannot be permanent revolution, and nor can it be to stick one's head in the sand. It must be a halfway solution in which flexibility is the watchword.

If the institutions of a country are important, then so are the attitudes and conventions of ordinary people. These, too, will come under some strain. Fundamental beliefs ingrained through generations will be challenged, indeed are already being challenged. The concept of a job for life, especially using craft skills, is getting less applicable by the month. The concept of jobs coming to people rather than people moving to jobs (a cherished idea in Britain) is fading fast. Parents are becoming less able to understand their childrens' school-work and thus are less able to provide reinforcement at home. The convention of secrecy and confidentiality of matters such as medical records and personal financial transactions is being eroded. Computers and computerization come into a head-on collision with the innate conservatism of most societies.

As we shall discover in the course of this book, these 'dark side of the moon' effects are balanced by the brighter side — by the benefits and potential benefits that could accrue from the use of new systems to people. It is possible to go even further than this, however. The costs or disadvantages may be inevitable but are capable of being minimized or even negated completely if the appropriate and often sympathetic counteractions are taken in time. In other words, if handled properly, the computer and all its developments and impact should prove to be a force for good and have beneficial effects on all forms of society. This will not happen automatically; rather like some marriages there will need to be a lot of work and a lot of give and take. This is because the basic underlying fears will not go away.

Art is often a better signpost to how people are feeling than opinion polls or general elections. The 1982 series of *Plays for Tomorrow* on BBC television were set at the end of the twentieth century and beyond. Almost without exception they painted a gloomy future—increased individual isolation, increased boredom or hedonism, increased vandalism, and so on. Earlier literature like Orwell's *1984* or Huxley's *Brave New World*, classic though they are, are hardly the signposts that most societies would wish to follow into the future. Even motion pictures like *Rollerball*, and in its day *Modern Times*, moved away from the rosy glow of Hollywood into a soulless and brutalizing future. When we laugh at these matters as we did in *Modern Times* and the kitchen in Jacques Tati's *Mon Oncle*, perhaps this means that society is coming to grips with the future and it is a sign of hope, although it is more likely to be a recognition of desperation. Overall, society would appear to be resigning itself to a rather unpleasant or uncertain future without much of a struggle.

Atomic weapons and nuclear power now preoccupy more people more of the time than any other single issue. Computers come a poor second. Yet the public nightmare is to have the two combined with each other. Nuclear power provides the major fear of no future, let alone an uncertain future, whilst computers not only control this potential Armaggedon device but could also lead to a less than human existence. These primeval fears are at odds with a consumer-based late twentieth century civilization and can only be exorcized by examining the problems likely to occur and then taking the appropriate preemptive action. Stressing the benefits alone whilst allowing the disadvantages to overtake an unsuspecting population can only lead to some form of social catastrophe.

There are questions to be asked and the answers must be given. However, as in so many cases, the right questions will be crucial. History is littered with the right answers to the wrong questions; the French Revolution resulted from a series of such mismatches. The questions in this instance are neither trivial nor are they of detail. They are fundamental, indeed, almost philosophical. There are at least five of these in broad terms and within them hundreds of smaller questions, and all are predicated upon the proposition that the technology itself is neutral and that it is people who take the decisions and thus determine the outcome. In truth there are millions of possible interrelated outcomes affecting not only individual societies but also acting on a transnational and even transcontinental basis. People of all nationalities will sooner or later have to ask themselves these vital questions. Some have already started to do so.

The first question is, who controls the computers and the systems? This is the relationship between those who see computers merely as a tool capable of doing any variety of tasks for any number of motives (for short we can name them executives) and those who actually have to make them work (the specialists). It is often fraught and contains the possibility of misunderstandings at very serious levels. Whilst this question could be looked at in both economic or political terms these will be subsumed under the other questions.

The second question is, who benefits from the new systems? This is an overtly economic and political poser and not one confined only to computers. Since mechanization and the industrial revolution, this question has been asked and answered thousands of times at elections, meetings, demonstrations. What makes it so vital today is the widespread nature of computer use and the depth and width of its penetration.

The third question is about change. Who should adapt — the systems to the people or the people to the systems? Who should take the decision — the executive, the specialist, or the people themselves? If the people, what mechanisms are there, or can there be, to make their views known and to get the appropriate responses? The computer presses around the world debate 'user friendly' as against 'user hostile' equipment and systems and this argument will have to be included. Another way of putting it would be to ask whether the new systems are too important to be left to the specialists. In other areas, especially nuclear physics and more recently genetic engineering, the answer to this has been 'yes'; these areas *are* too important to be left to the specialists and political control has been exercised.

The final two questions are about the paradoxical nature of electronic computers and can be summed up as: are they a force for good or are they a force for evil? These questions embrace political systems and political control, secrecy, work and its availability, armaments as against other production, and possible legal controls.

How these questions are asked, let alone answered, is quite another matter. They could be raised within the generality of political intercourse, but this would not only not commend itself to politicians who know little and care less about these problems but would bore the generality of the population. It could be done using the mass media, but both the popular press and the media networks would probably fight shy of such an esoteric subject. The result would be that only off-peak programmes or minority taste channels would carry the debate, along with what is generally known as the quality press and the trade press. Given this, it seems that the most productive method of starting the debate is to do it within the computer profession itself. Other professions have taken a pace back and looked at themselves critically. Doctors, lawyers, and scientists of many disciplines have questioned the morals and ethics of established practice and analysed the probable consequences of new practices and techniques. This should also happen with those who make, design, implement, and work with electronic computers.

There is a school of thought that suggests that 'progress', however defined, cannot be halted and, moreover, must be a good thing. It is a very mechanistic approach, believing that more means better. What it ignores is quality. Computers are quite capable of enhancing the quality of life as well as delivering more goods and services at an ever-faster rate. It is in this precise area that we must get computer people involved, and through them politicians and other groups of interested people. Within individual countries such matters are difficult enough to raise, especially when the system is so closed as to allow little or no open debate on such matters. Across boarders, with the potential of satellites and laser communications, the problems become even more daunting. Will we have permanent jamming by some countries or will we have information havens in the same way as we now have tax havens? Will we be overinformed? How will we control the communications on an international basis or will there be no control at all? Will the spread of transnational programmes, propaganda, and information lead to a lessening of differences between different societies or will it provide a reaction so that existing differences are widened and reinforced? What use will the lesser developed countries make of computer technology; is it an appropriate technology for them in their present state of development? These plain yet complex questions will arise in the very near future.

Within any one society, however, computers will impart their own imprint. It is undeniable that they are fundamental in the sense that not only do they change the way we do things in themselves but they also act on other unrelated matters in a way which speeds up their changes. It was recently estimated that in the 1980s the half-life of a computer-based technological breakthrough was only five years. This imposes as much stress on computer and electronic professionals as it does on the society which receives the results of these changes. In such circumstances there may be a receptive audience amongst computer people for they, like everyone else, will find previous certainties disappearing.

It would be a tragedy if, as in the bulk of science fiction, a Frankenstein type of society actually developed, for there is no absolute need for it to do so. Yet even in these early days of the computer wave, the mass symptoms of stress (or as it is more fashionably known, alienation) are occurring. I have alluded to riots and civil disturbance but the increase in drug taking, whether it be narcotic, hypnotic, or of the prescribed tranquillizer variety, is disturbing. When it is realized that this is running parallel with a worldwide increase in alcohol abuse, an increase in terrorism, the growth of fundamentalist religions, the growth of psychologically based remedial contact seminars, and an increase in the stranger quasi-religious sects, it is clear all is not well. People are running away and hiding behind physical or spiritual placebos because the world in general is just too hostile, dark, or complex for them.

Nuclear weapons are often blamed for this malaise and there may well be more than a grain of truth in this. Yet the nuclear threat, undesirable and threatening as it may be, does not generally affect an individual's dealings with other individuals or institutions. These are the factors that people find difficult. The current technologies bring more services into the home but this also has the effect of cutting some people off from relationships with others. The growth of bureaucracies and the increasing size of companies and other organizations make individuals and families feel vulnerable. In too many societies the community grouping which imparted stability is breaking up, which is especially true of urban centres around the world. The computer has played its part in these changes so far and its role has not on the whole been helpful. Whilst standards of living, whether measured by consumer goods and services or health and education, have obviously risen in industrialized countries over the last twenty years, it is perhaps the quality of life which has been most neglected. This represents the challenge to the next generation of electronic computer designers and professionals.

Despite the hankering of some people to return to the 'good old days', which incidentally were never that good for the people living at that time, there will be no turning back, no chances of a successful 'Luddite' approach. The golden age of threepence for a packet of cigarettes and crispy bacon will never return and never was golden; the slums, rats, and diseases are always quietly forgotten. We have, however imperfectly, begun to live with the computer and although there have been some casualties and many mistakes, it has not proved to be a fatal exercise, as yet.

The nostalgia boom, however, continues apace. Whether it be retrospectives of not particularly brilliant films or films recreating the apparently simpler and happier recent past, the art world plays its part yet again. A large number of people each year not only dream of the idealized agrarian society but attempt to put it into practice in Welsh farmhouses or Arizona ranches. Regrettably for most of these people, reality supervenes quite quickly and only the hardiest and most philosophically committed manage to last the course. Whilst the 'flower power' drop-out syndrome of the middle to late 1960s has gone, in reality it is only the commercialized romanticism that has vanished; if anything, the underlying causes of that movement have actually hardened.

People desperately want to be happy but the circumstances of life always seem to conspire against them. Death, illness, accident, divorce, unemployment — all come into conflict with the idealized world as portrayed in films or the advertising industry. When computers are then used to create systems that are not comprehensible intellectually and have the added disadvantage of removing even more control from an individual's ambit, it can only add to the insecurities already manifest.

Of all the tools ever invented, the computer is the one that needs the most sympathetic management and handling. Ordinary people find it impossible to argue with a computer. Even experts find this a problem, yet they find themselves having to do so in matters like allegedly unpaid bills or when querying an account. People need human contact and human argument and this element must be accepted by those who design and build the new systems. People make up societies; without people societies do not exist, and we ignore this truth at our peril.

All tools are man-made to aid human beings in their daily endeavours. As such it is mankind which theoretically controls the machine. As with many of the other major breakthroughs, the control can be exercised in a way which, by almost common consent, is counterproductive. The remainder of this book will explore what computers are, their uses, the people who use them, their potential, and, most importantly, the different paths that different societies have taken and can take when using them. The choices will be made by people — if they are given the chance and the information and confidence to do so. It would be a bitter irony indeed if the computer with all its potential actually widens the gap between the rich and poor countries or, indeed, damages the fabric of industrialized countries. Optimism must prevail, for if nothing else the human race is optimistic — it has had to be. Time and again, plagues, wars, floods, earthquakes, and volcanoes have wiped out the endeavours of mankind, but its resilience and resistance have proved to be remarkable. Societies can and will use computers to their advantage — providing these societies insist on it being so.

Chapter 2

The Pre-cradle to the Grave Technology

COMPUTERS ARE THE UBIQUITOUS TECHNOLOGY AFFECTING the citizens of an industrialized society from pre-cradle to the grave. Their penetration into the fabric of such systems has reached far and wide and by now is almost certainly irreversible. Everyone is affected in one way or another, although in many instances one has to look hard and analyse exhaustively to discover how or where. The wonder is that so few people know anything about them or even realize that they are there. The computer is the backroom tool *par-excellence*. The advent of home computers and high street computer shops have made little difference in this respect as yet.

One of the basic reasons why, despite its importance, it has not really impinged on public consciousness, except in a romantic or idealized way, is that it is disseminated so widely. Each time a computer or a new system is introduced its effects are limited and, moreover, low profile, in the sense that they are rarely highly visible like a new motorway or an aeroplane. Computers themselves are scarcely televisual and the systems they spawn or control are not visual at all. For example, an electronic office telephone system looks just the same as an old-fashioned system other than the switchboard and as a result television rarely concentrates on this form of programme. It prefers instead to use robotics or other large building devices on which to peg high technology computer-oriented programmes. From time to time we do get a flash of a computer, perhaps a large police installation, but generally in the context of computer privacy or some such subject. It is rare for the computer to be used in its normal working environment to explain what it does and what it contributes to the organization in which it is used. It is as though computers have been introduced through the back door at the dead of night for some nefarious purpose — none of which of course is true.

31

Few people understand the motorcar, or television, or even the telephone; they certainly do not understand them well enough to repair them or explain them to others. Computers are thus not unique inasmuch as the generality of people do not comprehend them — the difference is that at least people can see and use the other products but can generally do neither with computers. People are on the receiving end of them knowingly and unknowingly, wittingly and unwittingly. Yet a recent BBC television series on computing was immensely popular, showing the desire that people have to understand the machines.

Most states in the world have two parallel economies: the formal and the informal. The formal economy is measured in government statistics and controlled through various legislative devices and subject to taxation and other constraints. It involves the world of business, government, and other services. Most people who work, do so in this economy. Within it, it is very difficult to think of any process which does not, or within the next ten years will not, use computers somewhere or somehow.

The cash only or informal economy is, by definition, not really measurable. In some countries, notably Italy in Western Europe and many Lesser Developed Countries (LDCs), it is assumed to be of more than passing significance. The growth of an informal economy tends to be inversely related to the growth of the formal economy. It includes crime, 'moonlighting', prostitution, and a range of similar activities. The computer is unlikely to be used to any extent in such pursuits except perhaps in the criminal area. When we suggest that it is a ubiquitous machine, this qualification has to be borne in mind — it is in the formal sense but not in the real world sense.

In this chapter, for the sake of convenience and analysis,

society will be divided into sections or sectors. Whilst this is a legitimate exercise it has to be recognized that this neat compartmentalization does not hold up at the margins in real life. There are blurrings and fudgings at the edges as sectors overlap or fade away. Quite often the computer has a dual impact affecting the consumer at one end and the workplace or government at the other.

Industrialized states are nowadays vast interrelated complexes of people, bodies, institutions, and physical assets — roads, railways, etc. They appear to have developed a momentum of their own rather than being places within which human beings can fulfil themselves. It does seem that the anthill complex has taken over in some respects. People in these societies tend to want to live in peace; tend to demand more goods and services each year; and tend to want their children to do better than they did themselves. These basic drives make up the rising expectations in society. And rising they certainly are. Examples of this can be found everywhere: in the health sector, recent advances in medicine and surgery have given new hope to people who, in the past, would have died or lived in pain. Such advances, however, tend to cost a great deal of money, especially in the early stages of their development. Thus, whilst it is possible to perform bone marrow transplants for children suffering from certain forms of leukaemia or a-plastic anaemia, the demand is greater than the availability of hospital beds or skilled personnel and back-up facilities. Yet the expectation is that these children can be cured and when this expectation is dashed there is clearly disgruntlement. The same argument of course applies to renal dialysis, heart transplants and many other highly publicized treatments.

Within the generality of society the expectation of consumer goods and services and consumer choices is high. Thirty years ago a black and white television receiver would have been an up-market product — nowadays almost the entire population expects to own or rent a colour television set and shortly this will also encompass videorecorders and videodiscs. Well over 50 per cent. of the British population have bought their houses or flats and more expect to do so, whilst the number of people using a car for themselves has grown year by year. The demand for services in the private sector has risen as visits to hairdressers, for example, become habitual for more and more people each year, and once this pattern has become established it is very difficult, if not well-nigh impossible, to break. Education for children and services like libraries, garbage disposal, good roads, and lighting from local government are now expected at a high standard, whereas not too long ago almost anything would have been accepted. Computers have been behind many of these advances for without the computer the expectations would not have been formed in the first instance or met subsequently.

The momentum of society appears to be unchecked, even in economic depressions when fewer people than usual can afford to indulge their whims. The urge to acquire, and to acquire the so-called 'positional' goods, is strong. Positional goods are those prized by some people basically because most people do not have them. They can vary from types of food to private aeroplanes, and many of the computer-related products and services come into this category. Price reductions make these goods unattractive to positional goods lovers by allowing other people into the market. This in turn has an effect on 'taste', as those who set fashion tend to be the type of person who prize exclusivity. As one of the major effects (in theory) of computers is to enable prices to fall by increasing productivity and efficiency, there will be a change in the patterns of fashion. It may well be that handcrafted goods and personalized goods and services start to attract even more people than they do at present. Whilst this may be an interesting by-product, it is not going to be (nor is it) the most fundamental of changes. The need to provide more goods and services more quickly remains the unchallenged priority over the range of activities in an economy.

It is possible to divide and subdivide a country for analytical purposes in many different ways, each of which has a logic of its own — geographically or demographically, by sex or religion, by economic activity, by age, by political persuasion — these are just some of the divisions. From the point of view of computer impacts none of these appear to be mutually exclusive although each of the categories will be affected in their different ways. Any division of a country or society is of course artificial; as we have noted, society is nothing if not interrelated in its various aspects. Whilst it is therefore a less than satisfactory technique, in that many of the dynamic effects are lost or need extra work to bring to the fore, it can, when used with care, give an otherwise inchoate picture some resolution and definition. It is for this reason that I shall use subdivisions rather than an *ad hoc* approach based exclusively on anecdotes and hearsay.

The arbitrary distinctions that I shall use are health, work, leisure, homes, government, products, defence, education, and 'others'. A cursory glance at these clearly shows the interactions: government and defence, health and work, products and homes, all spring to mind immediately. At a secondary stage a government controls products through all kinds of economic and political actions, as well as the education and health impacts on products (and vice versa). Wherever possible these indirect effects will be elucidated, if not quantitatively then qualitatively.

One major problem in analysing the effects of computers upon society is the comparative lack of relevant government statistics. This is partly because it is so difficult to define a computer and this is compounded by the fact that the technology itself is so new. A second reason is that governments do not keep good 'supply side' statistics; they concentrate on the demand side.

Over the last 30 years most industrialized states have attempted to control their economies by intervening on the demand side of the economy, using taxation, incomes policies, etc. They have not, by and large, intervened unduly on the supply side and thus have not seen the need to collect adequate statistics. On the other side of the coin, specialist manpower statistics are also deficient because some of the jobs are so new and also because as computing becomes decentralized so it becomes more difficult to define a computer worker. For example, is someone who uses a terminal (intelligent or otherwise) a computer person, or is someone else who does airline bookings and operates almost exclusively with an 'on-line' terminal a booking clerk — or what? Within large traditional mainframe installations there is no dubiety on these matters although job titles are, to be charitable, flexible and only too often less than informative. Precise figures on who does what, on which machine, and to whom, are thus difficult to obtain, if not almost impossible.

It is becoming clear that computers are now part and parcel of the very fabric of industrialized societies. The new levels of expectations could not be met without them. 'Quality' newspapers now advertise them for personal use and office equipment and systems products are advertised at peak television times. Their use and their acceptance as an inevitable fact of life are now virtually complete. This is not to say that 'all is for the best in the best of all possible worlds' or that social problems of one form or another will not be stimulated by their use. It is, however, quite remarkable that this 'pre-cradle to grave' technology has been accepted with so little disturbance except in individual and isolated terms. So many uses are now taken for granted — if not always appreciated. Comedians can still get a cheap laugh when referring to computer mistakes and a few times a year there are newsworthy snippets which are built up around the 'gas bills for ten million pounds sent to aged widows living without gas supplies' story.

The national press and television stations around the world are fascinated by technology in general and computers in particular and the microelectronics revolution in the most particular. Many papers have started 'technology columns' over the past three years but a large number carry pieces which are unintelligible to all but the initiated. Conversely most of the television programmes not only oversimplify the technology, they sensationalize it and often attribute powers to it that do not as yet properly exist. The existence (or lack of it) of voice-controlled computers is a classic example. If these media outlets indicate an interest, indeed fascination, about the subject amongst readers and viewers, then the computer press itself indicates the depth of computer penetration in society.

In 1981 there were 88 different journals dealing with computers in the United Kingdom alone. This was six more than in 1980. In the United States there was a staggering total of journals in 1981. Computer industry personnel are clearly voracious readers, although most of these journals carry hundreds of classified job advertisements which are the attraction to so many of their readers. Overall their style, if not their content, is very different: they run from the irrelevant and flip to the 'po-faced' and dull. The fact that not only have they all survived, even in a period of economic recession, but have expanded in number is a fair indication of the coherence and sense of identity which this virtually infant industry has built up in a short space of time.

Equally informative is the number of new books published on computers. In 1981 there were no less than 484 new titles and 393 new titles in 1980. Whilst many were intended for the profession itself, many others were aimed at a wider public and students. The thirst for knowledge on the computer and general microelectronics area is far from being quenched, despite this total information barrage. Some people believe that computers will be the basic technology of the future and are seeking as much knowledge as they possibly can. The percentage of the total population doing so is still small, however, and quite obviously self-selected, which results in the majority of the population being in a state of ignorance, blissful or otherwise. Still, the signs are encouraging, for the more people know and understand the more they will feel comfortable in tomorrow's world.

In 1981 in the United Kingdom there were roughly 1,500 separate computer departments varying in size, type, and reason for existing. The departments were in over 9,000 different locations and contained within them almost 32,000 digital computers. It must be stressed that not included in these figures are text (or word) processors with computing ability, intelligent terminals, or, for that matter, the home computers which are now increasingly used in small businesses. Between 1980 and 1981 there was an increase of over 5,000 computers in major installations, representing a growth of over 19 per cent. which in the context of the deepest post-1945 depression is a staggering achievement. However, the number of separate locations grew by less than 3 per cent. This argues that existing departments are expanding in size or that there have been mergers between departments, or both. This trend towards bigness or merger is one which, although inevitable, given the technology itself, is now counterbalanced by the growth of microcomputers and the growing number of systems which can be decentralized. Indeed, between 1980 and 1981 there was an increase of over 3,000 intelligent terminals in the United Kingdom, which is only about half the number of new computers, which argues that the option of decentralizing is not being taken up as quickly or as widely as many experts predicted.

The entire industry is waxing whilst others around it have been contracting, which means that to a limited extent it is recession proof. Growth in some of the areas, especially in the microelectronic/computer industry in America has certainly slowed in response to the economic downturn. Even in the legendary growth area of Silicon Valley, California, the latter-day Klondike, unemployment has reached down and plucked some high fliers from the skies in mid-flight. The basic truth, though, is that as an entire industry it has weathered the storm better than most and its infrastructure is if anything still strengthening.

In 1981 there were no less than 310 companies recruiting computer staff within the United Kingdom. There were over 2,000 suppliers of equipment of various kinds and nearly 1,000 service companies, an increase of over 60 per cent. in two years. Courses offered by private consultancies and classes in subjects varying from computer art and music to systems analysis and computer sciences are proliferating all over the world. It would, however, be instructive if the drop-out figures for such courses were made available publicly. As a result of all the media coverage and the perceived central position of computers, it has become a respectable topic of conversation even at the politest of dinner parties. Indeed, the odds are that the hosts (be they a dowager, duchess, or a self-made businessman) actually want to know whether their sons or their daughters can get into the profession, or perhaps how an installation might benefit them in the running of their estates or businesses. The intriguing thing is that less than two years ago the subject of running a computer tended to provoke glassy stares and a swift reach for another large gin and tonic — it was a combination of 'trade' and boredom. Now it is a profession and a 'sexy' one at that.

Computers in their widest sense go beyond the large installation or even the home computer linked into a domestic television set. Nowadays they control production lines or machine tools and are built into all sorts of domestic products and, if the definition is stretched to include integrated circuitry, a wider range of products and machines such as calculators, watches, cookers, cars, and games. It is this last step which takes us into the future, away from the fixed ideas of large computers and into the realms of science fiction. These integrated circuits, whether with fixed programmes (dedicated) or programmable, are a form of computer so let us look at the broad areas where they can be used. The details will be covered later in the book.

Health services are obviously one of the most vital parts of any society; like food, shelter, and clothing they are one of the basic needs. Medicine, in all its forms, has made remarkable advances in a very short space of time; the mortality and morbidity statistics demonstrate this quite dramatically. Antibiotics are taken in billions of grammes per year and have controlled most bacterial diseases which were such killers, yet did not get onto the market until after the Second World War. Diagnostic techniques, drug therapy, radioactive therapy, and all forms of surgery depend upon technological advances. Computers have been a mainstay in these advances and more recently have been used in a more direct form. Medical research has depended upon computers, as has epidemiology. The ability to sift through apparently unrelated data and find common causes and threads and trends have resulted in work establishing the link between cigarette smoking and lung cancer or heart disease and between genetic defects and pregnancies in the forty plus age group. The sheer volume of statistics would have been so great as to make these analyses virtually impracticable without a computer. Clinical trials on animals or plants or humans can be evaluated if not short-cut by computer analysis. Medical records, appointment systems, and the day-to-day smooth functioning of a major hospital are all now increasingly dependent upon the use of computers, as are the new 'on-call' computer systems for doctors and nurses.

New medical techniques are now becoming computer based. The monitoring of patients in intensive care and the scanning devices for pre-natal observation of the fœtus or for prophylactic cancer checks are, within financial contraints, being done on a routine basis. Open heart surgery, new anaesthetic techniques, dialysis, and many treatments now involve the computer in the equipment used. The latest advance has been in computer diagnostics. A patient tells a computer visual display unit what his or her symptoms are and a rough diagnosis is then fed to the doctor. The interesting feature of this, as yet experimental, system is that patients appear to be more honest and less reticent when confronting a machine rather than a fellow human being. This may be because the people tested had to approve of their participation beforehand; it remains to be seen whether there is as favourable a reception amongst the population at large. In terms of health care there is little doubt that computers and microelectronics will have a great deal to offer in the future.

For the first time the concept of the 'biochip', an organic microelectronic device, is being taken seriously — the pessimists might say that Frankenstein rides again but the optimists might look to the possibility of the eradication of crippling diseases. Like other applications of this technology and the way it is controlled, society or people should determine the outcome.

There have been massive increases in both the quality and quantity of health care available to people in the recent past. As a result the health care sector has changed out of all recognition. New companies manufacturing new machinery have emerged; the types of work done by health service employees has changed as has the education and training available. Difficulties due to these advances have arisen, however. Governments find it increasingly difficult to give a clean bill of health to the plethora of new drugs; new ethical questions about life, birth, and death and when and how they occur remain to be solved. The computer, as always, does not have one single impact; it has multiple direct and indirect effects on a variety of institutions. Taken to the extreme, one can legitimately enquire whether it will be possible to continue a high level of pension payments when computer use allows more people to live for a longer time. Financial and health matters are linked by computer technology in a subtle, not always easily divined, way.

Much public attention has been drawn to the impact of computers on work and the workplace, be it in the health services or any other sector. This has concentrated upon the amount of work available rather than on the type or quality of work. The earlier generation of computers had unexpected work effects. The immediate view was that they would replace people and diminish the number of jobs. In fact the precise opposite happened and there was a substantial addition to aggregate jobs in almost every industrialized country. There were many reasons for this happening, none of them ever likely to recur, and, moreover, recent research has suggested that the process of job loss entails a twelve to fourteen year lag.

The major reasons for the job creation were that few people understood what computers were as compared with the expectations of what they could do. Organizations bought large installations because rival organizations had them. They were status symbols—the modern equivalent of a corporate fountain—and as such represented a triumph of computer sales and techniques over commonsense. By the early and mid 1960s the fist computer boom was well under way but many large installations were working at less than 40 per cent. capacity. Costs of software were seriously underestimated. If things went wrong, and they did so with frightening regularity, the data processing manager pleaded that there were not enough staff—and there was no senior manager or director to gainsay this. Staff levels and costs accelerated and the quality of staff was distinctly variable. On top of this neither directors nor senior managers appeared to realize that computers not only required information but required the information to be specific and in a standard form. The new information systems had to be put in place whilst at the same time business had to proceed as usual. This meant at times a virtual doubling of staff. Hopefully, from the point of view of efficiency the lessons have been learned and the mistakes will not be repeated.

By the end of the 1960s the computer bubble had burst, rationalization and redundancies were legion, and a large number of organizations either designated a very senior manager or director to oversee the functioning of the department. The later and newer generations of computers have the advantage of being cheaper and integrated with a leasing system whilst the information systems are now broadly *in situ*. Software is still a problem but is slowly dropping in real price terms and becoming more reliable as bespoke programme amendments can be made more easily.

Various forms of computer technology are now used in the workplace across manufacturing industry and offices, warehouses and research establishments, retail outlets and transport organizations, as well as a variety of miscellaneous concerns and departments. Computer control systems abound in continuous process plants such as those used in the petrochemical industry. Production line speeds can be controlled to avoid unnecessary bottlenecks and surpluses and robotics and automated machine tools are appearing more frequently — their novelty has worn thin. Components used in products are changing too, which makes a marked difference to the manufacturing process itself as well as making production engineering a more important science. Generally speaking, the day of the complex subassemblies of components is over, especially where electro- or thermomechanical devices are concerned, and the era of the integrated circuit has now dawned. Across the length and breadth of manufacturing industries the computer terminal and visual display unit is making its presence felt and in some instances, notably steel production and electricity generation, large plants with large computer installations need very few people to run and maintain them.

More people work outside of the manufacturing sector than within it in the industrialized world, as the public and private service sector grows in all countries. Computers have been more in evidence in this sector (especially in offices) than anywhere else, even from their earliest days. Computer staffs have been on payrolls throughout this time, although for both geographical and other reasons they have not often mixed very much with the generality of other staffs. This is partly because many large computer installations are in completely separate buildings, even different parts of the country and well away from the other staff, and partly because there has been some tension between the two sets of staff. This latter reason appears to be diminishing. Whilst it existed a lack of communication was the basic cause, with a combination of the use of different jargons and conflicting functions creating the problem. The computer has of course had indirect effects on individual and group relationships in the offices which have changed their work and payments systems. These will be covered in a later chapter.

Computers themselves are changing, becoming smaller, lighter, and often easier to operate. This has resulted in an increasing take-up of them by enterprises like small circulation magazines or journals for postal distribution to subscribers. Banks and supermarkets, stores and hotels use them for stock control, billing, and invoicing, and whereas these jobs were once performed manually by many people, now fewer people provide a more efficient service. Government, local government, and public utilities like gas and electricity use literally banks of them, but by and large these are the older type of larger computer. The spread of terminals to points in these organizations remote from the mainframe computers is gaining momentum and as it does so the number of people at work having contact with computers and having to understand computer techniques increases, even though most of them would not describe themselves as computer personnel. The world of work has changed irrevocably as a result of computerization but the changes to date are small compared with the potential for change over the coming decades.

The development of robotics and control systems, linked machine tool production lines, and ultimately the fully automated factory is well under way. The office equipment revolution has started but the systems which will link the bits and pieces together are still rudimentary. Until these are not only developed but also linked into an electronic telephone system the radical change will not happen. The possibility of people working from home and of importing and exporting clerical work could change the way that office blocks are designed as well as the patterns of transport and housing facilities. Very few, if any, formal workplaces will be immune, even if at present they appear to be so. From the electronic cash register in the corner shop to the telephone-linked terminal in a rural-based travelling library, the computer will be truly ubiquitous in work environments.

Without exception, industrial societies are very work orientated so that the time we spend not working is regarded as residual. Leisure as a word carries connotations of hedonism and sinful time wasting which reinforces the view that it is a subject not to be taken very seriously—by serious people. Computers, though, are very much in evidence in the leisure industries and affect us directly and indirectly as consumers in a whole variety of ways, some of which are taken for granted to the extent that we have forgotten the computer is there at all.

Obviously television games and the new forms of slot machines in arcades, whether they are for gambling or for sheer enjoyment (like *Space Invaders*), are based on computer technology. It is a relatively new phenomenon and has a very high public profile. However, our theatre and holiday bookings and the theatre itself rely on computers although we rarely see them at work, and this applies to uses such as the scheduling of air transport too. Computers are used in television programmes, especially sports coverage where they provide a variety of statistics almost instantly, as indeed they do in the coverage of elections. The databases and information systems now available on domestic television sets are based on computers. Museum cataloguing and security systems (especially in art galleries) and the theme parks like Disneyland with their life-like figurines are all computer controlled.

The major growth area in the leisure industry has been television and with the advent of videorecorders and videodiscs this has been reinforced. When widespread cable television arrives in Europe the trend to home entertainment will be boosted and consequent changes to other forms of leisure activity will follow. Whether this form of passive recreation rather than active, in the sense of doing something and making a conscious effort to leave the home, is a good thing socially will be discussed later in the book. The depth of penetration is so deep that even the traditional cricket scoreboard has succumbed. The implications of much of these technologies in terms of copyright law have yet again not been fully realized at present, but those that have been suggested that the law itself will have to be amended.

An increasing amount of leisure time is thus, despite increased car ownership and public transport, spent within the home and it is here that computers and electronics are making the fastest inroads. The home computer, television and its accessories, some new cabling schemes, Prestel, and teletext systems are here now. Consumer-durable (or 'white') goods are increasingly dependent upon computers and integrated circuitry. Washing machines, cookers, freezers and toasters, clocks, vacuum cleaners, and television sets themselves, all incorporate electronics, if only in the newer models. Children's toys, even the control mechanisms of electric train sets, are now computerized; indeed, some toys like spelling and arithmetic games sell well on the grounds that they are computers in their own right. New and improved household gadgets such as intelligent bathroom scales or ultrasonic toothbrushes are threatened too.

The house (or dwelling) itself and its construction has not yet incorporated computers other than in one-off experimental houses. However, in terms of design, computers now play an active and increasing role. It is not only possible but probable that within this century new houses will not only have a central computer control system but a wiring and switch system based on computers and microcircuits.

The overlap in these arbitrary divisions is seen most clearly between the previous two categories of leisure and home and the next which is products. Obviously all the household goods just mentioned are products and indeed so are the computers and the office equipment and robots referred to earlier. Many of these are amended products, that is to say, they existed previously but are using computers or electronics to improve the product, or to make it more reliable. Items like washing machine timers come into this category. Cars and trucks are another area where these amendments will be important. Cruise at constant speed, tyre pressure monitoring, petrol level monitoring, and emission control are not flights of fancy; they are slowly becoming standard. Cars, and inexpensive ones at that, now talk to the driver. The amended product creeps in without any startling impact on the consciousness of people. They accept a known article and just marvel gently (if at all) at the new option.

New products like television games are in a different category. They often need some time to be accepted in the market-place and whilst television games can rarely be described as threatening, many parents certainly rue the day they were invented. Other breakthroughs such as electronic surveillance devices are not viewed in quite the same sanguine light. New products for new markets also have to be differentiated from new products for old markets. For example, the digital watch (one has been developed with a tiny television receiver included) was a new product but for an old market. In contrast, the videorecorder was a new product for a totally new market. This distinction has, as we shall see, great importance when looking at the effect of computers on the total amount of work available.

It is really no exaggeration to speak of a time not far away when almost all electrically driven products will have a computer (broadly defined) incorporated within them. Many of the other products we use at one time or another and which are not basically electronic will incorporate them too. The march of the computer has only just started as far as products are concerned, because their size, reliability, and price have only recently been suitable.

Governments are very heavy users of computers. For no other reason this is because they are generally charged with the maintenance and production of statistics both for their own planning purposes and for publication. Whilst it has always been possible to fulfil this function using non-electronic means, the computer has given governments a chance to extend their statistical coverage, refine the statistics, and produce them more quickly. Whether the statistical series are on manpower and employment, output, expenditure or whatever, their regular production now means that there is a media check on government in a way that was not possible only some twenty years ago. The more centralized the government system the more need there is to use computing power both in terms of day-to-day control and overall strategy.

In Britain the great departments of state keep and maintain a huge stock of computing power and employ computer staffs of various grades. Local government, too, is a very heavy user of computers, as are the public utilities like the gas and electricity services. Within central government much of the computer work goes on without the public's awareness. The Department of Health and Social Security (DHSS) has a computer file for everyone who has a National Health Service number or pays or receives National Insurance or Social Security. In this respect the size of this filing system in the United Kingdom dwarfs any other, including that of the police. Whether it is in tax collection, both direct and indirect, rate bills, bills for services, or merely to facilitate the smooth organization of sections and ministries, government is becoming highly computerized. In every industrialized country governments are absorbing new powers and duties and extending their regulation and control; the impact on society of the computer is reinforced in this way, although with the lowest profile possible.

Defence is (other than tax collection) the one factor that all governments have in common and it is often the most expensive item in any one government's budget. In the United Kingdom, defence expenditure is over 5 per cent. of the total Gross Domestic Product (GDP), as it is in both the United States and Greece — in anyone's language a huge chunk of money. None of these percentages include the infrastructure, without which the defence effort would fail, such as the Civil Service or some of the research and development in military hardware and software. Much of this latter development is in, or is using, computers.

Not unnaturally, this is not an area which generally impinges on public consciousness, partially because until the weapon or defence systems are used few people know of them and, secondly, because the Official Secrets Acts or their equivalent make much of the information unobtainable. Communications and early warning systems exist openly for public morale purposes, although their details are not widely known. The actual military hardware: rockets, missiles, and guidance systems do not receive much public attention until they are used. The Falkland Islands war was a classic example, as was the Israeli incursion into the Lebanon. In the former instance, who had heard of Exocet missiles before the war and, in the latter, who knew that a defence system had been developed against SAM anti-aircraft missiles? As communications and guidance systems are now the key to military defence (or success), the computer and electronics become ever more important.

Another strand is strategic planning where computers are used to analyse data, check defence and battle plans, simulate wars, and, overall, act as an aid to the general staffs — a painless way of playing at war and thus to be encouraged. Such installations and their uses are generally highly secret. The public does, however, learn about defence in roundabout ways. When a flock of birds confused both radar and computers and the US Air Force went onto a red alert, people realized that not only did such mechanisms exist but that they were not infallible. It is interesting to note that great play was made of the fact that war did not break out and that the 'fail safe systems' actually worked. Films such as *Doctor Stragelove* bring the conjunction of computers and defence into the public realm in quite a different way. Overall, however, the entire matter is shrouded in secrecy and half-truths, yet a paradox remains. Most people need to feel secure yet do not want to know what it is that adds to their security — if indeed the systems do this — and moreover do not feel competent to challenge experts or governments on the matter of computer analysis or control. Providing that they are assured (rightly or wrongly) that human political judgement is the final arbiter they feel reassured. Defence uses (along with security) represent the ultimate in covert computer and electronic power and control.

Education is virtually the antithesis of this situation. Where and whenever computers are involved in the educational process people know about them, be they young people, their parents, or both. There is a slowly dawning awareness that computers are a potent aide in teaching, although their use is not very widespread as yet. Programmed teaching, based on either books and computer material combined, or a simple system of progressing through a series of answers, is thought by some educationalists not to be education at all. They claim that people (especially young ones) learn the tricks but do not learn the subject. In systems where examinations depend on the regurgitation of facts and little or nothing else, such a method of teaching is appropriate and if it is not, but nevertheless computers lead us towards it, what is to be done?

Computers can of course do far more than this, whether they are in the form of toys or in schools. Within universities much research could not reasonably be undertaken without computers, especially in the disciplines of the natural sciences, economics, and mathematics. Of course the computer itself is now the subject of courses in its own right and these vary from sophisticated degree level computer sciences to the training type of course in basic 'appreciation'. It is highly probable that the computer will play an increasing role in the educational system at all levels and for all ages. From working out timetables in large schools to curriculum development, they will have administrative impacts. The growth of videorecordings will carry teaching into the home, as does the Open University and Open Tech, and both of these depend on electronics and computers.

Rather like medicine, it is an interesting analytical area. Both areas of life almost certainly need the reassurance of human contact, whatever advances the technologies may bring in terms of efficiency. We would do well to remember that new technological systems need careful thought if, as we shall see later, they result in people having to change in response to the systems in a way which increases general alienation. This is not just a United Kingdom problem, nor, indeed, a European or North American dilemma; it is one of worldwide significance and embraces the concept of 'appropriate technology' for the developing as well as the developed countries.

There are other less definable uses for computers in society which make an impact on our lives and on which we depend now for our living standards, both quantitatively and qualitatively: e.g. the control of transport, especially air transport and the simulation machines, which range from games to home golf lessons to training bomber pilots. Lasers in medicine or entertainment, defence, or simply for eavesdropping, are generally computer linked or controlled. Television and cinema depend heavily on computers, while the printing of books and newspapers, the subscription to your favourite weekly, the football league match schedules and football pools, the daily milk delivery and the soggy bread, traffic control and ironically traffic jams, political opinion polling, and computer dating bureaux are all computer aided. Gas, water, electricity — three of the basic elements in an industrialized consumer society — could not now be delivered without computer use so without computers such societies would fail.

Computers now embrace and coddle society in general. They are literally pre-cradle to beyond the grave along with much of the in-between. The pre-natal testing and screening of foetuses and the statistical records concerning deaths and causes of deaths give us the polar positions: the middle covers most of life. Computers, as we shall see, actually make choices for us. The number and type of goods available and even the shape of goods are involved in this process. It is a hidden embrace and in essence one which has been effected with little drama and little publicity, although the public aversion to computers, such as it is, has stemmed greatly from those occasional mistakes — news is nearly always bad news. In a rather random and certainly disaggregated way the computer now represents a staple commodity, like roads, railways, or the electrical power systems. It is inconceivable that its presence will disappear (except perhaps to be replaced by something altogether more efficient), and equally unthinkable that people in industrialized societies will do without the goods and services that it makes possible.

However, computers do not work by themselves. Whilst the newer generations of equipment need fewer people to work with them, people still need to do all sorts of jobs on and around computer installations. In the United Kingdom it has been estimated that there are in the region of 250,000 people who would qualify as Computer Skilled Manpower (CSM). Whilst when compared with industries such as banking and insurance which employ over a million people this is a small number, the power, potential and real, that they wield is considerable. By 1985 it is estimated that the number of CSMs will have risen to near 400,000, although the estimate is based on an optimum take-up of the newer technologies. Of this 400,000 it is also estimated (in a report of the Electronic Computer Sector Working Party) that just over half will be professionals, and these include programmers, analysts, managers, and electrical engineers. The whole industry is thus very knowledge-intensive based — far more so than most other sectors of the economy.

As an industry, it employs more people than agriculture and will soon exceed the total number of people employed in shipbuilding, coalmining, or textile manufacturing. Rather like the more nationally based professions like medicine, accounting, and the law, the people in computing tend to be mobile both geographically and between industries and companies. Most of these people work in the installations of computer users but around 10 per cent. work in the computer services industry and roughly 50,000 in the computer manufacturing industry. In services, over 90 per cent. can be described as professional staffs, but in manufacturing the percentage is roughly the average for the CSMs as a whole. CSMs are defined as 'manpower which requires a minimum of some months instruction or its equivalent. Data preparation operators, who do not necessarily require such lengthy instruction are also included.'

The number of different grades commonly found amongst computer workers in the United Kingdom is quite large. The NEDO report on computer manpower uses seven main grades whilst the *Computer Users' Yearbook* uses twenty-one different grade levels in its salary analysis. Given that the whole of the Italian labour force is subdivided into only seven grades from top to bottom, there does seem to be an excessive and artificial splitting of functions amongst computer personnel — a standard procedure when complex wage and status differentials are at stake. The seven broader distinctions are: computer managers, systems analysts/designers, software (systems) programmers, applications programmers, computer operators, operations support (data controlled), and data preparation people. As in so much human endeavour, the complexities arise from the difficulties of rigid definition and the blurring of one large function with another. Thus, there are six analyst or analyst programmer grades alone. In general terms, however, the hierarchy (both social and financial) is in the descending order outlined in the seven main categories — managers on top and data preparation operators at the bottom.

As a general rule of thumb it is assumed that the less expensive the computer installation the fewer computer skilled people work it. The cheapest installations, worth, say, less than £20,000, have no CSMs whatsoever. As the new generations of computers arrive and their price falls, so this rather arbitrary figure will have to be revised downwards. Equally, it is probable that this change in computer technology will bring with it a growth of service agencies who will design and then look after new systems, especially the smaller ones.

Overall, roughly one person in a thousand in the United Kingdom can be described as computer skilled and approximately one other person in a hundred uses a terminal, word processor, or other piece of computer/electronic equipment for at least part of the time. Yet very few of the other 98 or 99 actually know what a CSM does. This is not a function of the relatively small number of these people in society. There are but 120,000 doctors, 21,000 dentists, only 'x' soldiers as few as 'y' judges, yet everyone knows what they do. It is the esoteric nature of the technology itself that promotes this ignorance — one that is all the more important to dispel as these jobs are so important to peoples' everyday lives. The seven main categories can be allocated the following duties, although it must be remembered that not only do some of the job functions blur into one another but also that one employer may call a programmer an analyst whilst another will call an operator a programmer.

Computer management is concerned with the smooth running and delivery of services by the computer installation. There can be technical managers and operations managers, as well as an overall data processing manager in the largest of the installations — those with between 400–600 personnel.

Computer managers have to display all the skills of general management although they must also have a more than adequate specialist knowledge. In some rare instances a computer manager can be promoted to board level. As a manager, however, he or she has the normal staff selection and discipline functions, budgetting duties and morale functions whilst fostering cooperation between sections and subsections is a major feature of the job. Finally the manager must be aware of all the new technological developments as he or she will almost certainly be the only senior staff member able to advise those in ultimate authority of what is available and what can be achieved. Of the jobs available in computing, managers are the only category where employers expect at least five years service or other knowledge-related experience before appointment.

Systems analysts or systems designers are next down the ladder. They are also occasionally (and more familiarly) known as organization and methods analysts, or business systems analysts. Quite simply, their job is to develop new systems, e.g. increase productivity, reduce costs, improve the service to customers, etc. Whilst most of the analysts deal with computer systems, not nearly enough have an adequate grasp of computers or programming, so that a gap between theory and practice may emerge with disastrous consequences. Analysts should have logical minds, too. They are expected to collect and then analyse the facts before designing the new system. It is here, when specifying what program the programmer should write, that potential problems can and do arise. The new system then has to be implemented and the appropriate training designed for the staff, whilst later the system must be monitored and weaknesses eliminated. Some organisations, mainly the larger ones, will employ analysts, but an increasing number of users of systems, especially smaller ones, buy in the services from consultancies. In essence a system analyst acts as a link between the computer installation and the overall users of the whole system.

Systems designers tend to deal more with information (they are also known as information analysts) than with clerical, administrative, or operational systems. As this generally requires an overview of the whole system, these people tend to have better computer skills than other analysts. The job, however, also requires considerable analytical skills and the combination of these two factors makes them highly priced in the labour market.

Software or systems programmers are somewhere in the grey area between analysts and programmers; indeed, some organizations label them analyst programmers and graduate trainees are often placed in this category. Within a computer installation the operating systems (controlling the day-to-day running of the installation) and the programs translated into the appropriate language by 'compilers' as well as the standard programs come within the competence of this grade of computer worker. As a group they will have to know all about the operating system and will link with the manufacturers in correcting or improving or simply adding to the capabilities of the installation.

Applications programmers simply do what their job title suggests. They program the machine to deal with specific problems. Generally speaking they work under a systems analyst or, indeed, a senior programmer — rarely on their own.

Computers need operating, that is to say, someone has to load the tapes and disc drives, put paper into the printers, and look after and store the tapes and discs. The jobs are done by computer operators who have sufficient skills to use the central console of the machine. Computer operators are the people seen working when passing a well-lit office at night, as, typically, in any larger installation there is 24 hour working. If one were to look at computer staffs in conventional terms, operators are the skilled and semi-skilled workers, as opposed to the professional and managerial workers.

Operations support, the last category, is divided between people controlling data and those who prepare data. Rather like a large office block which cannot work at all without a switchboard operator, operations support staff are vital to computing. Without standard data in the proper form, computers do not work at all. The similarity goes further: neither are highly regarded either in status or money terms. A data control clerk handles all the data entering the installation and has the responsibility for ensuring it is in a correct form. A data preparation operator is the person who uses the machine to put the information checked by data control into a form suitable for a computer.

Where do all these people come from? Managers and analysts tend to be graduates although no data are available as to the precise percentages. Because they are graduates and because the intake into universities and polytechnics in the United Kingdom is very socially oriented, these people are overwhelmingly from the higher social classes — groups A, AB, and B. However, this is a peculiarly British symptom and does not apply so strongly to other European countries or to North America. Programmers are either bright school-leavers with somewhat higher than average qualifications (and have stayed on till 18 at school) or graduates of some description — often in mathematics or computer sciences. Operators and support staff tend to be school-leavers who left at 16 but had some examination successes. Overall it is a knowledge-intensive industry. As one would suspect, the proportion of women working in these jobs increases the lower down the payment and status scales one descends. There are very few female managers of any description, let alone in computers, slightly more analysts, and considerably more programmers, but they do make up the majority of the support staffs.

Within the entire industry as a whole there are more highly qualified (and paid) people in the consultancies and software houses than in the large free-standing installations or in the manufacturing sector. This should in theory, and does in practice, mean that these smaller companies offer services that manpower non-availability constraints for the users themselves. It is also an industry which has traditionally attracted young people and where the age distribution has been far more skewed towards the 21 to 44 age ranges than the generality of employment. However, this has been partly because it was itself a young industry and people are now growing old within it. The middle-aged disillusioned clerk is now paralleled by the computer programmer who wakes up one morning to find that at the age of 45 he has a great future behind him.

Computers and the people who work with them have become more efficient and structured in the short space of fifteen years. Education and training programmes with some standards in which others can have confidence have replaced the eccentric and often appalling early courses. Financial and personnel control have replaced the early freewheeling attitudes. The machines themselves, if not the skills in programming, are more reliable. Computers and the computer have come of age remarkably quickly. Without such rapid progress the technology itself would not have increased and nor would society have tolerated the effects as well as they have done. The age of the 'megamistake' is almost over — in terms of defence, anyway, we all have to hope and pray that this is so.

Chapter 3

What Computers
Are—And Will Be

CHAMBER'S *20TH CENTURY DICTIONARY* (1971 EDITION) defines a computer as 'a machine or apparatus, mechanical, electric or electronic, for carrying out especially complex calculations, dealing with numerical data or with stored items or other information, also used for controlling manufacturing processes, or co-ordinating parts of a large organisation'. The *Oxford English Dictionary* (shorter edition) defines a computer as 'one who computes' and it was not until 1973 that the definition of a computer as a machine rather than a person appeared and then only in the Addendum.

As arguments about definitions are notoriously time-consuming, deep, bitter, and often sterile, the definition above appears to be more than adequate. It does not of course present a comprehensive list of what an electronic computer can do, especially as the state of the art and technology have improved so much as in the intervening ten years. A United Nations Organisation agency once spent two years in an attempt to define a scientist and to distinguish technicians and technologists from scientists, and thus delayed an important report for what in hindsight proved to be for no very good reason. Regardless of whether a device should really be called a computer or an integrated circuit, if it is capable of being programmed, i.e. have instructions fed into it, then for the purpose of this book it shall be a computer. However, many integrated circuits are pre-programmed dedicated computers and will be treated as such. To progress otherwise would significantly and unnecessarily complicate a difficult enough series of problems and concepts — in other words, computers are what we think they are!

Obviously, computers in an historical sense are new. Most analyses of the history of computers tend to start with the calculation functions of the abacus or the 'predictive' uses of the ancient megaliths like Stonehenge. Whilst this is quite legitimate, in that the calculation functions were those that initially stimulated the development of electronic computers, there is a distinct qualitative difference. The development of a memory endows a machine with an added dimension over previous mechanical or electronic devices. Memory is perhaps an unfortunate word in this respect. Within human experiences the brain, memory, and the spirit are words which convey an essence of aliveness, awareness, and animality. To attribute this word to a part of an inanimate object, and a machine to boot, elevates that machine to a high level. It does more than that, however. It endows that machine with the sense of aliveness which accounts for the awe in which it is held by non-initiates. Nevertheless, the history of the computer is really the history of a search for quick and reliable methods of performing calculations and other mathematical operations.

Mathematics is probably the only truly non-empirical science or art that exists. Its subtleties and elegance are lost on the overwhelming majority of people and mathematicians describe their work as being in a language. Within the pure sciences (and certainly applied sciences) there are tedious and lengthy explanations and calculations that need to be performed. Astronomy, physics, engineering, and econometrics all require the solution of difficult simultaneous or differential equations, operations which take up valuable time. The value of the time is even greater when given the scarcity of suitably skilled people in these fields. However, other, perhaps less rarified but no less important, people have needed to use numbers. Merchants and their clerks, the people who controlled kingdoms, their budgets and their logistics, insurance actuaries, churchmen controlling assets, and statisticians of all kinds, have all looked for aids in their work.

The abacus, invented in China in roughly the year 3000 BC,

is still in use today. Using beads on a wooden frame, simple arithmetic operations were carried out with great speed by proficient operators. The megaliths literally dotted around Northern Europe or Stonehenge in Wiltshire, and in Brittany, were almost certainly placed in positions enabling calculations of heavenly body movements to be made. A strange proposition is that sophisticated mathematics was needed to site the stones in the first place. Indeed, at later dates the Pyramids in Egypt, Mexico, and South America must have required engineering skills which themselves depended on sophisticated mathematics. The Romans used pebbles or 'calculi' to count and no doubt the Greeks and, slightly earlier, the Phoenicians and Etruscans had similar devices. Little is known of developments in this field until the seventeenth century—it is probable that with literacy and numeracy at a very low level those with the skills were unwilling to let others have a share in them, or much of a knowledge of them.

Napier, a Scotsman, is commonly held to be responsible for the first breakthrough. First he invented logarithms with which generations of schoolchildren have subsequently struggled. He followed this by inventing a series of rods or 'bones' which were used as an aid to ordinary calculations. The bones were originally intended to perform long multiplication but were later adapted to do square roots and division. Both card and mechanical forms of this invention were subsequently made. These techniques were successful to the extent that they were used for at least two centuries after Napier's death. The next step along this route came from the seventeenth century French mathematician, Blaise Pascal, who produced a mechanical adding machine. Numbers were appended to six cogs which appeared at six windows. The user 'flagged' the numbers needing to be added and the machine automatically did this up to (but not including) one million.

In contrast to Napier's method, the machine was a commercial failure. In the light of the current wave of technological changes the probable reasons are interesting. It was expensive relative to the wages (or cost) of a clerk, so the employer had but a marginal incentive to purchase one. The clerks themselves were obviously worried that the machine could put them out of a job so resistance came from both ends of the equation. Some time later an Englishman, Thomas Moreland, developed a pocket-sized edition of the machine which proved to be somewhat more successful commercially.

The next breakthrough was in fact the odd one out, in that it had nothing whatsoever to do with numbers. This was the development of the punched tape and was used by another Frenchman, Jaquard, in a new form of weaving loom. This loom, which was capable of providing very sophisticated patterns and designs received its 'instructions' through cards punched with holes. These holes were the only areas in which a needle could get through and thus the pattern was formed and the colours chosen. It was a novel, not to say brilliant, idea but the use of this technique had to await a singular man of genius. The early nineteenth century saw the entry of this man, Charles Babbage, who is generally acknowledged to be the father of the idea of the computer.

Babbage first invented the 'difference engine' inspired by the idea that astronomical calculations based on the existing tables could be performed automatically. The engine, which was accurate up to twenty places, solved polynomial equations. It was a very complicated machine and took the next decade to develop and build (with the use of government funds), which again is a relevant factor when considering modern computer developments. Having made the machine, Babbage set about building a bigger, newer, and more flexible version, the 'analytical machine'. This differed from the original concept in three significant ways. The first was, that rather than perform just one function it was intended to perform many, the second was that it was to be mechanically driven — by steam — and the third, and probably the most significant, was that the input to the machine was to be on punched cards — Jaquard's invention was about to be put to new uses.

With help from Lord Byron's daughter, on both technical and morale boosting grounds, the engine was developed. Its features were most impressive. It could handle fifty-digit numbers and could add two such numbers in a second and multiply them in around a minute. It is, however, the similarity between the analytical engine and modern computers which is so startling. There was an input device (the punched cards) and a printed form of output. There was in effect a memory or store which contained one thousand tabular lists and the calculations were performed on cogs and wheels. Not only was there a punched card input but it was a dual one. One set of cards told the machines what calculations were required, the others the numbers that were to be operated upon and where the result should be stored. In hindsight it was an overambitious project. The technology of the time could not cope with the precision needed and as a result the engine itself was never fully built. Its value, however, lies firmly in its ideas — Babbage was the Leonardo da Vinci of computers. Strangely enough, a smaller and simplified version of the engine was produced and used to compile actuarial tables, but the machine itself never fulfilled its potential.

Herman Holerith provided the next step and again it was a giant one. He used electromechanical means to power his machine. This all started when the administrators of the 1890 United States Census realized that the collation of the census might well take them into the 1900 survey! They decided on a competition to find the swiftest and most accurate machine to do the job. Holerith used punch cards along with electric power and his machine won the test hands down. When used, it took but six people to determine the size of the United States' population. It is not only for this that Holerith became famous. Being the exception rather than the rule in this catalogue of pioneers, he was an excellent businessman and set up the Tabulating Machine Company, which became International Business Machines (IBM), the largest computer firm in the world.

The twentieth century saw the first possibilities of computers, initially in a theoretical form. Yet another mathematician, Alan Turing, presented a document entitled *On Computable Numbers*. This discussed the development of a general and learning computer. In the 1930s, a German and an American began to build on the conceptual framework and started to develop computers. The German was Zuse, who built a series named somewhat mundanely Z_1, Z_2, Z_3, and Z_4. He was underfinanced and the machines were made in a somewhat Heath Robinson fashion. The Z_1, however, worked in binary, i.e. in numbers reduced to either 0 or 1, and used a keyboard as the input device. The Z_2 used electric relays of the old Strowger telephone exchange equipment type and Zuse replaced the keyboard by 35 mm film punched with holes — a return to the Jaquard principle. The Z_3 and Z_4 computers were developments of these basic themes.

In the United States, Howard Aiken of Harvard synthesized the work of Babbage and electricity and with the lubrication of money from IBM started to develop a computer based on the ill-fated analytical engine. This line of investigation followed closely but was separate from Zuse's work in Germany. In one of life's odder quirks, Aiken was promptly called up by the Navy, which proved a blessing in disguise.

The Navy realized the strategic value of the work and as a result efforts were redoubled as Aiken was seconded to work with this project. It resulted in the Harvard Mark I. By all accounts it was a most impressive machine. Over fifty feet long and eight feet high, built in stainless steel and chrome, and with almost a million components within it, the effect was mind-blowing. However, little is known about its capacity or ability. For IBM, it proved to be a magnificent publicity ploy and identified it with computers.

It is suggested that the world's first electronic computer was Colossus, built in Britain in 1943 in order to decipher German war codes — a system called *Enigma*. Colossus lived up to its name. It had over 2,000 valves and an ability to scan over 5,000 characters per second on paper tape. Several more were built before the War ended but the machines could do only one task: computers they were; programmable they were not.

At the same time, but without contact with each other, a team from the Moore School of Engineering in the United States were also working on an electronic, all-purpose computer based on electronic valves. The computer, named the *Electronic Numerical Integrator And Calculator* (ENIAC), took four years to build from the planning stage and was completed in 1946. It had almost 19,000 valves and because of this became extremely warm; the cost of the electricity supply was outlandish. It differed from modern computers in two major respects. It worked on the normal decimal rather than the binary system and was not really programmable in practice without substantial and time-consuming changes, in this respect differing little from Colossus. It was only at a later date that the idea of the stored programme took root; that is to say, the programme (or instruction to the machine) was stored in the machine itself. This development is widely attributed to Von Neumann, a physicist who saw the potential of computers in helping with the calculations needed to produce nuclear weapons.

A larger memory, a binary operation method, which stored programmes and electronic valves together led to the first commercial computers and moved the science away from individuals in universities. Both Britain and the United States moved into action. In Britain, Ferranti built the world's first commercial computer in 1957, and in 1953 the retail and wholesale food chain, J. Lyons (more famous for its Corner Houses and Nippies), had installed the first computer, named Leo. In America, IBM and Bell Telephone started along the same route but with considerably more financial backing than in Europe. By the early 1950s IBM were marketing a range of machines for commercial rather than military or university use. They were large, expensive, unreliable, and at times appeared to display petulance. There was, however, still one piece of the jigsaw to fall into place and when that happened, computing took off. This was the invention of the transistor in 1956. The development and sale of computers increased dramatically at this point, whilst the integrated circuit has added an extra dimension to this growth.

Both the size and cost of computers have diminished and these rates of change have been accelerating in recent years. Many analogies have been made on this score but probably the most dramatic is that if cars had developed in the same way as computers in terms of price and performance, a Rolls Royce car would cost £1.35 and do over a million miles to the gallon. The other common description is that the power of a thumbnail-sized integrated circuit chip would have required a computer the size of the Albert Hall in the 1960s. Both of these ingenious and attention-grabbing comparisons are broadly true. Over a very short period the development of computers has been nothing less than astonishing—

certainly nothing like it has been seen previously, either in mechanical or biological evolution.

A complex web of events has stimulated this progression. Valves had to be replaced because they were bulky, consumed vast quantities of electric current, generated immense heat, needed specially prepared rooms in which to operate, and were unreliable — they broke down. The transistor changed all of this. At the same time computer production companies were being commissioned by the armed services all round the world for machines which could work on strategy, as well as provide control systems for the ever more powerful weapons. The arms race and cold war released massive amounts of government research and development monies which the computer manufacturers were only too pleased to accept. The growth of large companies and the trend towards more government control over new areas of society gave a civilian and civil market side to the military developments.

The space race rather than arms was responsible for the second wave of change. The Americans decided to put a man on the moon. This meant comparatively light payloads and therefore smaller rockets could be used; it also meant having to miniaturize both equipment and computers. The development of the semi-conductor integrated circuit, generally on a silicon chip, was the key which opened the door to this form of space exploration. Yet again, it was financed by government through its agencies — neither private companies nor entrepreneurs could have provided the necessary finance, nor could they have mobilized all the resources as efficiently. The computers needed to be very sophisticated so as to aid the design of the craft as well as plan the routes, orbits, life support systems, and all the other systems needed for these complex operations. The miniaturization of the electronic working parts of the craft was adapted for more earthbound uses both within computers and also in general integrated circuitry for use in such diverse products as washing machines and telephone switchboards.

The basic formulation of the computer, however, has remained unchanged. From Babbage's hand cranking and then steam, to telephone switch gear, electronic valves, transistors, 'chips', and 'bubbles', only the motive power and its immediate delivery have changed. Certainly speed, size, and overall power have changed, but the basic ideas and formulations have not altered. There is nothing magical about them. In many ways computers are less astonishing than heavier-than-air flying machines or television pictures; they do not challenge physical perceptions of the world around us. They are, however, powerful machines and people realize this fact. Whatever their size, their price, and the sophistication of the equipment, computers have basic elements in common.

Many books, articles, and commentators have compared the computer with the human brain. Whilst fundamental analogies can be made, e.g. the fact that both the machine and the human system work by using electrical impulses and information has to reach both before actions are taken, the overall analogy is quite misleading. The brain not only receives messages from external and internal sources but is also creative in its own right. This is not merely a matter of identifying geniuses like Beethoven, Tiepelo, or Shakespeare. It applies to all people, from craftsmen to housewives. The ingenuity and flexibility of the human brain is exemplified by its ability to react to totally unexpected external events—events which could not possibly have been foreseen, nor, indeed, been programmed into a computer. The analogy also falls foul of the matter of emotions and moods; the brain copes with happiness or sadness and, more pertinently, turns them into appropriate actions—often irrational. Rather as with 'memory', the conjunction of the computer and the brain raises worrying thoughts in people as they consider the less objective and less functional elements of the brain and then read them across to computers. It is unnecessary and, overall, quite damaging for the comparison to be made in sweeping terms, although in individual actions valuable lessons can be drawn—e.g. in chess-playing computers. The confusion arises because of the debate as to whether computers are intelligent or, put another way, whether machines 'think'.

Alan Turing, the person whose paper on computable numbers started the development of the computer on its present course, invented a test to determine whether or not machines think. The idea was that one person was isolated in a room with two computer terminals, one of which was operated by another person and the second by a computer, both in other rooms. Conversation, jokes, and questions were passed to and fro. If there was no difference between the two social intercourses then the computer had passed the thinking test. To date no computer has done so. It is worth noting that this test was devised in the 1940s before the practical, as opposed to the theoretical, basis of these machines had been established. It would be a foolhardy person indeed who would claim that the test would never ever be met. However, human arrogance is such that many people hope that it never will be and, moreover, the state of the art at present is not such that it can be met in the immediate future, although the 'fifth generation' proposals will bring computers closer to doing so. Computers, however, work in essence on a simple basic set of ideas, even if they are conceptually difficult machines.

The electronic computer has three basic elements: a control unit, a logic and arithmetic unit, and the memory. The rest of the computer system resides in outside factors—the so-called peripherals and the software. Because electricity works on a charged or not charged basis, it is logical to put all the information into a computer in a form which can be described as either black/white or yes/no. This is done by converting our normal numbering system into what is known as the *binary system*, where every number can be represented either by 0 or 1. The system of numbers which we normally use is based on the number 10. All that the binary system does is to base the number on 2. It is again a simple concept. Schoolchildren of seven and eight can cope with it quite well. An example is as follows.

Take a number; 845 will do. The system works on powers of ten, viz. a unit is a single number — 5. The 4 is really 4×10; the 8 is really 8 one-hundreds or $8 \times 10 \times 10$. The binary system uses numbers up to 2, i.e. 0 and 1, in the same way that our decimal system uses 0 to 9. Thus the number 3 in binary is 11, and is explained by adding together 1 and 1×2, which equals 3. The number 17 is $2^4 + 1$, so is represented by 10001. Any number can be written, added, subtracted, multiplied, or divided using this system. All information fed into the computer is converted into binary, whether it is a word or a number or letter. When using the computer the person does not need to know the system — it is converted internally. The information we give to a computer is called the 'input' and the information we get out is called the 'output'.

The input unit puts the information into the computer. It can be a punch card system, although this is now being phased out. A standard punched card has eighty columns. The appropriate information can be put onto the card (in code form) and then channelled into the memory of the computer through the input device. The current most popular device is a keyboard with a visual display unit (VDU). The message, or instruction, is 'typed' into the unit and appears on the screen for the person to check or change. As in this instance the VDU also takes the messages from the computer back to the person, the whole unit is both 'input' and 'output'.

There are two other input devices. The most widely used is an 'optical reader'. The most easily noticed manifestation of this is the special numbering on the bottom of bank cheques or the 'bar coding' on items that are bought in shops. Voice input is the other method, although this is still really the stuff of science fiction and likely to be so for some years to come. Some computers and systems can respond to a very limited vocabulary at present and some can respond to a specific person's voice — also with a limited vocabulary. The technical problem to be overcome is that people not only speak in different ways and with different accents but the computer recognition device has difficulty with the ends of words. People tend to swallow the ends of words and that is why a classical Shakespearean actor declaiming a speech sounds so strange and theatrical — the word ends are always pronounced clearly.

Once information is in the machine, something has to be done with it. The computer is controlled by the 'control unit'. This unit takes in the instructions in their proper sequence, interprets them, and then initiates and controls the subsequent actions or operations of the computer. It may be that the information is sent by the controller to the memory of the computer and nothing else, or various calculations or other operators have to be made, or, quite often, both. In either case the memory is called into use. This is because the various instructions as to how the calculations or material are to be performed are stored in the memory unit. The memory stores information in the form of an electrical charge and the cells within it can be either positively or negatively charged; thus the binary system with only two characters — 0 and 1 — is essential. Each charged cell is called a 'bit' in computer jargon;

a very truncated form of Binary digIT. Eight bits equal one 'byte' and this most commonly used item of computer jargon is used as the main measurement of memory capacity. Computer journals are invariably full of new devices offering 20 megabytes, etc., which would mean a memory capable of holding 20,000 bytes or 160,000 bits of memory.

Before the computer can get to work it has to be programmed. Not surprisingly, this is done by programmers. Programmers use computer languages with which they communicate not with each other but with the machine. A program, to be more accurate, is a program of instructions. Without a program it would not be possible to put any information into the computer. Even if there was some form of input program alone the computer is still useless without other programmes to make the computer work. There are many languages. Some are difficult and others relatively easy, or, put into jargon, there are low and high level languages. BASIC is one of the lowest of the levels — others, such as COBOL, are languages in common use in business and large installations, whilst FORTRAN is essentially a mathematical language. These languages were developed to meet the needs of different incompatible computers and also to get some degree of uniformity.

There are approximately 500 languages in existence at present, some of them like ADA (a language being developed in the United States with the Department of Defence's cooperation) being extremely controversial and difficult. To get the program into the computer a machine called a *compiler* is often used. This is a piece of software (i.e. it is not a part of the main machine and it converts the language into a form suitable for the machine in the appropriate code). *Software* is the name given to the programs that can be used with any one computer system. There are literally millions of such programs, most of which are provided by the computer manufacturers themselves. They can be a massive additional expense to computer users depending upon the functions the computer is expected to perform. Each program will enable the computer system to perform a specific task and can be amended or individually written to suit individual requirements. Most often the term software excludes individual programming; however, the growth of 'software houses' selling consultancy services and systems packages is extending the traditional meaning.

Some of the general kind of software programs have to be explained first, as without them the computer cannot work. *Housekeeping packages* control the input and output operations, the transfers, and parity checking amongst a range of functional tasks — there may be so many they have to be kept in a separate library. *Operating systems and programs* are used to control the other programs and are central to the actual working of the machine. There are *processing programs*, *debugging programs*, and *utility programs*, all of which can be used at various times to test or control additional machinery. Once the machine has the programming in place in terms of its operational capacity and also in terms of what it is supposed to do, e.g. control another machine or prepare the wages, an instruction is then fed into the computer. The message first gets onto a 'register' of the control unit which tells it what the first part of the program should be and where it is stored in the memory. An address is located in the memory (this is precisely what it sounds like) and the instruction is then channelled back into another register or the control unit. This continues through the total instruction, which in all probability is activating a program already in place in the machine using the programs in the control unit. These latter programs make sure that the correct circuits in the logic unit and the memory are used, that the calculation (if that is what is to be done) is performed, and that the result is entered into the correct part of the memory. The control unit makes an electronic note of this new memory address and also comes onto the next instruction to be performed.

Having made the computer do something it is now necessary for the results to be made available; this is done using an 'output unit'. Rather like input units, these can be of various types. The most common used to be traditional printers, but new forms are now being used. These can vary from the old-fashioned telex or typewriter methods to the relatively new ultra fast 'daisy wheel' and 'ink jet' varieties. We have already noted the use of VDUs but they can also utilize graphics as well as numbers and words, and so can graph-drawers and electronic oscilliscope devices. The use of graphic representations, in three as well as two dimensions, especially when holographic means are used, is growing in certain disciplines, e.g. engineering or architecture. Smaller computers (especially home computers) use tape as both input and output carriers, but this has limitations. Microfiches using microfilm and card punches are also used. A 'banking' storage system is also necessary from time to time and these systems are often called libraries. They are especially useful where masses of data need to be stored and only a portion is needed at any one time — the police and insurance company installations are typical of this. The data are kept either on tapes or discs.

Discs (generally called 'floppy discs' or 'floppies') are the fastest growing forms of input and output devices. They slot into 'disc handlers', which act in a similar way to gramophone players and can be found attached to most of the newer microcomputers and word processors.

The input and output diaries and storage devices are called

peripheral units or 'peripherals' and are defined as machines operated under computer control but within the computer system itself. All of the items we have discussed in the input/output range are peripherals. A terminal, which may be remote from the computer in the sense that it may be geographically distant (even on another continent) and connected by a two-way telecommunication link, perhaps via satellites, is also a peripheral. Some terminals are known as 'intelligent terminals', which means that they have sufficient power and circuitry to act independently of the main computer, albeit to a limited extent. A computer system is thus made up of the 'hardware' (the apparatus), 'software' (the programming, etc.), and 'peripherals' (the extra machinery needed). In essence, there are two forms of computers: one is known as digital and the other as analogue. The difference is in the manner in which they operate.

Digital computers act on data which are in a number form (hence digits). Analogue computers work by using physical quantities as analogues for the numbers, which only works when all the proportions between the numbers and the physical dimensions are kept constant. An example of this in a non-computer environment is the wristwatch powered by a silicon chip but using a conventional dial and hands, rather than a digital display. Analogues are used in engineering, electrical engineering, etc. They have a special advantage in that they take inputs which vary with time and perform operations on them; the resulting output from the computer can then be used to control a machine or process. In other words, the computer responds to changes so that a study can be made of a process in operation, or a control system can be built up at the same time. The analogue has neither the massive memory nor the extensive numerical abilities of digital machines; its strength lies in its analytical and 'real time' abilities. 'Real time' is the sort of system one sees in airline booking operations, where the booking changes the analysis of the computer by almost simultaneously changing the variables. More and more systems which affect consumers are based on 'real time'applications.

Computers are not only getting smaller, cheaper, and more powerful, they are also communicating with each other or with peripheral terminals more easily and more quickly. The telephone system has been the obvious method of such communications but difficulties have arisen. One such is a combination of the non-availability of lines, especially during the busy day-time periods, and unreliable connections even with lines reserved for computer purposes. Another is that the ordinary telephone system works on an analogue basis whilst computers use digital communications. A converter or MODEM (short for MOdulator/DEModulator) has to be used which turns digital into analogue and then back to digital again. The new electronic telephone systems in Britain known as 'Systems X' solve these two problems at one and the same time. The exchanges with microprocessor-controlled switching will handle calls more accurately and swiftly, whilst the system works digitally all the time so that text, voice, and graphics go down the same lines at the same time. 'Clever' exchanges and switchboards will soon be standard. Satellites add an extra dimension to this communication system. Fast global communications grow as the number of telecomm satellites increase. This joining together of telecommunications and computers (known as convergence) is known in computer jargon as 'information technology', and in the United Kingdom the year 1982 was designated 'IT'82' and several millions of pounds of government monies were poured in to increase the awareness of the population in general. They needed to. A survey found that over 50 per cent. of people did not know what information technology was but over 70 per cent. of the same sample thought it was essential for UK industry!

New advances in computers depend upon the size of integrated circuitry and microprocessors, which in turn make computers available to hitherto unknown and unthought of areas. This stimulates advances in software, which subsequently create new services and new uses, so that the whole area becomes a self-fulfilling prophesy of growth. A quick look at the computer press of any country will make these advances quite clear, both in respect of the new small computers being developed and the new applications for which the software is being designed: programs to write programs, many types of local area networks for linking computers together, new systems to link together incompatible machines, new control devices, new and better storage facilities, new software packages to run large or small companies, new integrated circuits on bubbles and grooves, new semiconductor materials, and, above all, immense cut-throat competition between the manufacturers of the products.

The silicon chip revolution has spawned almost as many books, films, video, and television programmes as it has new products and gadgets, but it is the industry of the chip itself in which we are most interested in this chapter. Silicon Valley, the area of California near Caltech and Stanford University, is now the envy of the world despite the fact that the bubble has burst and companies are contracting and laying off workers. Other Western countries are desperately trying to encourage the development of their own version but to date with only marginal success, although the Thames Valley in the United Kingdom could claim to be host to more small 'high tech' businesses than most other areas. Names that have created their own mythology faster than any others in the history of productive businesses, like Texas Instruments and Motorola, Intel, and Mostek, are bandied around the magical, charmed circles of those who are in the know. Japan appears to be most likely to take over (if any one country does so) from the United States. Its style of business and management, its Confucian style of society, and its combination of available skilled people and at present stable political system, makes it ideal. Taking a lead in the fifth-generation computers is the Japanese aim and one which is not at all out of the question.

The fifth generation of computers is more powerful, smaller, and easier to use than any of the previous generations, but it does require an advance in silicon chip technology so as to mass produce at an extra dimension of power. It will have voice input and output, visual sensors, and in all respects will be the breakthrough to science fiction that has been promised, indeed anticipated, for so long. Furthermore, it attempts to bring the working process of the machine into a form more like the working process of the human brain. The machines will work concurrently rather than consecutively.

Announcements of new startling changes and inventions are made at almost daily intervals. The microwriter is one which attempts to replicate the functions of a typewriter but without a keyboard — intelligent bathroom scales are another! The Josephson junction, which at first sight (and analysis) would revolutionize the working and construction of a computer, needs temperatures of near to absolute zero to function properly. Science fiction continues, as it is now suggested that computers could and should be assembled in space because of the low temperatures out there.

Intelligent or 'clever' machines continue to proliferate. Clever typewriters or word processors with their own computing capacity are combining with clever telephones and switchboards and exchanges. Clever television receivers linking with view-date systems are bringing these technologies into the home. Computers themselves are now within the price range of most people so that home computing is a fast-growing hobby, and advertisements for home computers are now moving away from the 'quality' newspapers and journals onto television, thus reaching a far wider section of people. Price is the key to this spread; few people actually know what to do with the machines when they get them and many never discover their uses — in other words, computers are becoming 'impulse buys', available in cheaper stores and stationery shops. The combination of games with these computers has stimulated software producers to such a degree that millionaires are made after a mere twelve months and are bought out by larger companies within two years.

One of the major problems confronting the computer industry in general and users of computers in particular is that various pieces of a system are only compatible with each other. Other items of equipment, be they hardware, software, or peripherals, cannot be used with those of other manufacturers. This, combined with an overall lack of protocols or common standards, has worked in favour of the large manufacturers and obviously against small firms. Compatibility between two computers is when a program can be run on both, without alteration; incompatibility obviously means that this state of affairs does not exist.

There are two main areas of incompatibility. The first is physical. Computers have plugs and manufacturers have unique plugs. Thus different computers cannot be used together and neither can peripherals. The second area is in coding and languages. The internal codes of a machine will only enable it to work with equipment of the same manufacturer. These codes are changed at regular intervals by some manufacturers and from time to time certain machines become obsolete. Some 'software houses' specialize in writing sophisticated programs in an attempt to transcend this problem and a considerable amount of research is being undertaken, especially within the European Economic Community (EEC), to develop a universal language.

The EEC is a crucial area in the future development of computers. The relevant part of the Commission wishes to develop a community-wide computer industry but attempts to do so have floundered to date. There is a manufacturing capacity in Germany, France, Holland, and the United Kingdom, but these all pale into insignificance when matched with American and, more recently, Japanese output of machines. The EEC have come across the stumbling block of compatibility in this field. Many large users have to use IBM or Burroughs or Univac peripherals and new models of hardware, or completely write off all existing equipment. The way the game is played at present, there is a *de facto* captive market once the initial installation has been purchased: consumers are trapped into product ranges. Amongst other things this runs counter to EEC rules on trade between member states. A similar situation arises with internal German law which refuses to allow beer which does not conform to stringent manufacturing standards, standards which only the Germans can fulfil. This gives the German brewing industry a virtual monopoly over a very large market and the EEC is fighting this. The EEC argument on the computer side is that the practice of securing peripherals and software by mainframe manufacturers is a restraint on competition and trade. This view has resulted in the appropriate division of the Commission attempting to take the world's largest manufacturer in IBM to the European Court on similar and related issues and IBM threatening to take the Commission to court too.

Because manufacturers adopt this commercial ploy there is an argument which suggests that innovations are correspondingly held back. The smaller the firm the more innovative it is, at least that is the general rule of thumb in most sectors of an economy and within the computer industry this is even more the case. The big technical advances based on microelectronics were started and then fuelled by small companies in Silicon Valley. It is highly probable that a large corporation with its own inbuilt checks and balances and with a large bureaucracy could not have stimulated the changes — let alone have followed them through. Because 'incompatibility' strikes hard at smaller companies, it inhibits this innovative tendency, except in the limited area of trying to find ways around the incompatibility.

Mainframe computer manufacturers compete for the large 'plum' contracts. IBM is head and shoulders above other manufacturers in terms of turnover, range, and, some would say, services and back-up. Within all the major industrialized countries they hold a dominant position, even though some, notably France, prefer to order their large installations from their domestic manufacturers. Many countries do have 'favoured sons' companies; e.g. Britain has ICL and Ferranti, Germany has Siemens and Nixdorf, France has CII and Delarue Bull, and Japan has Hitatchi and Mitsubishi. Within the United Kingdom the register of mainframe installations produced by the *1981 Computer Users' Yearbook* lists sixteen different manufacturers. Of these, twelve are foreign owned. The large manufacturers are transnational corporations in the true sense of the word.

IBM, Burroughs, Honeywell, etc., all pride themselves on having plants in many countries and, in theory at least, can often claim to be nationally based companies. When the Falklands conflict was raging between the United Kingdom and Argentina, one British installation in a foreign-owned company needed certain IBM printers but could not get them at first because they were manufactured in the Argentine. The UK customs and excise lists of computer peripherals imported into the United Kingdom show that they come from the oddest places. Oman and Muscat, Niger, Zaire, and El Salvador do not readily spring to mind as computer equipment manufacturers! It could be that some of this equipment is used: it could also be that equipment is shuttled around the world in crates taking advantage of favourable tax and tariff situations. It may also be a method of more conventional 'transfer pricing' which is where a transnational company sells itself items across national frontiers at a price which suits its own global policy, rather than the price at which it would sell them to other manufacturers or consumers.

Despite the fact that new, smaller, and cheaper machines are coming onto the market daily, there is still a burgeoning mainframe industry. Because of this there are charges of skullduggery, especially of industrial espionage. This is clearly most sensitive in the areas of compatible plugs, rather than the newer miracle machines. If, for example, manufacturers could find the new plugs for a new IBM range, they could undercut the IBM peripheral market—let alone the mainframe sales. IBM have a very strict security system and has brought cases against other manufacturers who have lured away their key personnel and offered them large benefits so as to tap IBM's secrets. Whilst these cases have never needed to reach a court, many have been settled to IBM's satisfaction. Indeed, according to the *Wall Street Journal*, senior IBM staff who leave now have to sign forms on which are listed all the technical and marketing information to which they have been exposed and 'positive vetting' *à la government* employees takes place. In the latest of these *causes célèbres* IBM is charging both Hitachi and Mitsubishi with industrial espionage.

The newer generations of computers are built into general office equipment and although the more traditional manufacturers like IBM and Siemens have moved into the field, the smaller companies have carved a niche for themselves. Systems computers controlling telephone systems, text processors, free-standing mini-computers with disc drives, and facsimile transmission machines, all play their part in modern work station development. There is less of a compatibility problem in these instances as each item is so much cheaper than a mainframe computer, and most manufacturers offer complete system ranges. Names like Wang and Texas Instruments, Apple, and Tandy do not figure at all in the more traditional computer areas. It is becoming the exception rather than the rule to walk around an office or a drawing office or factory and not see a visual display terminal anywhere.

Computer design is so complex that those engaged in it have not only to have an excellent knowledge of the technology but also a high degree of flair and imagination. The industry employs a great number of electricians, electrical engineers, and electronic engineers, but it also employs a large unskilled or semi-skilled assembly workforce. This is why LDCs are used so heavily for the assembly of components and subcomponents; little training is needed, the wages (and thus costs) are low, and quite frequently there are no real unions to speak of. It is becoming a highly fragmented industry in the classic Adam Smith sense.

Computers will become smaller and cheaper. They will be built into other machines or buildings and sooner or later (probably later) will be voice controlled and have voice inputting, although voice outputs will be perfected sooner — indeed are readily available today. Machines can now be programmed to play chess and to do algebra, which argues for at least a sense of intelligence, if only dependent intelligence. Machines can learn to avoid repeating mistakes and to rank various pieces of information. As the technology progresses so these functions will increase in number and in depth — vacuum cleaners learning the layout of a room, for example, and robots capable of the more science fiction deeds. Little of this will happen tomorrow or even the day after tomorrow, mainly because there are always considerable lags between an idea or concept and the ability of a manufacturer to make it cheaply and make it reliable. Not only will these things happen but the beauty of the technology lies in its uncertainty and unpredictability. Who knows where computers will lead us, who knows in what unimagined areas they will be used, and who knows who will make and control them?

Chapter 4

Work and Computers

M OST PEOPLE *WORK TO LIVE*, BE THEY SUBSISTENCE farmers or lakeshore fishermen, or people working for a wage, a salary, or themselves to pay the bills for the wherewithal of life for themselves and their families. This is the usual explanation of work and as with so many economic and social truisms is only partly valid.

People also *live to work*. This is a phenomenon known as the work or protestant ethic where work has a value of itself, transcending money or goods. For most people work imparts an identity as well as self-respect, but the strange thing is that despite the fact that people feel they need to work, many do not actually like doing it all that much. It is rather like drinking senna pod tea because we think it has good effects yet few people like its taste.

We all spend a lot of our lifetime actually working. An average man can expect to spend forty-nine years (from the age of 16 to 65) at work. Roughly forty-six weeks are worked each year and on average (including overtime of one type or another) forty hours each week. This adds to more than ninety thousand hours of work in one lifetime. Other than the time we spend sleeping, this is by far the largest slice of our time used in doing one particular thing. Work, or to be precise paid employment, within an industrial society is thus a very important factor in our lives. This importance varies in theory as to whether the work is for survival (crop growing, hunting, igloo building, and so on) or whether it is to buy the second motor launch or a villa in Marbella. Whilst this statement might sound realistic to a person from another planet, it has no real validity. The importance of work nowadays is absolute and universal. For the purpose of this chapter, work will be defined as paid employment, including self-employment, although as most people realize gardening or other hobbies can be described as work, and quite hard work too at times.

One cannot describe the impact of computers at the workplace or on work in general without describing work and work systems. In most countries fewer people work than those who do not. Pre-school children, those in full-time education, the chronically disabled, the retired, and married women who choose not to enter paid employment (and who do not register as unemployed either) give a ratio of 23 to 33 in favour of non-workers in the United Kingdom. By definition the retired have at one time or another worked. By tradition those in full-time education expect to work some time in the future.

Work systems vary enormously. For most people they impart a discipline inasmuch as there are fixed working times, a routine for getting up from bed and getting to work at a specified time, doing a routine job and then leaving work at a specified time — predictable and for many people boring and decidedly unfulfilling. Most people hate having to cope with getting to and from work in rush-hour periods, yet, because flexible working practices are still in their infancy, such inconveniences have to be tolerated.

Those who dignify the sweat and nobility of labour are generally academics whose notion of sweat is a work-out in a squash club and of nobility, a browse through *Burke's Peerage*. It is very difficult to see any dignity in shovelling smelly chemicals, working in hospital laundries, or perhaps repetitively tightening four bolts on the same subcomponent on an assembly line. Some people may prefer to have jobs that are not mentally demanding but there are many who would prefer to be more stretched than their jobs permit at present. We have managed to split most jobs into their basic component parts, and they do not allow many of the responsibilities that individuals might wish to have, or indeed used to have. This process, initially noted by Adam Smith in his analysis of pin manufacturing, proceeded inexorably, if slowly, throughout the nineteenth century in almost all of the industries of that time. It has since accelerated.

Taylorism, or the science of mass production, first widely used by the Ford Car Company, brought the use of repetitive action into the manufacturing process in a standardized way. Efficiency from the point of view of the producer was enhanced considerably while the price of the product from the point of view of the consumer was reduced considerably. Those suffering were the people who had to work on the new production lines. The car suddenly became a mass good rather than a luxury item. In turn this gave rise to the gasoline and oil production industries and markets and filling stations, road building and repairing, vehicle repair shops, an extension of the insurance business — indeed, the car, or to be precise the mass production of the car, stimulated millions of jobs. By and large this fulfills the tenets of classical economic theory. Many of the technical changes of the nineteenth and twentieth centuries had similar effects. The development of electricity followed by radio, television, and other consumer durable goods has again created millions of jobs around the world. The same is true of petrochemicals, pharmaceuticals, the aerospace industries, and the extension of financial services to more and more people.

Many of the newer industries and processes have not been appropriate for the application of Taylorism. Some of the jobs, indeed, were few and far between as the processes, especially those in industries such as petrochemicals, were most capital intensive. Continuous processes such as these, the new fibre industries, and the batch processes like steel and aluminium production all became more productive and efficient. Job opportunities started to decline in the manufacturing industries in the United Kingdom from the early 1960s onwards. Unlike many other industrialized countries the United Kingdom employs relatively few people in either the agriculture or mineral extraction industries and the numbers of people so employed have fallen substantially since the 1950s. Eltis and Bacon, two Oxford economists, pointed out that over this period employment had been maintained by increased opportunities in the service area. Being political, the Eltis and Bacon thesis was really aimed at what they considered to be excessive job creation in the public sector service area. If this is being uncharitable to those researchers, it was certainly picked up by Right Wing politicians to prove this self same thing. The substantive results, however, stand by themselves — there has been a dramatic shift in employment patterns in the United Kingdom over the past two decades but within the context of an increased labour force overall.

There are two major points which emerge from this analysis of post-war policy. The first concerns the nature of the work itself. Jobs of all descriptions were created — unskilled, skilled, and professional, and all the subtle shadings in between. Direct production jobs, office jobs, backroom jobs, scientific and technical jobs, drawing office jobs, servicing and sales jobs — it was a jobs bonanza. Universities expanded after the Robbins Report; the Beveridge concept of the Welfare State was put into operation and the new polytechnics, technical colleges, and the National Health Service all combined to create a myriad of new job opportunities. Throughout Western Europe the Marshall Plan gave the opportunity for increased investment, increased consumption, and increased job creation simultaneously. The Cold War and the arms race provided yet another economic stimulus. With these new jobs went new differentials and new promotion patterns, new job evaluations, large industrial relations and personnel departments, demarcation areas, grey areas; a complete new industry —

industrial relations — came into being. Few people actually enjoyed doing all these jobs but they were done nevertheless. When throughout the 1970s and 1980s the law became more entrenched in work matters, the industrial relations industry grew even faster and larger. Job protection, through the industrial tribunal unfair dismissal procedures, maternity leave provisions, health and safety provisions, new laws on closed shops, recognition, and discrimination (sexual and racial), have all changed the environment surrounding us at work fundamentally and swiftly. There are now bureaucracies supervising bureaucrats and as a result changes are harder to make and shocks created by changes themselves create even larger waves.

The second of the points is that many of the new jobs are more easily replaceable by computers or systems than the older craft or 'whole jobs'. In theory computers can be programmed to do any repetitive physical or mental function; indeed they can be programmed to replicate literally thousands of such tasks performed by any one person or by groups of people. The theory, however, has to be sublimated to the realities of both technology and finance. It clearly only pays a potential user of a new system to use that system if its cost is such that it is less than the cost of the people it replaces, within some specified accounting period. Equally, the new system must be able to do what is required of it. Thus capital or leasing costs and electricity costs all have to be balanced against the salaries and overall cost of keeping the existing staff levels. From the point of view of the manufacturer of these systems enough of their products have to be demanded for economies of scale to reduce the price at which they are available. The whole process of 'take-off' thus needs several people ordering equipment almost simultaneously — rather like the mid-1960s and mainframe computers.

As most people do relatively repetitive jobs it follows that new computer systems will put the jobs of most people at risk sooner or later. Whether this repetition is manual, as in painting or welding where a robot could do the work, or whether it is administrative or clerical, where an electronic filing and retrieval system replaces the people, is of little relevance — both types of job will ultimately disappear. The relative cost of the new hardware and systems compared with the cost of labour will basically determine when and where the replacement will come about. This leads to one odd conclusion which is at odds with the present received wisdom, or perhaps ambition.

It is quite clear that the lower paid the jobs the less financial incentive there is for an employer to replace the people doing them with a computerized system. As the majority of people who do low paid jobs tend to be doing the boring, repetitive, dirty, and unpleasant jobs the notion put about by various computer devotees that the new systems will release people from these unpleasant jobs is just not true. At least it is not true to the extent that these will almost certainly be the last of the jobs to be replaced. As most of these jobs are manual jobs robots would be the replacement tool, and these tend to be expensive. Far from there being an altruistic reason for this job replacement it is certain that there will be a set of purely commercial decisions and these will not take the quality of jobs or their dangers into account in any way whatsoever. The new systems will be used to replace the existing highest cost systems or perhaps the least efficient of existing systems, or both. Certainly matters such as quality control, consumer satisfaction, and accuracy will play as great a part in system design and implementation as will mere costs.

In total, then, many of us are doing jobs which are at risk of being replaced by some form of computer system because so many of us do repetitive jobs and, moreover, jobs which have been split into ever smaller specializations. As computers and robots can work 24 hour days, tend not to have hangovers, and have an almost 100 per cent. record of reaching the desired quality there can be no doubt as to where the trend will finally take us.

There is also another category of people whose jobs will be threatened by new computer-based systems. These are people who take decisions but whose decisions are always based on known factors or parameters. An example of this is in chess playing. A computer can beat all but the very best of chess players; decisions have to be made by the computer but within a finite set of options. If, however, the chessboard is upset and the pieces placed on different squares and no-one tells the computer, then the computer will lose. An external factor has crept in. The same sort of criteria applies to people in jobs. Many administrators and middle managers take decisions, but only those on the information they have been given. Computers themselves, as we shall see later in this chapter, are responsible for much of the information rationing which constrains managerial decision making. If externalities do not creep in then sooner or later it will be easier, more practical, and cheaper to have computer systems taking decisions. In managerial terms, only those senior people who have to take account of externalities, possible oil price rises, wars, earthquakes, droughts, and so on, will be proof against replacement.

This will also apply to people having to use imagination or creativity in their jobs. Artists, writers, musicians, chartered accountants (who practice a branch of creative writing), and doctors (who use psychology as much as drugs or surgery) are all the sort of people who will be immune from systems replacement. They will all use computers as adjuncts to their work, although the work of their ancilliaries and assistants will alter markedly. Even those working with computers will not be totally safe from replacement. The new generations of computers need fewer, even no operators, and whilst programmers and analysts will be needed for some time to come, programs to write programs are now being developed and analytical computers cannot be that far removed in time.

The early wave of computerization created far more jobs than it destroyed. This is most unlikely to be true of any of the new computers or the new systems and technologies stemming from them. The reasons for this are severalfold. Firstly, the newer computers need fewer people both directly and indirectly to work with them. Secondly, the technologies come into use all over the economy at roughly the same time. Libraries, factories, town halls, and local supermarkets all use the same basic technology but different software. The result is that few if any traditional sectors of the economy will need to increase their demand for labour. The technology itself will be used basically on the supply side to increase efficiency and productivity. Its use as a stimulus to demand like the motor car or the artificial fibre industry is very limited. This is because, to get an aggregate addition to demand and thus employment, new products for new markets are needed, *not* new products for old markets or amended products. For the volume of work available these distinctions are far from academic—they are crucial. As this computer technology is in essence concerned less with products and more with increasing the efficiency with which they are made and distributed, the distinction takes on a vital importance.

New products or services for new markets obviously add to aggregate demand and thus most often to total employment. The mass-produced motor car, television set, or videorecorder production all come into these categories. There are some job losses, even in such cases. Coach and wagon wheel makers, for example, died out with the advent of the car while cinema and music hall employees were made redundant by videorecorders. Nevertheless, the production of the new systems themselves — computer games, the cabling of houses, the setting up and maintenance of data bases — are new things for new markets. A new good or service for an old market tends not to do so well in employment terms. An example is the digital watch, a totally new and cheap product. More people could afford to buy these watches so more were made and sold. Yet the total number of people, including those packing and transporting the watches, is now less than the number which used to make traditional watches. The difference is that the old watch needed one thousand different operations. The new ones have but five basic components to assemble. Finally, there are the amended goods or services and these will certainly be the most common manifestations of the new computer systems. They will range from the addition of controls for cruising at constant speed in cars to better timers and cycle control systems on washing machines and cookers. In between will be the new telecommunications equipment, which to the ordinary user will appear to be an amended product, and a host of automatic magic eye or sensor devices, attached to existing products. Few, if any, of these changes will stimulate the buying of a new product before the old one would normally need replacing, e.g. changing the car every two or three years. Only the few people chasing positional goods will trade in an article early to get an amended version. The new product for the new market will be the only provider of new jobs over a considerable period if free markets are left to their own devices and no planning or government funded jobs takes place at all. It is quite clear that any government could, if it wished, create jobs. These might be, however, at the expense of increases in efficiency from computer implementation. Planning to preserve jobs is possible although there may be hidden costs.

The quantity of work that may be available is only one aspect of the problem, albeit a very high profile one at present. Computers and computer systems also affect the type of work available, how the work is done, what training is needed, which skills are needed, and which disappear. In an industrialized world committed to a strong work ethic, unemployment is one of the greatest fears. The fact that most computer systems will provide an increased amount of goods and services but will use fewer people in the process is now quite widely accepted even by those who originally pooh-poohed the idea. However, this does not necessarily mean there will always be high unemployment. Shorter and different working lifetimes, community-based enterprises, and a reevaluation of the work ethic, combined with financial security, could solve most of the problems alongside an expansion in the caring and person-to-person sector. Even so, a considerable time-lag will be present between the loss and creation of jobs — say twenty years.

To say that all this represents a series of important and fundamental political commitments is very much an under-statement. Yet the scale of the potential problem requires such a series of political approaches. There are few more extreme sets of political differences in industrialized countries separating the political parties on the left and right than those which concern the distribution of income and wealth. Yet the optimum take-up and use of computer-based technologies could exacerbate existing income and wealth maldistribution and thus widen political differences. This divisiveness will be discussed in Chapter 14. Overall, however, it is possible to minimize some of the worst aspects that computer technology can visit upon an indstrialized country in terms of available employment. Of these the possibility of a large minority of permanently unemployed people, most of whom will be socially and educationally underprivileged, is the most disturbing and potentially destabilizing aspect.

As more computerized systems are introduced, so the working day, week, month, year, indeed, lifetime, will shorten. There is an impetus on this matter on a pan-European basis even now, without the stimulus of new technologies to prod it along. Working days are becoming flexible and the new computer systems are making new forms of flexitime practicable. Some company employees work a four day week rather than five days, and in Germany there is an experimental flexiyear working system running at two computer companies. The employees are given a task schedule for the approaching year and they can complete it when they feel they would like to. If they have families they may take the entire summer off as a holiday or if they are keen on skiing they may take the winter. Retirement is occurring at earlier and earlier ages. For example, Shell retire their senior employees at the age of 55 and in parts of Europe people doing strenuous or dangerous jobs like underground mining or deep-sea trawling retire after 30 years of service, no matter what their age. This sort of approach is also taken by the armed forces and the police in many countries. A combination of job-sharing, of semi-retirement, and of quasi-work will all have a part to play by the end of the century in coping with the lack of available jobs.

The assumption so far is that all the technologies will be used to increase efficiency and productivity but without any compensating expenditure. In theory, but regrettably only too rarely in practice, it is possible to use the resources released by the new systems, generally people, to increase services to the public or to other companies or bodies. This was certainly done in Japan where new television sets required less servicing and fewer people to manufacture the sets themselves. The solution was to retrain redundant manufacturing workers to become service engineers and provide an almost instant 24 hour repair service to consumers. This happens to be an on-cost to the company and thus is not something that Western accountancy-hagged companies would countenance doing easily. In turn this means that those who espouse the use of new computer systems on the grounds that clients will get a wider range of services are almost certainly wrong in Western societies—especially in the United Kingdom. The United Kingdom is not a service-oriented society. One only has to look at the standard of cleanliness in 'fast food' shops and compare them with their US counterparts to realize that British people are not complainers. Who asks for their windscreens to be cleaned in UK petrol stations or objects to queueing for all sorts of things which neither Northern Americans nor other European people would countenance for one moment? Without a revolution in attitudes, it is unlikely that jobs will be created in the private side of the service sector within the United Kingdom. Entertainment, especially in part and television may prove to be the exception.

Health care, education, social care, and aiding the mentally and physically handicapped are quite different matters. These are jobs requiring person-to-person contact as well as *care* in the broadest sense of the word. Literally the whole of any country's GDP (gross domestic product) could be spent on either health or education. In the real world far more money could and should be diverted to these two mainstream and fundamental disciplines, both of which impart human dignity. To do so, however, would require a basic rethink of public expenditure and taxation; indeed, it would require a decision on what to do with the fruits of this new computer revolution and again this is a subject broached in Chapter 14.

It is unlikely in the extreme that there will be enough jobs to go round with the same definition of work and jobs as we use at present and without a change in attitudes to the Third World countries, at least for the rest of this century. There will be jobs — it will not be a jobless society even though the Japanese have just developed the personless factory. Some commentators believe that all of mankinds needs and demands will be fulfilled by using only 10 per cent. of the population. We are more likely to need 60 per cent. of any one industrial population to meet the needs of the society in which they live. Many jobs will always need to be done by people, although there will be a different range available compared with today.

Our grandfathers believed that one trade, profession, or skill would last them a lifetime. Our parents found this was not quite as cut and dried as it had seemed. Skills like bricklaying were suddenly less in demand as pre-site construction techniques developed, and even the skills of carpenters, woodworkers, and other craftsmen started to be less highly prized. Nowadays highly skilled engineers are being replaced by not just numerically controlled machine tools (NCMs) but also by extremely sophisticated computer controlled and linked machine tools. One highly expensive machine at an aeroengine factory can perform eighteen different skilled functions and reduces machining times from over two weeks to thirty hours. The generality of skilled and semi-skilled jobs will be reduced in number, too. Many of these are found in factories, plants, and offices and are the most easily replaceable by electronic systems. Whereas our forefathers believed that the one skill or trade was sufficient for the security of their children, it is now widely accepted that people will have to train and retrain several times in a lifetime, often in totally different disciplines. Nowadays doctors, dentists, computer scientists, indeed, industrial relations specialists, have to go to regular refresher courses merely to keep up with the current state of the art. What will now be happening is that many 'arts' will have even shorter lifetimes—rather like a mayfly today compared with great-grandfather's giant tortoise. People will need to be far more flexible.

Unskilled jobs like street cleaning and cleaning of almost all types, unskilled office jobs of a 'pop round and chat' variety, and jobs like supermarket shelf stackers, hairdressers, night-club bouncers, barmen, waiters, and waitresses will all be with us, although it is possible to envisage total self-service food establishments. The creative, imaginative, and artistic jobs will remain, too, as will the high level decision-making jobs. Jobs within and around computer systems should increase overall, both in terms of manufacturing the products and in the preparation of the software, and in designing the new systems and servicing the new systems and data bases. Traditional skills will be replaced by new skills but often with fewer people involved overall.

By and large the new jobs are likely to be of three distinct types by the end of the century. The first is the knowledge-intensive job built around the professions and computers themselves, the second the unskilled job, and the third the creative and seasonal jobs. The central and conservative pillar of industrial life over the last century, the skilled artisan, is likelier than most to be the *dodo* of the twenty-first century. It is a worrying prospect that the training and educational facilities needed to cope with such changes amongst those who have always been described as 'the salt of the earth' are just not available, nor are they really being thought about in sufficient detail. In short, there is likely to be a polarization of job opportunities and, moreover, one loosely based on social class but with one significant difference from the normal class analysis. The new working class, the bank and insurance clerks, local government clerical staffs, and civil servant executive grades, none of whom tend to think of themselves as working class, will be greatly affected by the new system introductions.

Computers are said by different people to either enhance the skills of people or de-skill jobs. Overall it would seem on present evidence that more jobs are de-skilled than enhanced and this is probably because the use of the new computer systems has been designed to increase productivity and this is often at the expense of job content. Many trade union movements, notably the Swedish L.O have de-skilling as their major preoccupation. Typing can be very soul-destroying but so can operating a text processor; what matters is the degree of flexibility, responsibility, and type of job that has to be done. In short, skilling and de-skilling need not be a matter of the technology alone; the organization of work is at least as important. Certainly many skilled engineering jobs have been de-skilled as qualified people become mere machine minders, and this has applied in industries as diverse as cabinet and furniture making and steel manufacture.

The impact of computers has also affected the traditional apprenticeship system. It once took seven years to train a craft engineer and five to train a craft furnituremaker or bootmaker. Training now lasts only two years and, in truth, many young people can be taught to use the new cutting, shearing, and other machinery, mainly computer and laser controlled, in a year and sometimes less. In turn this has an impact on the wages of young people as they get paid an adult rate as soon as they do adult work. In Germany and France, where apprenticeship schemes include life sciences and wider vocational matters, this is not a problem. However, in the United Kingdom with its narrow definition of indentured training it is proving to be an industrial relations problem. Yet again it is the use to which computer systems are put and the job training designs around them rather than the system itself which determines the outcome.

One group within the United Kingdom, CAITS (the Centre for Alternative Industrial and Technological Systems), is committed to using new robotic/mechanical/computer systems to create new skills for working people, and groups both in Germany and the United States are following suit. For this approach to succeed requires that the new systems are not used solely for increased productivity and in turn this presupposes a society dedicated to a combination of socially useful products and a less strong profit or efficiency motive. This may not be a lost cause. The mass-production moving-track principle has been abandoned at Volvo in Sweden without significant profit losses although, regrettably, also with less favourable worker responses than anticipated. At the same time, however, a manual spot welding line was replaced by a robot line which reduced the number of welders from one hundred to twenty.

Another major factor when discussing job skills, is the 'macho' syndrome. Research in Germany was conducted into changes in the print industry, with especial reference to skill rather than job loss. With the exception of the employers all agreed that there was too much job loss. In truth, the researchers had the preconceived idea that they would find a high level of de-skilling among the remaining jobs. In practice they found that every single operative (and they were all men) believed that their jobs had been downgraded and that they were now using fewer skills to do the jobs with the new computer-controlled setting equipment and presses. The researchers, however, thought that if anything the workers needed greater skills: that more skills were required to use computer terminal inputs as well as their trade skill knowledge of pigment thickness, colour tint, etc. What the men were actually objecting to was that their new skills were used in jobs they considered either effete or women's work (keyboarding, for example), whilst their old skills had involved lifting heavy weights or moving hot lead (male skills). Skills often are what people perceive them to be and not things that can be assessed objectively, especially when the ego is involved.

Work systems obviously change when computers are used to break down and analyse the various functions undertaken by departments or individuals, unless of course by some happy chance the optimum system was already being used. Even the computers themselves are likely to be able to improve upon their own previous productivity records. One major group of people whose jobs have changed and will change are those of management of all descriptions. Foremen and supervisors, the first-line management, are changing. Historically their job has been worker management and they have needed interpersonal skills which were developed on the shopfloor from which they were recruited. The new systems will mean that foremen will need to know more about technique management and are more likely to be technicans or trainee graduate managers. The one escape from the shopfloor for most manual workers, the promotion to foreman, is becoming and will soon be a thing of the past.

Britain has a set of very amateur middle and senior managers in contrast with those operating in other European countries, Japan, or the United States, who are professional both in training and outlook. The amateur mentality has filtered down through the university, especially Oxbridge, system and the coverted all-rounder syndrome of the UK civil service. It has meant that qualities such as the ability to sift through masses of extraneous knowledge and information has been important, as has an all-round knowledge of the business or enterprise in general. Computers, however, can split information into appropriate parcels so that in any large corporation a manager now only receives the information pertinent to the department he (rarely she) is in charge of, and the departments with whom the manager will have to deal.

There is thus a strict form of information rationing which actually makes management a less adventurous and entrepreneurial occupation. It also turns management into a form of Taylor-type production line, whose repetitive decisions are taken based on information supplied from the centre. It is interesting yet again to note that the new generation of computers would allow managers to build up their own information centres, but it appears that those already at the centre are unwilling to let this power go easily. Within the United Kingdom this constraint upon managerial power increasingly means that the better qualified people take a more jaundiced view of business management than ever and that as a desirable career it comes very low down on the list — a position which is dropping steadily. This in turn has repercussions on industrial relations in general. As managers themselves receive little information so the amount that they do get is guarded jealously and unions in Britain get less information about the running and the future of the enterprise in which they work than any other union movement in Europe. UK managers use the phrase 'managerial prerogative', behind which they hide their anonymity and inferiority complexes. In turn this leads to a gratuitous strain on management/union relations; overall performance is affected and managers become even more defensive.

There is one final interesting thought about the new

information and communication systems and British managers and that is the use of the keyboard attached to a text processor or work station. British men, unlike many in other industrialized countries, are not taught to type or use keyboards at school — it is thought that such activity is for girls, not boys. The exception of course is when the keyboard is attached to a mainframe computer, when the persona of power 'Captain Nemo' at the keyboard of his organ takes over. Whilst in the long run this is a deficiency that will disappear, in the shorter run it will mean that some male managers will not be able to use the new systems and as a result the systems will be designed to bypass them. The managers, not their secretaries, will be redundant and the secretaries likely to take over some of the managerial functions — my prediction would be at low rates of remuneration.

The computer will have almost universal work effects on an industrialized society. Some services, notably personal services, which at present are somewhat less than legal, will probably be immune — little else will be. In manufacturing industry robots, computerized machine tools, computer control and flow systems, and computer materials handling systems will not only mean fewer jobs but will also mean that control and variations will pass from individuals to a system. The mere fact that integrated circuit components will replace conventional electro- and thermomechanical components will result in job loss amongst those who make the components, subassemblies, and assemblies. As the components overall will be smaller and lighter and have fewer subcomponents in them they will need less invoicing, billing, warehousing, and transporting and as the production process becomes truncated so the need for foremen and managers will be reduced. An example of the sheer scale of this is seen in the sewing machine where one microprocessor has replaced 350 moving parts.

Computer-aided design and manufacture, known as CAD.CAM, is changing the jobs of draughtsmen and engineers out of all recognition. One problem that has been revealed is that there are too few engineers who know about computers and vice versa in the United Kingdom although in France there is an almost embarrassing surplus of such people. Even in Japan, the innovations in engineering are outpacing the abilities of their design staffs. Silly situations then arise when professional engineers feed information into a computer terminal in order to act upon a three-dimensional representation of, let us say, a jet rotor blade; breaking points, etc., can thus quickly be established. However, the engineer cannot change the computer programme and is in fact trapped by it, so that new ideas or concepts cannot be tested. Until engineers, analysts, and programmers are able to communicate with each other these difficulties will remain and not only will engineers become bored and leave their jobs but in the interest of efficiency new ideas may well be lost, or new hazards remain undetected. Boredom is no longer the prerogative of the unskilled production line worker; the middle classes are catching up too.

In offices work is more likely to change more radically, although perhaps not quite as quickly as in almost any other area. Certainly warehousing transport management and retail work are all changing, too, but offices, including the offices of these other areas, are ripe for change. Other than computers the only major new addition to basic office equipment over the last twenty years has been the photocopier. The computer is only now starting to become part of general office furniture rather than a backroom tool. The word or text processor is the most high profile of all the current new pieces of technology but it is most often being used as a typewriter substitute. They are merely typewriters with editing and memory functions and a screen. By themselves they change offices marginally. There may be fewer keyboard operators needed because a given amount of correspondence, contracts, or other typing can be done more quickly. If there are many repetitive standard phrases that can be called from the memory this adds to the advantages of instantaneous correction and the efficiency increases again. There will also be a change of relationship between the keyboard operator and the originator of the correspondence and at times this will by-pass the traditional secretary if the typing is done in a typing pool. The office manager will become the key person in this respect, both allocating the work and keeping the peace.

The future lies in a far less paper-filled office. It lies in intercommunicating word processors where messages are tagged for other processors, screens, or printers, for storage and then recall for storage in mainframe or minicomputers, and all can be controlled by systems computers. Once the telephone system becomes electronic on a universal basis this will virtually mean that the telephone and text processor becomes the same machine in the same workstation and paper is used for formal and legal purposes only. The electronic office obviously has work effects but, less obviously, the major ones are not those that most feminists believe. Keyboarding skills and typing skills will still be in demand. Jobs at risk will be telephone operators, filing and postroom clerks, and general clerical and administrative staffs. There will be new and different jobs. Work teams will be built around workstations but not attached to any one station and will be linked by systems managers who will also have personnel functions. Overall, however, there will be far fewer office jobs. The Nora/Minc Report in France and one in Germany by Siemens independantly estimated 30 to 40 per cent. fewer office staff would be needed by 1985. The majority of these will be women because society has arranged that women do most of the clerical jobs. The new computer systems will also make it more practicable for people, especially women, to work part-time or to job-share. It is also possible, indeed probable, that clerical work will be performed increasingly from home. *Citibank* in New York and Rank Zerox in Britain are both using this system and a halfway house of local or suburban 'office shops' are also possibilities. In the United States stockbrokers are now working from home and dealing from home using terminals plugged into the Wall Street data base systems. Once the electronic telephone system is in operation both of these options become easy and cheap. Both are possible at present either by purchasing an intracompany electronic telecommunications system or by using the existing telephone cable system. In the United Kingdom the whole process is likely to be advanced rapidly by the interactive cabling of all urban housing — an experiment that is at present being partially performed in Le Touquet in France.

Offices are the main breeding grounds, although not exclusive ones, of hierarchies and promotion patterns. They take on an extreme importance, often out of all relation to the running of the establishment, although obviously quite in proportion to the aspirations of individuals. Computers have in the past disturbed, and no doubt will continue to disturb, what have been traditional pyramidal patterns. A new system means new skills and abilities suddenly becoming more important to the employers than the older, more traditional ones. More often than not, newer, younger, brasher people use the new skills and systems, and the older, more experienced people get shunted onto one side. This is partly because there is a retraining problem amongst older employees and partly because as new skills are needed quickly, they are recruited from outside the organization. This leads to great resentment amongst career staffs of, let us say, the age of 40 and upwards. They had always believed that if they did their job adequately, kept their noses clean, then there would always be a level to which they could legitimately and confidently aspire. Once these beliefs have been shattered the traditional deferential loyalties amongst such staffs break down. This was clearly shown in the banks, insurance companies, and local central government when mainframe computers were introduced and the frustrated career staffs led the march into the relevant trades unions.

As promotion patterns change and relationships between managers, secretaries, and typists change and blur, so the hierachies within large establishments change. Part of this change is financial. The differentials between different jobs obviously move as new jobs interpose themselves between older ones and more totally new jobs appear on the horizon. In turn this means that job evaluation systems, so beloved of various consultancy firms, have to change too. If there is a continual introduction of new technologies and consequent changes in the responsibilities of various job grades, so the scheme will have to be in a state of continual evolution and flux. The jealousies that can be generated by a combination of thwarted promotion (felt to be unjust) and a loss of dignity in hierarchical and financial terms can only be described as industrial Othelloism and the result regrettably is the same in industrial if, fortunately, not in physical terms.

When mainframe computers were first introduced there was a certain degree of hostility between data processing staffs and the regular career employees. Much of this was created by the tensions just referred to between those thwarted in mid-career and those they felt responsible for their misfortune. In reality it was senior management with whom they should have been angry. The tensions were compounded by an almost complete lack of knowledge of each other's jobs and responsibilities, compounded by the use of computer jargon by the data processing staffs and the normal in-house work jargon of the career staffs. The final straw was that there were totally different payment systems. Traditional staffs had their normal job-evaluated payment systems but the shortage of skilled data processing staff and what was felt to be an inability to place computer skills within normal job-evaluated systems ended up with computer staffs getting paid more than the other staffs felt they should be paid. The fact that computer staffs tended to be mobile between companies and industries whilst the career staff tended to be centred on a single company, let alone industry, was another distinguishing feature.

This has now changed somewhat. Not only have computer staffs fallen behind recently in matters such as increases in remuneration and conditions of service but there is now more of a realization of each other's problems — a recognition that has taken some ten years to build up. Another factor of course is that computers are becoming widespread, as are computer terminals and all forms of visual display units. This presents difficulties in defining a computer professional in large organizations such as the civil service. As more people see and hear of computers, so the hostility between the two sets of employees has tended to diminish. Large computer departments are now often geographically separate from other parts of the organization, banking and the civil service being cases in point, and, as the adage goes, 'distance lends enchantment'. It is thus a problem likely to diminish over time.

Many things happen at the workplace. People work, although to read some of the more disreputable British newspapers this is a minority habit; people socialize, eat in canteens and restaurants, feel ill in rest rooms, and have affairs (hetero- and homosexual). The workplace is important and computer systems help to make it more pleasant for all concerned. In simple terms things like drink and food delivery machines, computer-controlled air-conditioning, heating, and lifting systems can be installed and controlled. It can also play a large part in health and safety procedures and tests.

Computers and microelectronics have revolutionized sensory equipment in that small particles or amounts of gas can be detected more easily and accurately than ever before. Whilst in theory this should improve human well-being, it is another matter to get employers to spend money to install such equipment, despite the fact that it could be a technology which saves lives and reduces industrial injuries. The sensory guard equipment that can now be used on machinery of all descriptions can be automatic and computerized. There could even be mechanisms devised so that machinery and chemical mixes are varied and changed in order to minimize any potential health hazards. Monitoring of personnel as well as the physical environment is also something which computer systems can perform extremely efficiently, and indeed regular screening and body scanning is now a distinct possibility.

A new branch of industrial study has emerged, *ergonomics*, surely one of the ugliest words in current usage; yet despite its lack of elegance ergonomics is an important matter. Most of the newer computer systems rely upon pieces of equipment placed in traditional office environments, with ordinary lighting, lack of space, uncomfortable seating, and desks. Many visual display units, however, need a special environment, in that conventional lighting reflects off the screens or the desks are at an angle which makes viewing the screen painful, especially for the neck and back. The type of screen, its colour and the colour of its type, its flicker and intensity, are all part and parcel of this problem. There are many combinations of colour, intensity, and screen type which have been recommended by various organizations, manufacturers, users, and unions. What is certainly the most important thing to do is to have the staff who will use the new equipment, help buy the equipment, and, if and when appropriate, design the entire system too. These actions are being taken within the more enlightened companies and perhaps companies where trades unionism is strongest, and in all areas where it has been tried the 'run-in' period has been smooth, even if not totally trouble-free. This is more than one can claim for some of the systems that have been imposed on staff, some of which are not in use at all — the equipment is still in its original packing cases in the basement! Office design built around the new modes of work and the new equipment will change the features of offices as radically as the Victorian clerks' office changed from the quill pen, high desk, and stool to the modern open plan office. There will be concerted efforts by unions and staff associations to avoid any potential health and safety hazards that may be inherent in the new computer technologies such as eye, radiation, and postural problems.

Computers generally need standardized information. Within an organization dealing with a lot of such data is yet another bonus, but organizations dealing with a significant number of exceptions to the general rule can find such generalized information counterproductive. This is truer in personnel relations and personnel departments than elsewhere. Certainly the ability to put employees on a computer roll and have programmes classifying them in various ways is obviously useful to an employer when used ethically or even unethically. Personnel departments have to deal with the individual problems of their employees, often at times of stress, and the computer readout on those persons may be a shade worse than useless in such circumstances. The tendency to treat computer readouts as some form of *eleventh tablet* falls foul of the simple fact that human beings can change their minds, be irrational, and often do not provide the information with which the computer should have been fed initially.

Standardization of information and techniques gives employers one considerable advantage and that is the ability to monitor and control the amount of work done in any one day. A text processor or a laser beam material-cutting machine not only measures the work successfully performed but also logs the amount of time and effort the operator is expending on the employer's behalf. To the machine a visit to the toilet is exactly the same as time spent necking behind a filing cabinet — the jargon calls it *machine down-time*. Robots used alternatively to humans on a production line are designed to have similar pacing and checking effects. Most workers resent this intrusion into their worklives and agreements are being made all over the industrialized world to stop the use of those controlling and checking mechanisms. Such action does not always work, as the introduction of the tachograph into UK lorries and trucks has shown only too well. Today, computer technology is also playing a considerable part in recruitment policies in two distinct ways. The first stems from the personnel register held by companies. If they wish to make an internal promotion, literally a quick push at two or three buttons will give a long shortlist which can be refined, as senior management refine their own requirements.

The requirements could be for a person aged between 27 and 35, married with two children (this always adds stability, employers reckon), experienced in widget watching and with a BSc in general architecture. In the likely occurrence that no such person exists within the enterprise, the senior people will probably go to an agency or consultancy specializing in such people. They may of course advertise in the trade press but generally for appearance sake only if the job is a senior one. The outside body will also have a computer bank of people and will attempt to match up the employers' requirements with one or more of its own clients. The UK State Professional and Executive Register uses the same system and the Job Shop chain is starting to become computer linked. However, given mobility difficulties, this latter development is unlikely to be cost effective.

The second impact of computers on recruitment is at the interview stage itself and represents a far more insidious and dangerous principle. The interviewee is surrounded by four or five interviewers who each ask questions. Some are concerned with the technicalities of the job, the person's experience, and so on, whilst others appear to be totally random questions. No one interviewer has a monopoly of either type of question. After the interview the answers to the apparently random questions are fed into a computer which supposedly has the correct answers to these questions. These will then indicate loyalty, responsiveness, honesty, imagination, and so on. The problem is that the answers are fed into the computer by a person with all the human failings and quirks and the answers themselves may be incorrect. But even if they are correct they only provide a clue to a person's ability or character if that person is within an average range. Supposing they are not and they give a correct but unusual answer — the computer will mark them wrong even if they are right. An excellent illustration of this is in the German award winning film *Kaspar Hauser*. Kaspar at one point is asked by a psychologist the old question of how one would find out whether a villager came from the village where everyone always lies or from the village where everyone always tells the truth. After a while Kaspar replies, 'I would ask the man whether he is a tree-frog'. His interrogator insists he is wrong, because the school of logic states that there is only one single question that can elicit the correct answer—and this certainly was not that question. Yet Kaspar was quite correct, his question would have worked. However, would it have passed the programme interview test? I fear not. Indeed, people with wit, imagination, and the ability to think laterally will not do well at such interviews. The ideal corporate person might emerge, but this, in a world crying out for radical change and for positive decision making, is totally counterproductive. In personnel terms the computer will select *grey* every time.

Computers and computer systems will thus change the nature of jobs in the short, medium, and perhaps even the long term, and reduce the number of available jobs. Just to give a flavour of what we may all experience over the next few years, consider the following system: job scheduling by computers with no people available to ensure that slippage does not take place; an *automated planning and executive control system* (APEX) that plans and monitors job deadlines and restarts; a *job mix optimizing system* that looks at current workloads and calculates the optimum use of machinery for the operator—a kind of critical path analysis, except that it is dynamic, not static. Other facilities now available are complete automation for production schedules and distribution, a scheduling program system that includes the whole of a production workload, and a system which automatically works out and then initiates, controls, and tracks production and *supervises manual activities*. These packages obviously change the role of all people, from managers and professional engineers and architects to floor sweepers and skilled and unskilled plant or office workers.

As I have sought to demonstrate in this chapter, few people are or will be immune. The salesman now using a computer in his suitcase to automatically order and log and invoice each sale to each retailer straight onto the head office computer is really doing a different job. The day of the cycling insurance salesman is numbered—Prestel and office terminals are taking their place. Cash dispensers put bank tellers' jobs at risk, as do credit facilities and credit cards, and in the United States crime makes the holding of cash a physically risky business.

As will be seen in Part II, the impact on jobs *could be* the chance of a new renaissance and an opportunity to restructure society so that work and leisure coexist rather than compete. As we shall also see in Part II, the computerization of jobs could mean a drift towards some form of totalitarianism—Right or Left. As with most other effects of computerization the choice is ours—not the system's, nor the machines. Interestingly, work is one of the areas where there are organized collective bodies, the trade unions, which have far more power and clout than consumer bodies or other voluntary organizations. Given that the introduction of computers is so diffuse as to make one single opposition issue unlikely (as opposed to nuclear power opposition, for example), the impact of computers on work in all its aspects is the one major area where dissent may be shown practically. This is because it is not a diffuse issue to the workers in any one place; it is a simple, single, and easy to grasp threat—just like the threat of war, but viewed from the workplace.

Because of this dichotomy union members all over the world are pushing their leaderships into policies for control of computer technologies. The International Labor Organisation in their 1981 meeting had an undefeated motion which stated: 'The basis of union policy in this field should not be to prevent, but to exercise rigorous control . . .' and goes on to state: 'Employees must be guaranteed influence on how and where computerisation and electronics are used.' Even the Japanese unions are now worried after a survey which showed that new technologies cost 31 per cent. of jobs in the audio/video business during the period 1976/79. From print to engineering, government employees to metal workers, all of the international trade union bodies are concerned. It may be with job loss, with youth unemployment, with job de-skilling, or with the lack of training, each separate country has its own preoccupations and priorities. Computers are proving to be the industrial counterpart of the general concern over nuclear power; they are arousing passions and are providing a threat, yet it must be reasserted only when viewed from the workplace in one limited sphere.

Chapter 5

Consumer Impacts I

BOOKS AND PLAYS ARE WRITTEN AND FILMS AND TELEVISION programmes are made about the human condition — love and death, birth and courage, personal crises and national traumas, anti-war or pro-justice and liberty. These epic and vital matters concern the moralist, philosophers, and creative artists who together overtly represent the cultural values of societies at any given moment in time.

There is, however, a completely different set of values, although some would deny that they are cultural, and these are represented by, as a proxy, the advertising industry. This industry attempts to persuade people to buy things, to want goods, and to need services. Objectively there is nothing wrong with this providing that certain standards are set and adhered to, mainly in respect of truthfulness. This second set of values ranges over the esoteric, upon which the cultural set tends to concentrate, across to the desirable and barely attainable, down to the foothills of the mundane and simple. From the *dream machine*, be it a Ferrari motorcar or a cooker with *everything*, to lavatory cleaners and baked beans, the advertising industry and its clients make their presence felt in the media. Books have to be bought or borrowed and it needs an active mental and physical effort on the part of the people concerned to do so, while paintings have to be seen in art galleries and visits to theatres and cinemas are external activities. However, much of the advertising *comes to us*; we become passive receivers rather than actively seeking out the information conveyed by the advertisement.

Advertising intervenes in programmes on television, indeed in the middle of a programme, so that at times one has to concentrate hard to distinguish between the programme and the start or finish of the advertisements. It comes in magazines and papers bought for purposes other than looking at advertisements. It comes on street hoardings and public transport, sports arenas, and even on sporting apparel. The latest phase is the free journal delivered to the home or given away at railway stations which contains 90 per cent. advertising. A great deal of effort, talent, and subtlety goes into trying to make people want things. When, with the gift of hindsight that all historians have, the mid-twentieth century is analysed, the consumer and the goods and services consumed may well be found to be the key to this period's motivation.

Even today, consumption is seen to be very important. John Maynard Keynes suggested that demand — in which consumption of goods and services by individuals or groups, corporate bodies, or government plays a very large part — was the crucial element to be controlled or manipulated in the economy of an industrialized state. We have seen that through the twentieth century consumption has created employment and that this in itself has satisfied one of the basic drives of this time. It is, however, not a static phenomenon. If it were we would neither have needed nor created an advertising industry. Fashions change, scientific and technical advances create new products and thus new demands, and people have rising expectations.

It is oversimplistic to suggest that rising expectations merely mean either more of the same or, indeed, more choices. Rising expectations affect what we want on several levels. We all believe we should live longer, in less pain, and overall more comfortably than did our ancestors. We all want our children to do well and, if possible, to do things we did not manage to do — or arrogantly that they should do what we do, only better. This does not include the general fantasy of sons scoring the winning goal in the Cup Final for the side father supports, or daughters dancing as light as thistledown at Covent Garden, rarely but occasionally vice versa. It is a real world, non-fantasy set of ideals for the next generation. Rising expectations involve other people. What they do and want constrains and defines what their neighbours do or want. Perversely the positional goods addict will take the diametrically opposed standpoint to the population in general (as discussed in Chapter 4). The population in general will try to get as many of the goods and use as many of the services as possible. This is qualified by income groups, family structures, and the fashions and desirability of products and services. These vary from country to country; indeed, within quite small distances there can be markedly different tastes even within one country. Bitter beer basically is drunk only in Britain, the rest of Europe and North America appearing to prefer lager-type beers. Yet within various areas of Britain not only are there fierce arguments about whether Northern, Southern or Scots bitter is preferable, but also areas where cider is the most common drink.

Consumers and their expenditure are very much a twentieth century phenomenon and, in some respects, very much late twentieth century. Certainly it is only with an industrialized waged society that goods and products are in the market-place in sufficient profusion to make them so important. Consumerism and the protection of consumers, often against themselves, is really less than twenty years old, yet its existence demonstrates the importance we now place on goods and services. We need to protect ourselves against buying wrong or dangerous things and more and more we need to be reassured that we are buying the best things available at the most competitive prices. We keep up with the Jones's and even try to keep a step ahead of them, and to do this we need to buy the latest, rent the latest, or, at the least, prominently display the most expensive bottles and bags in the garbage. This may sound cynical but not when one considers the strength of the drive to acquire material things in this part of the twentieth century.

To motivate people into buying products, the advertising agencies use sex, security, class, and dreams—the most powerful weapons in a positive sense. Though we all know that using the right mouthwash will not really deliver that beautiful girl seen on the train every morning into our arms, can we take the chance, supposing it can? Negatively, advertisers use ridicule and exposure: the six-stone weakling, the man who forgot to insure his house, the man passed over for promotion, and so on. These images and inducements are heavier than those used by politicians or even psychologists, and as computer technology grows so these techniques will grow. This is partly because, as we shall see in Part II, computers themselves have set and will increasingly set or even create entire markets, let alone single products, and partly because computers themselves will have to be advertised in subtle and often very different ways so as to humanize them. This is especially true of a period not more than a decade away when the 'service and high tech' image will have lost its glamour and may, indeed, be counterproductive.

Overall, though, it is because computers will enable goods and services to be available to people faster, cheaper, and earlier. Competition, even within a single company, will intensify and consumers will be wooed more ardently than ever before. This chapter is about the improvement in quality, quantity, price, reliability, and delivery of the goods and services that computers have made available in a direct way. It is this series of improvements that will lead to the expansion of advertising and other marketing ploys.

Neither this chapter (nor, indeed, the next) is supposed to be an exhaustive list of computer applications as they affect consumers. Rather, both chapters will use examples to draw out arguments and expose areas of impact. Indeed, given the rate of change in computer technology anything written on a definitive basis is heroic in the extreme as it is likely to be out of date before it is in proof form, let alone published.

In basic terms computers have enabled consumers to have certain benefits. Whether these are sufficient to balance the benefits to the producers and suppliers or the hidden costs involved in computer use will be discussed in Part II. Indeed, whether such costs and benefits should or even can balance is a legitimate question. Here we merely look at the benefits and note some of the costs.

Compared with people, computers are very fast. This means that an advantage to consumers is that some goods and services reach them faster than they would if the systems underpinning them were manually based, as they used to be. In the realism of services such consumer benefits are easily noticed and found. Booking an airline ticket, be it through an agency, airline office, or at the airport itself, is now easier, quicker, and more reliable because airlines use *real-time* computer systems. This enables the computer to adjust itself to the changes that each booking or cancellation makes to the availability of seats on a plane. In theory this must give a better, faster, and more reliable service, but this is not always the case, the problem being one of corporate opportunity to make extra profits. There is really no excuse for overbooking other than budgeting for a small percentage of late non-attenders, because all the booking outlets are linked into this instantaneously adjusting computer. Yet overbooking there is, and in some countries — notably the United States — in fairly dramatic terms. Indeed, one might almost say that computer use has made it easier to overbook and thus give consumers a more unreliable service than they would otherwise have had. At least one American airline, Braniff, has attributed part of its bankruptcy to competitors taking its passengers and thus deliberately overbooking themselves. The compensation that had to be paid by US law to incommoded passengers was worth while in the long run, given the elimination of a major competitor.

Air travel generally is facilitated by computerization. It allows for more accurate flight scheduling and the optimum loading of freight, and adds a dimension to our ability to plan long, interrupted journeys should we need multiple flights. In this respect Swedish railways have gone one better and now produce timetables which incorporate train, boat, coach, and air travel and all the connections between them; these are updated or changed at three monthly intervals. In the late nineteenth century *Bradshaws* (the British railways timetable of all the private companies and their connections, including ferries) was one of the wonders of the world—it has taken the computer age for it to be superseded. Airlines use computers to work out fuelling stops and schedules, especially given that there are different fuel prices at different airports, and also the weight of freight and passengers on their planes. Airlines have to use computers extensively, often linked across countries and continents. The consumers, passengers, those who meet or deposit passengers at airports, and those who send or receive freight, benefit broadly from the ability of the computer, especially its analogue *real-time* ability.

Airports, at least the large ones, could not work nowadays without their computer systems. One set of information systems is that which services the airlines using the airport—a sort of data base for air travel—but which also allows confidential input and access. This can include basic weather information or provide sophisticated import/export programmes which liaise with customs and excise officials automatically; the speeding up of customs clearance can thus be substantial. Passenger information systems, mysterious though they may be at times with disembodied voices intruding upon waiting and often highly disturbed, nervous, and tired people, themselves depend on computer systems. The display units giving the news, too often unpleasant, are kept up-to-date on a minute-by-minute basis, taking information from planes in flight, airport ramps, fuelling stations, and other airports.

The airport itself has an infrastructure; indeed, large airports like Heathrow or Kennedy are more like small cities with amenities catering for religious, old, young, pregnant, fit, ill, hungry, thirsty, exhausted, and bored people. The amenities provided have to meet potential demands and are correlated by computer systems. These systems also provide fuelling for planes and the fuel companies are on-line with the airport system for coordinating airport buses and terminal loadings. When the main computer is *down* (jargon for not in use), some airlines claim they have only twenty minutes before coming to a standstill. It is thus not surprising to find that back-up systems are needed, but as these add to the costs, they are not entirely popular. It is most unlikely that the systems will, indeed should be able to, revert to being operated manually. Air travel from beginning to end is computer controlled and so to a great extent is the bit in the middle — the flight itself.

Air controllers use computers in every large control tower and this means that not only are take-offs and landings aided by computer but also to a great extent so is the corridor and the height at which the plane will fly on its journey. In America, the breaking of the Air Traffic Controllers Unions was greatly facilitated by a computerized flow control system which took care of flight systems and removed much of the human element. However, it is accepted in all flying circles that safety is paramount, and despite the use of computer systems there have been some near misses, one in Atlanta only being avoided by a last second human correction. In 1981, the Transportation subcommittee of the US House of Representatives found that computer malfunctions 'pose a threat to safety especially during peak traffic periods'; in particular, there was especial concern about the time taken to transfer to a back-up system when a failure takes place. This is one of the problems concerning computers which we shall analyse in Part II. There are no such things as infallible machines but it costs so much money to provide back-up systems (human, electronic, or both) that there is a reluctance to provide them, or to service them.

Modern civil aeroplanes are increasingly becoming flying computer and electronic carriers. Their communications systems are electronically based. New navigation systems are electronic and computer controlled, combining with land-based computer and electronic beacons. This capability, along with computer-based auto-pilot rudder equipment and at least three fail-safe back-up systems per plane, could herald the era of the pilotless plane depending entirely upon computers. Computer scanning in three dimensions of the structure of planes as large as the Boeing 747 is now being done on a regular basis for the engineering servicing of planes. Transport is an area which overall is dependent upon computers, although air transport tends to have a deeper and heavier dependence. In the main the consumer benefits by having shorter waiting periods, faster transfers, easier booking, and probably a marginally lower price, although this is difficult to prove. Safety has been improved but, as the US Report suggests, 'complacency can creep in which impairs safety' — computers can be counterproductive.

Land and water transport both use computers. The railway

systems of the industrialized world use computers to schedule and handle trains and to trace, track, and handle freight and containers. Signal systems are becoming automated and computer controlled both on the overground and underground railway systems, and these should add to safety. On subway systems like London's Victoria Line, trains can run without guards or drivers and have a computer-controlled signal system. In the United States the *people movers* (closed loops or electric trains) are entirely computer controlled, a perfect example being the 'train' which connects a hotel and shopping mall in the home of the motorcar — Dearborne, Detroit. The projected linear motor powered airport link to the centre of the city in Tokyo will also rely upon computer control and signalling.

Large cities have complex traffic problems mainly because they were never really designed for large overground transport movements and the viability of the underground transport system depends on subsoils, underground rivers, and so on. Cities like London, New York, and Paris have large commercial centres employing millions of people and a widespread suburban population; together these lead to millions of journeys over quite large distances on working days. Even larger cities (in population terms) such as Mexico or Calcutta have different but equally difficult traffic problems. The shifting of these millions of people requires trains, subways, buses and coaches, walking areas, cars, bikes, horses and motorcycles, and, to a smaller extent, boats. It would be nice to be able to say that computers have been used to coordinate these different transport methods and even to analyse and then stagger journeys to and from work. Regrettably, nothing could be further from the truth.

The railway and underground systems use their own computers for their own ends. Some suburban bus systems have started to use both computer scheduling and computer tracing of buses, that is to say they are able to locate each bus at any point on its route and as a result are theoretically capable of altering schedules and thus averting queues of buses not meeting queues of potential passengers, so common in London and New York. It is a simple system based on a combination of short-wave radio and tagged vehicles passing fixed transmitter posts. Overall, however, the universal large city problem is traffic — more precisely it is an excess of traffic especially at the rush-hour time of day. Very few transport authorities use computers to coordinate buses and trains and private transport: chaos is still the rule rather than the exception.

Computer analysis of traffic flows has long been used along with a primitive method of computer-controlled traffic signals in an attempt to prevent jams at crossroads. However, new technologies have opened up new avenues for this sort of scheme. A system named 'SCOOT' has been tried successfully in Britain, in both Glasgow and Coventry. Incidentally, it exemplifies yet another computer characteristic, the clever acronym. SCOOT actually stands for Split Cycle and Offset Optimization Technique. It is a real-time system, that is to say, the light sequence of groups of lights change given the relative density of traffic flows around those junctions, and is serviced by vehicle detectors in the road. Because it acts spontaneously to demands it will be useful in the densest traffic areas and London is to install fifty at the most congested junctions in the centre. This system is clearly in its infancy but equally clearly has great potential both for public and private transport users. The Dutch have gone a stage further and have linked motorway signals with the density of traffic in the city into which the motorway leads. Diversions and speed restrictions can thus be planned in advance and the driver gains considerably. Naturally it is a computer-based system.

Road hauliers, local authorities, and public bodies use computers quite heavily to coordinate and plan the use of their vehicle fleets and routes. Various computer programs are available for fleet maintenance, optimum fuel use and other matters, and route planning on a pan-European basis. Despite early faults, especially in the latter of the systems, both packages have been established and provide faster deliveries over the Continent as a whole. Better and more frequent garbage disposal, road repairs, and meals-on-wheels schemes can be provided on a local basis. Road users are just beginning to reap the direct benefits of computers although the indirect effects of efficient management and route and fuel planning have been in existence for well over fifteen years. Ship fleet owners have been using computers for load factoring, ordering, loading, and, indeed, keeping in touch with and if necessary redirecting their ships for quite some time.

Traditional business and economic theory prevails, in that these uses of computer lead to consumer benefits, faster deliveries, better services, cheaper goods, and a wider range of goods like fresh vegetables being available out of season — Australian strawberries in London in December or Californian carrots in Paris in January. In short, the distributive mechanism is speeded up for goods, and personal transport *should* be that much easier and painless. Transport is a very important service within and between countries and is a good example of how computers have become a vital part of everyday expectations in this field, although as with *all* other matters in life, from time to time these expectations are not met in full.

Before goods are transported they have to be sold and salesmen, wholesalers, and retailers all play a part in the chains between producer and consumer. Lest naivety appears to take over, it must be recognized that this may involve a single company rather than a succession of separate companies, even though the names of each company at each stage are different. This so-called *vertical integration* is a marked feature of industries like boot and shoe manufacturing and of retail sales. The job of salesman is changing as computers come on stream in the communications and accounting areas. Automated warehouses and stock control systems are being used in larger numbers and these, too, affect the jobs of salesmen as well as those working in the warehouses both quantitatively and qualitatively.

Salesmen nowadays have to make sense of computer printouts and have to be able to analyse the data obtained from them. Increasingly, at least in the better managed companies, the sales force is seen as part of the overall team and has to contribute to profits within similar constraints to those of their colleagues. As salesmen become more efficient and get around to more outlets more frequently and the distribution mechanisms interact with them equally speedily, consumers should reap the benefits. There should be fewer and shorter periods when retail outlets have run out of stock in some of their lines. The hand-held or suitcase computer terminal plugged into the normal telephone system through to either the head office or regional warehouse has been the main mechanism whereby suppliers, and occasionally wholesalers, can respond very quickly.

The retailers, too, have been changing. Mr Polly would not now recognize the stock, ordering, or invoice system. He would be unable to fill in modern tax forms and, perhaps saddest of all, would have to look long and hard to locate his type of shop. Supermarkets, hypermarkets, and chain stores now predominant in the high streets and department stores in the larger city centres. Most of these depend on bulk buying to keep prices lower than those in the smaller shops. Shelves are kept stocked by a sophisticated stock control system. There are several methods. The main one at present depends on a hand-held laser wipe which scans a coded label and in turn this records the number of these goods sold in a particular store. When an optimum number of cases have been sold they are automatically reordered from the central warehouse. This may then involve contact with outside suppliers. As far as consumers are concerned this method helps to keep a steady availability of goods. As far as the store is concerned it means that it does not lose sales through the 'sorry dear it will be in tomorrow' syndrome and also means that they can monitor closely the speed of sales of lines and new lines in particular. As we shall see, this may not always work in favour of the consumer, especially in the matter of ranges and choices.

The newer methods, however, are even more sophisticated and ensure companies have complete control of stocks. The point of sale terminals will rely on fixed scanners, more latterly holographic 'reading' of either special labels or the bar codes, or both. These computer terminals will not only provide automatic printed and itemized bills but adjust both the stocks at a shop storeroom and remote warehouse level. This obviously is a step forward—now the adjustment can be made on a shelf as opposed to numbers of cases. This further cuts the delay time in replenishing the shelves as they empty. Such fine tuning can mean almost daily visits by store vans from local warehouses. It also means that an even closer analysis can be made of the rate at which various lines are sold and their regional differences or an analysis of the importance of the position of goods on display. Point-of-sale computers thus have a market research function as well as a sale and stock function.

One strange side-effect of this trend is that it has caused bigger and better traffic jams. Because deliveries were made more often and as too few shops have service roads behind them the delivery lorries had to park on high streets. *Thus one of the more peripheral costs of computerization was urban traffic jams and resultant bad temper and delays in the delivery of the goods* (note: peripheral does not mean trivial). In recent years the costs of delivery have been so great that the computer planning of deliveries takes these costs into account and the number of deliveries has decreased.

There are variations on these themes. *Unipart*, a car component and accessory chain of shops, has to carry stocks of not only British Leyland products (their parent company) but also of most other makes of car. To do so would really be impossible in respect of both the sheer bulk of stock and the cost of doing so. Most Unipart shops are linked into the central warehouse computer and can not only identify parts for customers but can also order them automatically through their terminals, so reducing the time the customer has to wait. Car sales firms are linked by computer so that a garage in Brighton, for example, may swap their white car for a blue one with a Scunthorpe garage to suit a potential customer quickly. Insurance companies are starting to use the same techniques. One of them has computer terminals installed in each of its offices. Customers can browse through an interactive data base and then, having identified the policy which most suits them, order that policy. An interactive data system is one which responds to the questions put to it — it is based on a series of algorithms and the difference between this and a passive data base is very considerable. The policy order is then automatically placed on the head office computers, which then automatically bill the policy holder and issue payments when and if necessary. It is a very computerized operation.

Mail order companies, a significant if rarely written about sector of the retail market, have also become heavily dependent on computers. Orders can be fulfilled faster if ordering is done in a standardized fashion and the computer also records and then traces the items in the warehouse. Payments, often made on a hire purchase basis in this type of retail business, can be checked and traced more thoroughly and easily. The automated or semi-automated warehouse is not peculiar to mailorder houses but is becoming more prevalent across the generality of warehouses and stockrooms. Goods can be placed in the best position, analysed as to how quickly they come in demand, and can be traced quickly and accurately. Some warehouses or stock areas are becoming virtually personless as computer-controlled cranes and lifts move unerringly towards computer-tagged storage bins. Once again, consumers should benefit as goods and components can be traced and moved faster to fulfil demand. However, the theory may diverge from practice in that these storage and retrieval functions are only part of the cycle or mechanism through which consumers get their end products. Traffic congestion could well cancel out all the other benefits as far as speed is concerned. But accuracy should be greater and mistakes fewer, and together these represent a bonus in consumer terms.

Whether the consumer benefits in price terms in these areas is quite another matter. Most of the systems we have looked at are labour saving and most are cost saving over a shortish time too. In retail stores there are traditionally high profits made in some ranges and very low 'margins' on other goods.

Only in areas of overall direct competition is there likely to be a cash benefit to consumers and then, perhaps as in petrol price wars, with only transitory effects. So far the best case that can be made for the price effects of computerization is that prices have remained constant or have risen less than they might otherwise have done. Indeed, petrol and gas stations are perfect examples. Most are now self-service with pumps electronically linked to the cash reception areas. This actually means that technology has put the onus on the customers, since they now have to help themselves. Computers have thus cut both jobs and customer service at one and the same time. What is significant in price terms is that there appears to be no correlation between the price of petrol in a manned or self-service station in similar areas, yet economic theory would suggest that differential pricing should exist. Indeed, the most ardent proponent of computerization would suggest that such a price difference would be inevitable.

This is not to say that there are never price reductions. Within the supermarket or hypermarket sector 'loss leaders' can be more easily sustained and widened if computers have cut costs and made it possible to keep up a constant supply of heavily demanded goods, without losing the ability to maintain the stocks of other goods. Some prices have been cut. The British Post Office, when it ran the UK telecommunications system, cut the cost of overseas calls after the introduction of computerized systems. Other new products fall in price, too. Overall, for the type of amended goods and services dealt with in this chapter, the 'cheaper price' benefit to the consumer is at best weak and at worst non-existent.

People do not always want things to be faster or more efficient. Two services, which the generality of the population would be only too pleased to have delayed and the system made less efficient, are general invoicing and billing and, in particular, tax statements. Not unnaturally these are precisely the areas that public utility managements and tax collectors world-wide have seen as the prime use for the computers' ability. Gas, electricity, telephones, property taxes, or rates are all now billed on computerized systems. Automatic metering leading to computerized statements is perfectly feasible and *in situ* in some places, especially involving water usage. It is, however, being held back overall due to a combination of high capital investment to replace existing meters and worker resistance—there would of course be considerable job loss amongst meter readers. There is no public psychological block in this change. There are no telephone meters in the United Kingdom (not even itemized bills) and we have to take the BT computers at their word—as we are all aware, to challenge one of the computerized bills is a task worthy of Hercules himself, in labour, nervous energy, and endurance.

Computerized billing has led to a loss of consumer amenity, in its way rather like the self-service petrol station. The problem of challenging a computer-rendered account is, as just mentioned, formidable. Even if it is proved that an error has been made the accounting system on which the computer operates cannot allow for a refund of the overpaid money. What is worse, some of the systems cannot issue an amended bill. This means that people have to either accept a credit note or wait for the next accounting period before they get a reduced bill. In either case the benefit lies with the providers of the good or service and the cost is borne entirely by the consumer, if only in terms of interest foregone.

Whereas in the past unpaid bills were followed by second or even third reminders before the nasty lawyers' letters arrived, this is changing. Some bodies, especially those sharing computer facilities (notably London Local Authorities such as Hackney), now issue only one rates bill which is followed by a summons—often after payment if this has been somehow delayed. Whilst payment stops court proceedings, the cost of the summons has to be paid in addition to the rates bill. There is no record of this method having reduced rates arrears in Hackney—indeed, the contrary appears to be true. Other bodies have just reduced the time between the first bill and the second and only issue the two—the cost of programming for three is said to be prohibitive. In these instances the consumer has lost a benefit. The argument that the aggregate of all the consumers benefit because bills are paid more quickly and regularly falls on two counts. The first is that consumerist theory makes the *individual* consumer paramount and the second is that no evidence exists that such aggregate benefits accrue. One might claim with some degree of legitimacy that the only benefit from computers in this field is to enable bodies to maintain accurate lists of debtors!

There are cost savings to bodies installing the computers, mainly in people terms, although these have never really been exploited fully, especially when so many installations are of the older and relatively labour-intensive variety. People or bodies pay their bills or react to invoices according to their particular circumstances and those are not determined by when they receive the bills. Cash flow problems or stock availability are the sort of factors determining responses. Given this, it is possible to question whether these older systems actually do any good at all. Possibly the most famous of consumer disutilities is what happened with the Swansea Driving Licence Centre, but this will be saved for the second part of the book.

Back in the consumer benefit area there are now all forms of computerized booking systems, e.g. train seat reservations, theatre seat reservations, holidays, hospital places, and so on. Most of our reservations in day-to-day life, like the hairdresser, dentist, or restaurant, are with organizations so small that they do not need computers as aids.

However, consumers are affected and often benefit in many other ways. When we buy, rent, or lease something we expect it to work and, moreover, to continue working, and often take it as a personal insult if the product continually misbehaves. In Britain there is a joke that a bad car is a Monday car—the workers had that Monday morning feeling; in the Soviet Union it is a Friday car—the norm had either been fulfilled so that no-one bothers or everyone rushes and botches the job. In either instance it is people who cause the problem. Quality and quality control are vital for the long-term success of products, indeed companies. A product soon acquires a reputation for reliability but once this slips and people say the product breaks down or rusts easily or is 'shoddy' and awkward to service, it is difficult to shift the belief that this is so. The 'rakes progress' of British Leyland is a classic example of this phenomenon.

Consistent quality, especially in sophisticated products such as cars and trucks, washing machines, and television sets, depends upon a combination of routine procedures carried out properly and a rigorous checking system carried out at all stages. Given that the differences tend to arise with the involvement of human beings, who as so many biblical sources have pointed out are fallible, it is the repairing of their mistakes or the prevention of their errors which will improve overall quality. Robotics and computerized machine tools, electronic testing equipment, and a more consistent set of operations and improved production engineering, mainly computer controlled, go a long way towards eliminating error and ensuring a high standard of quality. Consumers at the least deserve this—at the most demand it.

Computers and the newer microelectronic technologies should give better reliability and quality and thus less service problems and lower cost, and they do it by acting in various ways at various stages. Design, especially production design, has improved since the advent of the computer, which allows for very much faster draughtsmanship of new designs and thus a larger number of options can be tested in a shorter time. Whilst yet again the theory is fine, in practice the computer program may dictate the final design and the programmer the program. This may be, and indeed has been, to the detriment of the engineering. However, in production design there is little or no room for dubiety, providing the program is not in error. Improvements in this field have meant, for example, that only three operations are needed to put a car door in place, whereas in the past ten or more movements would have been needed. Not only does this reduce the chances of misplaced or damaged doors, but it also speeds up the entire operation. A second method of ensuring better quality is using machines rather than people — these can be robots or other types of machine tools.

Robots are as yet in their infancy. It was estimated that in 1983 there were 37,000 robots in the world, really quite a small number. Japan, the United States, Germany, France, Italy, and the United Kingdom were the heaviest users, Japan being the heaviest of them all. There are several types of robots, ranging from single-function small robots to large materials-carrying machines, as seen on television car advertisements. Robots working properly will perform their functions with a high degree of accuracy and consistency — they do not suffer from hangovers or backaches but whilst they also have no absenteeism they can and do break down. The more complicated the type of robot the more likely it is to go wrong, the larger materials-carrying moving robots being the least reliable. The single-function, static, welding or painting robot, or the simple static single-component holding robot where other components move, probably on a mass-production track, is the work-horse machine. If it breaks down there are fail-safe devices which stop the whole operation; the alternative is that a robot could continually perform a job wrongly which would of course be totally counterproductive from the point of view of the producer and possibly dangerous for the consumer. In human analogy terms, there is like a short-term strike — the whole line shuts down. However inconvenient this may be to the producer, it does protect the consumer.

One of the technology blocks holding back the development of robots is the late emergence of suitable sensors, be they tactile, audio, or visual. The 'fifth-generation' research may rectify this but towards the end of the 1980s rather than earlier. There is also a robot psychology. When BL introduced robots into their Metro body shop production line they did so with a vivid splash of publicity aimed at repairing their poor quality image. The argument went as follows: we are replacing workers by robots. As a marketing ploy it was successful, mainly because the robots were chosen wisely and, indeed, did increase quality overall — this has not always been the case. Machines controlled by computers are just an extension of the robot principle. Even the most brilliant time-served skilled engineer can make mistakes — the new lathes rarely do. They *may*, however, place stresses on the metal that can have unforeseen and dangerous consequences at a later date with buckling or an increased propensity to metal fatigue, although the newer machines are attempting to take this potential problem into consideration. It is vital that this is done. A fractured rotor blade could kill more than 400 people in a Boeing 747 in the worst of all possible scenarios.

Overall, robots and automatic machinery have tended to improve quality and reliability, but so has a third factor. Integrated circuitry based on 'dedicated' micro-electric computers has replaced many devices, especially electromechanical ones, in many products, and domestic electrical equipment is one such set of products. This was discussed in terms of jobs in the previous chapter, yet clearly there is a large impact on quality. Fewer parts mean fewer operations and this in turn means fewer potential places where mistakes can be made. Secondly, within each product, component, and subcomponent, there are fewer moving parts and thus clearly fewer chances of things going wrong. The new integrated circuits tend to work or not to work: there are few halfway houses or intermittent functioning, or 50 per cent. effectiveness. Servicing tends to be much easier and thus cheaper. A defective circuit, once identified, is replaced *en bloc*, rather than carrying out a long-winded though skilled repair performance. This applies across the range of domestic appliances, cars, work equipment, and so on.

Yet another way in which computers have been used to increase quality to consumers is by improving techniques and standards in physical measurement and testing its equipment. This applies in particular to scientific equipment, to temperature control, and to the test instruments which check the working parts and stresses within a product. In particular terms, almost the entire ranges of consumers electronics and cars are more reliable than ever before. They also have improved performances and additional features.

Washing machines have more varied cycles so that individual programming for different types of wash are now available. Cookers also have programmable systems allowing for different foods or dishes to cook at different times and to start cooking at different times. Television sets, videorecorders, and videodisc players are all used within the home and together these allow those who need to cook, wash, and do the housework far more free time and something to do with the time. Cars are another prime user of the dedicated computer or microelectronic circuit, examples being instrumentation based on digital non-moving components; trip computers which can monitor engine speeds and torques, fuel remaining, and mileage left at optimum speed; if information is fed in beforehand, data like estimated time of arrival at present speed; and so on. Automatic diagnostic systems are just starting to be used by the motor manufacturers. Ignition, carburettor, timing, exhaust emission, and transmission controls are not only feasible but are being installed in newer car models. Cruise at constant speed devices, tyre pressure and tread signals, and all the new uses should make motoring much safer and easier, but of course the former inevitably depends on people. All that can be done is to manufacture a car which, if damaged in a crash, minimizes the damage to driver and passengers. The benefits of computer components in cars are that they are easier to drive, more reliable, with early warnings to avoid major breakdowns and therefore requiring less servicing; cleaner and more environmentally acceptable both in terms of pollution and fuel consumption. In the future it may be possible to build in safety features which override a driver's propensity for errors, perhaps radar or computers reacting to the signals from other cars or computer signals from within the roadway itself.

The second idea is not new. It has been suggested as a method of 'taxing' cars which drive in the more heavily congested city centres or on the more heavily used motorways. Each car would have a computerized sealed meter (like a taxicab) which would pick up signals from implanted studs within the road. The more heavily the road is used the higher the tariff and the closer together the studs. Fortunately for town motorists no authority has been prepared to stand the enormous cost this would entail.

Consumers have also benefited in the less overtly commercial services like education or medicine, although some might challenge the word 'benefit'. There has certainly been change. At the administrative level, records, appointments, and rosters are all being placed on computers rather than traditional files. Whilst this is giving rise to very legitimate worries in the field of privacy (explored in Chapter 13), it is also giving rise to greater efficiency and a better use of limited resources. In medicine and surgery, computers are used to an ever-increasing extent to affect patients directly. The intensive care system is computer based, although it could be 'nurse based' — computers allow one nurse to monitor five patients simultaneously rather than five nurses monitoring five patients sequentially. Anaesthetic equipment can now deliver doses of anaesthetic controlled by the patients' own respiration, heart rate, body weight, and temperature, thus leaving the anaesthetist free to get on with monitoring the patients well-being. Examples of how computer control affects patients in hospitals are legion both in medicine and surgery: in diagnostics, through body scanners, the computer analysis of heart rhythms, all the new pathology laboratory equipment in haematology, in repair work with brain and eye, and so on. Surgery performed with lasers and computer-matched tissues for transplants and grafts are examples.

Less highly publicized but, nevertheless, as important — perhaps more so — is the role that computers play in the development of new techniques and drugs. In the pharmaceutical industry this has led to some startling break-throughs, although human genius has had to be the initial prompt, with the generic alpha and beta blockers as outstanding examples. It has, however, also led to the game of *molecular roulette* in which a drug company changes a single molecule of a known compound and patents the new substance. Quite often this has little effect on the illnesses that the overall population of drugs can treat. It can, however, if well prompted, give extra profits to the company and is a procedure that has brought some degree of disrepute upon some drug manufacturers. Without computers neither the breakthrough nor the roulette would be feasible.

Artificial limbs and the power packs on them could not have been developed as well or as quickly; contact lenses are immeasurably better because of new computer-controlled lathes and new materials developed with the use of computers. Computer-based aids for the disabled and geriatric are now available — automatic SOS phone signals, for example — yet most are very expensive, and what is worse the cost would have to be borne by those least able to pay. There needs to be some element of subsidy for these goods from government but even in the 'Year of the Disabled' in 1981 there was precious little of this available. As a result far less is being done in practical terms than is theoretically possible.

The educational use of computers is perhaps less well defined, appreciated, or indeed real. Computer programmed teaching has some adherents but appears to be more suitable to adult educational modular systems and specific or vocational ones at that. Learning is not the same as education and this perhaps is where the confusion arises. Computers can lead to adequate learning systems. At present computers play but a small part in teaching techniques, although intensive language laboratories now use them and, by and large, schools in most countries use them to teach about computers themselves. Even in the United States where the use of computers as a teaching aide is more advanced than in other countries, there is an interesting statistic. Of the top twenty teacher training colleges (or schools of education) in 1981–82, only eight have any requirement for computer literacy, and of these, in only one, Illinois State, do all students get some exposure to computers.

Plans for the increased use of computers in schools are growing. France and the United Kingdom are to have a computer in every school and the US Department of Education could spend as much as $25 million on a similar project. The intention is to increase computer awareness amongst children. The uses do not really include the teaching of other subjects using the equipment. One of the reasons for this is that we still learn reading and writing from books and our methods of memorizing are by literate and verbal means. Recent research suggests that visual and audio stimuli, on television for example, tend to be mutually exclusive — either the image or the words go in. What is even worse is that television now has such a hold on people, especially in the United States, that students have difficulty in concentrating for more than a few minutes at a time and thirty minutes at maximum.

This problem has been noted by the Massachusetts Institute of Technology. The Artificial Intelligence Laboratory has developed a simple 'language' which even pre-school children can understand and use. Nice friendly things called *Turtle* and *Sprite*, both shapes, can be made to move across and around a visual display unit, drawing things, rubbing them out, and changing them. Colours and shapes change and the vehicles for the change are friendly. *If* this approach is correct and succeeds and is taken up widely, then the blocks to learning by computer may disappear as the mechanisms become part of childhood culture. It has been suggested that computer games will fulfil this function. With but a few exceptions, the mathematics and language teaching games in particular, computer games impart little understanding of the technology, although they do give quite a high degree of manual dexterity and if played on a home computer some people might be tempted to play with the computer itself. A far deeper cultural change is required for computers to be used in general ways like education. The most disturbing aspect of this is the argument that the change actually means the end of conventional literacy — a sad prospect indeed.

Life is not all about work, nor totally serious matters. We escape from these in the entertainment world, or perhaps in a fantasy world, and often a combination of both. We relax and spend our spare time in many ways, some of which are very old like the theatre and others relatively new like the cinema, television, and video. In all of these, computer technology is not only playing a part but is setting standards which are becoming the norm to the extent that productions not using the technology appear to be shoddy and amateurish.

The theatre is special. The Greeks knew this and for centuries differing nations have steeped themselves in its magic. It depends effectively on its immediacy and that it is live and vibrant. It is a continuously evolving art form and, within that evolution, technology since the Roman Colosseum days has played its part. The design of the theatre, the ability to shift scenes quickly, mechanical aids such as lifts and hoists, or revolving stages and parts of stages have all added to our experience of the theatre and nowadays are expected treats. Even children expect the effects these gadgets can bring in pantomime.

Computers are now making an impact on theatre lighting systems. Lighting is a key part of the magic. The illusion that good lighting can create is often the difference between good and mediocre theatre. In a fair sized auditorium there may be literally hundreds of different lights, singly or in clusters, and in a complex production these may all have to be brought into action at a given cue. This is not merely a series of on and off switches, but dimming and changing in intensity. Few theatres are equipped with computers for lighting (or other purposes). London's National Theatre has a computer but the most sophisticated computer is the one in use in the Schaunspiel Haus in Hamburg—both are relatively new compared with the older city centre buildings.

Computers, especially microcomputers, are now used in touring shows or repertory companies to manage the sequences and the actual activation of theatre lighting. The cues are numbered on a sequence and the lighting pattern is plotted. There are, of course, manual overrides or by-pass sequences which can cope with the cast missing cues or lines, or tripping over the furniture. Floppy discs are used as the input medium and the activation is generally done with the use of infrared beam systems. The number of stagehands and electricians needed, given a very sophisticated lighting pattern, is far less and the work is really done by one person who is probably also capable of doing the programming—an eight hour job on average. One very sneaky use of computer lighting systems concerns the change of cue needed from time to time. On Broadway it is estimated that because a specified number of musicians, actors, stagehands, etc., must be in attendance, even if they are not needed, it costs $11,000 per cue change. With a lighting board system, a cue change can be worked in quietly for nothing, providing of course it was a lighting cue!

The actual content of shows can change with the use of computer technology, but we shall leave this until the next chapter as it involves new ideas which depend on the new technologies for their existence. Computer lighting sequences merely let a company do something better, using fewer resources than they would have had to use; indeed, the standards for theatregoers are now very high in these technical respects. The West End or Broadway can now be replicated in Derby or Stavanger with a high degree of accuracy and success.

Both the television and film industry use computers. Camera and lighting sequences in technical films, especially those using slow or fast motion photography are coordinated by computers and are increasingly becoming computer system controlled. The complicated title sequences we now see, especially those using split screens, multiple or broken images, or the fragmentation of the '4' of Channel 4 can now be controlled or formed instantaneously in a live performance by the use of special computer techniques. New equipment such as *Electronic News Gathering* (ENG) will make the dissemination of news and current affairs items incredibly faster, using fewer skilled people. Again, ENG depends on simultaneous transmission and filming, but without the normal outside broadcast facilities. At present little of this is being used in the industrialized world and not unnaturally the relevant unions are objecting.

The consumer also benefits in less direct, more technical ways. Editing, especially when there are hours of rushes, can be speeded up and made much more accurate with computer tagging facilities. The tinting and flying spot technique now available in the telecine process and the dubbing procedures are all computer controlled, enabling mediocre photography to be amended to first class or first class to amazing on a frame-by-frame basis; it is this the viewer sees, not the original. The scheduling of complete series, indeed the entire network scheduling, is now done on computers. There is little doubt that the consumer benefits, because the quality of the actual pictures of the programme are better than they would otherwise have been. Whether this is appreciated is quite another matter. Equally, whether the content is better is also open to question.

Even artists are using computers. A recent (1983) exhibition at the Tate Gallery in London featured a computer-controlled painting machine — it did not receive an ecstatic press.

None of us appreciate our national telephone systems. For some reason or another a group of strangers from another country can always be brought into animated conversation (given a common language) by three subjects: beer, national beer is always the best (US citizens tend to be the exception); sex; and the phone system. The national telephone system is always the worst. Horror stories of crossed lines, missed connections, wrong numbers, and the inordinate amount of time it takes to either get a telephone installed or have it repaired are internationally interchangeable. When the new electronic systems come into full operation, telecommunication systems should be faster, more reliable, and more accurate. Quite what will happen to the present international consensus is anyone's guess. Different countries are using different systems and protocol for their internal use and these are also at varying stages of development, so the grumbles will also be at different stages.

In the previous chapter we described the dramatic change that the electronic exchange will make to work and to the work environment. In consumer terms it should mean easier, cheaper calls and will open up new areas, like interactive teletex systems. It may indeed be the basis of a future videophone system using existing television technologies or lead to the development of new closed user groups of verbal and printed message passers as well as teleconferencing. It is not always quite as expected, however. New electronic switchboards are having teething troubles. Some are peculiarly erratic in that conversation becomes inaudible, words disappear, phones tend to ring spontaneously, and it also eats callers. Perhaps there will still be room for the international cooperative in telephone grumbling. Satellite transmitters will both relay and boost conversations in telecommunications all around the world. Where today we have radio hams contacting each other, the next few years will almost certainly see the development of computer buffs, whose installations will contact each other by satellite across continents.

In practical terms a better and more reliable system is likely to increase both business and personal traffic on the new telecommunication systems. Whilst this technology may lead to the first vandal-proof public telephone box, the growth in use will mean that fibre-optic cable rather than copper cable will have to be used if the system is not to run up against a physical constraint in its capacity. One slight problem here is that rats appear to find fibre cable quite delicious and it is a rather expensive way to satisfy their appetites.

It is really quite difficult to state confidently and without contradiction that any single change has improved matters for all consumers. It may have improved things for some people, yet worsened them for others, depending on individual and group circumstances, and in other instances the consumers may simply not have consciously noted the changes at all. This last category applies to printing, especially of newspapers and magazines. Some newspapers and periodicals are now printed by a process known as photocomposition rather than the old, traditional black and hot lead processes. Newspapers are converting, or trying to convert, to computerized typesetting, eliminating many of the traditional craft printing jobs and allowing direct input by journalists or editorial staff. Other and newer forms of printing like laser setting and ink jet printing are being used, often by remote control using telecommunication links and even satellites. Colour printing is also now computer controlled with shades and contrasts built into the programs of scanners and other very sophisticated and expensive equipment.

What difference does it make, however, whether the daily paper is printed in the new or old style? Does the reader care or even notice? There may be typographical changes but it is unlikely that these are due to the printing process alone. It is also nearly always the case that computerization leads to fewer editions, not more. It does appear that the reason for using the computer technologies is sheer economics. The cost of running a newspaper using the labour-intensive old technologies is said by the proprietors to be prohibitively expensive. This is a world-wide plaint. Germany, the United Kingdom, the United States, and France are all moving in the same direction, i.e. to use computers within newspaper printing. To the extent that if the proprietors are correct in that computer technology is the sole method of keeping the newspapers in existence at all, then the readers are best served by their use. It is, however, a slightly questionable proposition as to whether the economics of newspapers can be summed up in such a trivial, indeed banal, manner and whether one technology, even one as powerful as the computer, will prove to be the saviour. Other than this and better colour printing, consumers — the readers — tend neither to notice nor to care how the newspaper is produced or printed.

These are merely some of the places where computers have made an impact on consumers in industrial societies. There are so many more that a catalogue of them would fill the rest of this book. They range from library management to heating and ventilation control; from sports coverage on television with instant statistics (useless or otherwise) to shop and museum security systems; from mail order catalogues to magazine subscription lists. People and families have had their lives altered, perhaps marginally, perhaps greatly by the new systems. None of the changes outlined in this chapter have been totally new additions to society; rather there have been slight alterations to, or improvements on, already existing systems. What the computers can do, however, is to stimulate and then operate systems which would otherwise not exist at all. Of all their properties this is the one which sets them apart from the generality of other machines. It is here that their revolutionary propensities and power lie.

Chapter 6

Consumer Impacts II

THE MARK OF A FUNDAMENTAL TECHNICAL OR SCIENTIFIC change lies not in its cleverness, nor in its intricacy, but in the effects that it has on people and society. A genuine breakthrough stimulates many changes, some scarcely conceivable at the time the original thought was gestating. The people who developed gunpowder for fireworks would not have envisaged guns or bombs; indeed, without some form of super foreknowledge they could not have done. Thus the significance changes tend to be of the secondary effect variety, even though the primary or first effect was often designed and produced with the replacement of a good or service firmly in mind. This, for example, applies to the steam engine and the motorcar. Their development away from the original concept of replacing wind, water, human, and horse power into real community changes were unforeseen at the time. It is also noticeable that the development of these machines tended to be over long periods and to involve many different people rather than one person — as is the case with the computer.

The second form of technological breakthrough is one which develops without a specific use in mind. The theoretical physicists working on electricity and conduction and, in a later age, nuclear energy had no specific uses in mind. It is most unlikely that even in his most innermost and unrecorded thoughts Gauss ever thought of the electric toothbrush or blanket, whilst it was the politicians who led the drive to nuclear weapons rather than the scientists. In a way, the computer resembles both types of these changes. It was originally designed to replace clerks and to solve and perform arithmetical problems and operations. Its potential for other yet unspecified tasks was clear from early days, too, and in many specifics these have been justified. It is almost becoming a utility like electricity upon which other systems or functions rely. It is quite clear, however, that whichever way one looks

161

at a computer it has the right to stand alongside gunpowder, the steam engine, and the aeroplane as a truly major society changer.

The key to this entry into the 'technological hall of fame' is the products and services now available which would not have been possible had it not been for the computer. This is the distinction between the things mentioned in Chapter 5, where goods were made more reliable or perhaps cheaper and services more readily available and distributed both more easily and quickly. In all of this there was no net addition to human progress in a fundamental sense, nor indeed a net subtraction except in unquantifiable social terms; there was a quality/quantity shift. The computer, however, has possibilities that take it well beyond these uses and into the realms of science fiction where there are generally new gadgets stimulating new forms of social ordering. Whether these new and indeed potential changes will prove to be to the advantage of people overall remains to be seen. Many of the changes have not been in operation long enough to see their real effects and some have not yet got past the laboratory stage and into general use. Most consumers have clearly been affected, although if asked whether or how computers have changed their lives, many of the examples given would scarcely raise a mention.

This analysis is not entirely based on a distinction between replacement or amended goods and new goods for new markets. Rather like the car which at one point was a substitute for the horse and carriage yet literally changed the lives of billions of people, there are computer uses which started as replacements but soon developed into a new product. The production of bank statements for clients transformed into computerized out-of-hours cash collection is a recent example. This is the case where the parallel with electricity looms up —

the use of the computer is so wide, and when installed so deep, that there is a danger either of dividing the technology into segments or of attributing to it some mystique which it does not deserve. We could break it into manageable pieces so as to more easily digest the whole eventually, or invest it with powers above most others because we do not understand it; it, the computer, can be overpowering. Whichever way we are tempted, whichever of our senses is assaulted or offended by these machines, we must resist both siren songs. Computers are in essence a single technological entity, however they work, whatever their size or cost, and whether they are programmable or dedicated. Only when we realize this and then also recognize that the mystique surrounding them is man-made, will we learn to accept and admire, perhaps even love, the machine in all its forms.

By and large consumers are funny people. Every person believes most firmly that they are an individual and as such unaffected by the rest of the world and other people when they come to make their choice of goods and services. Market research, however, suggests that people *en masse* are suggestible, although they may only buy once if the product is poor; that advertising works; and that sample testing is an accurate method of predicting how and when a product will sell — rather like political opinion polling. This means that products nowadays invariably are tested in some way before being released onto the unsuspecting public, but even so there can be unexplained flops. A general depression and falling disposable incomes will always explain some of these mistakes, as indeed they account for some of the successes. Just to give a small example, one would expect monies to be spent on staple goods if incomes are falling, thus leaving luxuries or fripperies in the doldrums. In fact, whilst this is partially true people also like to cheer themselves up and so will buy costume jewellery at the cheap end of the market and cheaper brighter clothes, and often do so at the expense of trading down in food from, say, roast beef to stewing steak. To complicate matters, not everyone is affected equally by a boom or slump. Different income groups and thus consumption groups vary in responses. Some people can reduce their savings; others have no savings to reduce. Overall, despite a general pattern of consumption there are still risks associated with bringing out new products and in computer terms this can be illustrated by the following examples.

In the United Kingdom, Prestel is a much-praised although scarcely advertised view-data service provided by British Telecom to businesses and consumers in their offices or homes. It has amazing potential in that it is interactive and could revolutionize certain forms of trading and shopping as well as information storage and retrieval. This system, indeed, the non-interactive Ceefax and Oracle teletext systems could not exist without computers. They store, analyse, update, and retrieve information and, in the case of Prestel, process the system so as to satisfy consumers' questions. It is neither a coincidence nor an accident that the *Consumers Association*, the body that produces *Which?*, was one of the early subscribers. However Prestel has just not taken off. Despite the fact that games can be played, insurance ordered, theatre times checked, tickets ordered, and links checked with airlines, not to mention closed user groups for use by companies or government departments, there were less than 12,000 sets after eighteen months of commercial venture. What is worse is that less than 1,000 of these were in private homes.

Although it is very early days yet in the life of the videotext market, it is clear that just producing a good idea is not enough. Marketing and price have to be right and, moreover, the product has to be what is wanted by the consumer. From the Prestel point of view both the costs of the receiving set and the costs of the services using British Telecom landlines are very high. In addition, the slow access speed has been a deterrent, as has the need to use a complex alphanumeric pad. Clearly both the Consumers Association and the Norwich Union Insurance Company have faith in the system reaching homes eventually. Equally clearly, Canada with Telidon (a possibility for the US market) and France, Japan, Germany, Sweden, and Finland, which have 1983 as the latest date for public view-data services (there may be some slippage in this), demonstrate faith in this type of service. Nevertheless, as has been said, Prestel has been most disappointing in market terms and so have the two UK teletext services, Ceefax of the BBC and Oracle of ITV.

Neither of these services, nor indeed any ordinary teletext service, require special additional receivers and the cost of a teletext equipped television set is now only marginally above that of an ordinary colour set. Even so, the take-up of teletext equipped sets, either by purchase or by rental, has been very slow — only 180,000 sets after five years of availability to the public. Neither these services nor the BBC2 service incur any payment at the time of use, yet both are used sparsely even when installed. There is some sort of danger that we may be becoming overinformed and that teletext services, attractive as they may be to people who admire masses of information, will never be used to any great extent. Compared with using a book they are slow in their page searching and also suffer from the massive cultural barrier provided by the traditional book-based method of getting information which still pervades all schooling. Thus, despite ingenious and very sophisticated techniques neither videotext nor teletext have yet taken off. They have not captured the imagination in the same way that other electronic developments have done.

One of these successful developments, and not one that had been widely forecast to do extra well, is demonstrated by the rush by buy home computers. Many people buy them as toys and then rarely use them again, but sufficient buyers are serious enough to subscribe to all sorts of technical magazines. Some computer buffs are spending so much of their free time with their machines that their marriages and other relationships are being threatened — computer widows now rival golf widows. Whilst the price of one small UK-produced computer is absurdly low (at less than the cost of an expensive pair of shoes), and this is the largest selling home computer, there clearly now is more than price involved in this sales explosion. There seems to be a very deep-felt need for some people to attempt things on their own rather than have instant spoonfeeding, and, interestingly, this does not seem to be related to age at all. It is, however, related to sex, there being far more male than female computer buffs. Overall this is a market with an astonishingly high potential. It has done well without the benefit of extensive school computer use, yet this in itself will promote considerable domestic sales. The computer shop in the high street and then I techs around the United Kingdom would not exist without computers — naturally enough.

The difference in success rates between television-based data services and home computers is even more startling when it is realized how much effort consumers have to put into the latter compared with the former. With either videotext or teletext services consumers merely have to use a simple alphanumeric pad and wait for the appropriate page or pages to be found. In the case of Prestel this may lead through a series of questions and perhaps even the ordering of a product. However, the instructions are simple and based on a YES/NO question so as to move onto the next stage, and the pad itself is neither difficult to understand nor to manipulate. Home computers have a totally extra dimension of challenge and, to put no finer point on it, difficulty.

Whilst some of the hundreds of thousands of people who have bought home computers (as of late 1982) are computer professionals and a few are engineers or others who work with computers, most people have little or no idea what they are, what they can do, or where to buy them. Indeed, many are purchased as an educational present for children only to be used by their parents — a latter-day 'father and the train set syndrome'. The instruction book has to be mastered, sometimes unfortunately a PhD level task in itself, and also programming and a computer language, even if only BASIC has to be learned. Many of the men who become addicted have never used a keyboard and have to learn to do so. All the inevitable early programming mistakes have to be made, or at least there seems to be an inevitability about them. Home computers tend to be unforgiving of mistakes. Commas and spacing, which in grammar and in a conventional written sense can be treated in a somewhat cavalier way, are now critical. The whole program could well fail or go wrong if just one lower case letter is in the wrong place. Graphics add an extra dimension in which to make mistakes.

Quite what these home computers are used for is not always totally clear. Many of the household chores, bill paying, or even trying to get an optimum use of energy for heating and lighting can well be worked out on a conventional calculator. As the smaller computers cannot act as process control mechanisms without a very high level of software, this too is a non-starter. Games can be played and indeed it is quite easy to invent one's own unique game, so most small computer manufacturers provide discs or cassettes of various games and teaching games. Some people set themselves problems, analyse their horoscopes and biorhythms, keep a computer cash book/diary, attempt to analyse the week's random events, train schedule deviations, and so on. The home computer magazines are full of these kinds of ideas and people are actually using them — not in their businesses, not for real work, but for their own satisfaction. Perhaps some people are trying to 'beat' the computer, however that may be done; in any event they try to compete with it.

The major point, however, is that the technology which has led to a system in which the consumer remains relatively passive has had a slow start, whilst the development into active, difficult, and self-improvement avenues has burgeoned beyond expectation. This flies in the face of other experiences — of television replacing theatre and cinema, of videofilms replacing scheduled television programmes, and of book reading and buying diminishing. It appears, on the surface, to be a most interesting and quite aberrant comparison. Deeper down it does appear that people like the challenge of the one but do not really need the services of the other — they can develop with one machine but not with the other. Both are new products and obviously neither could exist without computers, yet the difference both in what they do, their market performance as measured against market expectation and human reactions to them, sum up the wide spectrum covered by this most ubiquitous of tools.

The data bases and extensions of Prestel into working, learning, and shopping from home are not ruled out in the slightest by their current slow start. However, there will almost certainly have to be a lot of rethinking of markets and, what is most important of all, what people actually want. The data bases, i.e. the teletext services, can be incredibly useful in business, research, and specific subjects such as toxicology or geology, but their uses for ordinary people sitting at home have yet to be explored. Television programme listings themselves, perhaps local statistics such as what books are in at present in the local library, could be welcome, but a printed news service or masses of stock market data, or food prices, do not seem to interest people. What makes this service even more unrealistic for the consumers at home is that it is competing with other forms of information. Local radio news programmes are at least as up-to-date as the teletext systems and have the advantage of the occasional in-depth treatment, give at least as good weather reports, and often far better traffic reports, especially *local* traffic reports. One problem with the present teletext arrangements is that they are national or at best large regional, whilst they need to be refined down to communities beyond the British franchise holders areas, rather like local stations in the United States.

The second challenge comes from the Prestel type of system. This not only holds all the information a standard teletext system can do but enables the consumer to focus firstly upon his or her specific enquiry and secondly to then do something about what has been found out. In other words it is a practical as opposed to a totally theoretical tool. At the moment there is a price constraint in the United Kingdom on Prestel, but this should diminish over time because more consumers using the service will make it more viable and, secondly, because the technology itself should become more efficient, especially the new telecommunication technologies and the routine cabling of houses. When this happens and local networks become the rule rather than a novelty, home shopping, home ordering, and, indeed, group communications or games could well rule home life in the 1990s. It will be a totally different (yet just as lucrative for some) gold rush through the remainder of the twentieth century. The combination of cable television and video cassettes could even make the parallel clearer and there could even be the second 'naughty nineties'.

Prestel or some similar videotext system combined with a house cabling programme (assuming of course that at least some of the cable capacity is interactive) would soon make basic teletext services obsolete except for specialist information. It will also open up the possibility of two separate strands of development, although they are not by any means mutually exclusive. The first is to use the cable for a direct multichannel broadcasting system and quite obviously this would not be using any interactive facilities — nor, indeed, many computer techniques. There is a fear that this form of broadcasting will have to concentrate on the more basic forms of entertainment, sex and sport. To this extent the report of the UK Hunt Committee of October 1982 actually reinforced these anxieties rather than allayed them. A deregulated system, especially if it is put to slot and coin television use, could both ruin sport watching for a considerable percentage of the population and at the same time put pornographers on a much sounder financial basis. Both are possible given the proposed system despite government opposition to them. Neither prospect makes proper use of the potential this system offers people, society, and communities.

The second strand of cable technology is taking it into links with other institutions in society. Provided the national telecommnication carrier was involved this could allow for a completely new range of services to be run from or to peoples' homes. Links between banks and individuals, shops and individuals, both on an account or free-wheeling basis, and a triangular link connecting the credit of the three parties, local authorities, hospitals, and schools, should be able to use the cable channels in practical ways, whether for the library suggestion made earlier or for the information concerning other services such as bus service problems or messages from the council. Being an interactive system, parents could be encouraged to get involved in schools, initially without having to leave home to go to a meeting — often a devastating experience for the inexperienced. Hospitals could call for emergency volunteers (blood donors) or simply try to arrange for community involvement for their long-stay patients. In the Teledon type of system it is possible for individuals to get into the network both in graphic and verbal or written form, and this development could stimulate clubs, quizzes, groups of interested parties coming together, and so on. The interactive component is being put to use within television channels in experiments in the United States. Debates are held or speeches made and viewers can register their approval, disapproval, or apathy instantly by using their selector devices.

Clearly this has national and local political implications of a very high degree. The matter has also been taken a stage further, or perhaps backwards, in that viewers can determine the ending of a play or, within bounds, the actual content of a play. Viewers are given choices: for example, do you want a play to be about (a) social workers, (b) giant pandas, (c) a sex-starved librarian, with the instructions to press the appropriate button. Either an entire identikit programme can be built up or the play stopped at various points so as to determine the next set of plots. The current experiment relies on majority voting, the most taking all. However, it is not inconceivable that enough pieces of plot can be arranged to virtually guarantee individuals their own identikit play and, if the parameters are right, an instant fantasy fulfilment system. It is not a system which allows for much peace of mind when it is analysed.

Cabling will obviously link closely with satellite transmissions and broadcasts and this will extend its range.

As users it is probable that companies and governments will be well ahead of individuals and households — business will use it more than those needing entertaining. It will, however, also have an effect on yet another computer-based technology, the videorecorder and tapes. The growth in VCR usage in Britain has been explosive, both of the purchased and rented varieties. There are two reasons for having a tape recorder in the first place. One is to record television programmes that will either clash with other programmes or that people know they are going to miss. Cable television will multiply the times this will happen, thus VCRs will become even more useful. In Britain the main use for VCRs will be to play rented or purchased videotapes of films. Some of these will be illegal, either in a pornographic sense or because they have been pirated and infringe copyright laws. The new channels will diminish the need for this sort of use, especially as the Hunt Report virtually gives *carte blanche* to those wishing to see any sort of film, however new, and no doubt there will be sufficient channels to satisfy most tastes. The victims here will partly be the VCR or perhaps videodisc manufacturers, but also, and mainly, the small high street shop that rents out the videocassettes. This if course assumes that the cost of pay cable television is low enough to make it financially viable overall and to take off amongst most households. Recent research suggests the opposite, in which case it is the cable channel that will be struggling. Videodisc without a recording facility is probably more at risk than tapes, although if the price drops sufficiently it may replace the conventional gramophone record over time. Indeed, disc manufacturers are putting their plans into cold storage at present until market conditions improve. Consumer dependence on the new aspects of computer power does not rely entirely on sitting in front of a television screen, although this may seem to be the case from casual inspection.

Visions of electronic shopping and banking may have some validity and suit some people, some of the time. Practical problems such as foolproof coding systems and adequate delivery services are needed, if only to allay the fears and suspicions that will otherwise hold back these developments. However, electronic banking comes in other ways, too, and one of these can be associated with shopping.

Electronics in banking has been in existence for some years. Banks were the early users of mainframe computers and the optical scanners developed primarily for cheque recognition have made these machines faster and more efficient. Yet these machines and the systems based on them (like computer-produced statements) are not what most people would define as electronic banking. This is exemplified by the cash dispensing machine which has stimulated a very strange syndrome amongst bank users.

A major complaint amongst city centre bank customers, other than the strange, truncated opening times, has been the queues at tellers desks, making simple cash transactions a lengthy time-consuming business. This has been especially true of banks dealing with large numbers of shopkeepers, thus handling much cash. Cash dispensing or cash point machines deliver a low maximum amount of cash to a customer when a card and the appropriate code number is punched into the machine. The statement is checked and all being well, i.e. the right number has been used and enough money or overdraft facilities are in the account, the money is delivered. From time to time there are stories of machines eating the cards but these are usually denied by the banks — even though the events did happen! The cash dispencer was intended for people needing cash at times when banks were shut or very busy.

It is not uncommon to see people queueing in the rain outside a bank waiting to use a machine which could possibly eat their plastic offering, whilst inside the warm, well-lit bank the tellers are having a chat. For some reason some people prefer the anonymity of the computer to the warmth of a teller. It may be that people are worried by what tellers may think of them if they are withdrawing only small sums of money, and only small sums can be obtained from the machines. Other than a thesis built upon these people just hating other people, especially bank employees, there is no logical explanation. The other form of electronic banking is still very much in its infancy and because it is so new the trials have not yet been evaluated. One Austrian supermarket and three French regions are conducting the experiments, although the Austrian one is based on a different principle to that of the French. A British system called *Homelink*, with the Bank of Scotland, Prestel, and the Nottingham Building Society collaborating, opened in 1983. Free consoles for large account holders will receive statements and transfer money between accounts and pay bills. Shops and instant debit facilities are also a possibility.

The Austrian system makes use of relatively orthodox-type technologies. Customers from one particular bank can present their bank cards and have an automatic direct debit from their account to the supermarket's account. The account is adjusted automatically at the bank.

The French system is wider, technically far more ambitious, and, if proved practicable, is capable of leading to far more applications. The French claim to have invented an electronic cheque book or file. Physically it is a plastic card with a microprocessor embedded within it. The memory is surprisingly large and is also controlled by the processor. The memory is divided into secret areas and other areas which can, however, only be accessed through a secret code. The secret area allows the customer to put in their own access code and the makers claim that should attempts be made to find out what this is, the card destroys itself. The accessible part allows the customer to see how much credit is left or to get a bank statement. Obviously, special point of sale terminals have to be used so whilst it is a wider experiment than the Austrian, it is still constrained. The operation is simple. The customer makes a purchase and places the card in the terminal entering the secret code with a hand-held attachment rather than a publicly viewable keyboard. A last minute fail-safe device of a button on the side of the point of sale attachment allows the customer to withdraw from a purchase if the price is too high or if the customer decides not to have the item anyway. The card is then debited with the amount of money spent and the store credited, and at any time the customer can use his card to find out what balance he has, either at a point of sale machine or in a viewer at the bank. Each card records and remembers more than one hundred transactions.

Clearly, especially for businessmen, such electronic banking has possibilities, if and when it can operate widely enough and in foreign currency. At present, clever though it may be, it is also clumsy and has few advantages over the traditional credit card or bankers card/cheque system. The system is known as 'delayed time' and the card is called the 'CP8'. Three other experiments using this card are about to start. Using *Teletel* (the French Prestel), a trial sample of 300 people in a Paris suburb will be able to use their cards and the videotext system to pay gas and electricity bills and place orders and pay for mail order goods. An educational experiment using the French teletext system *Antiope* will use the card to record and monitor the progress of handicapped people. Finally, doctors in a Paris clinic are using the CP8 cards to record data about patients with pacemakers. They can act as reference cards but, unless the patient has given specific or blanket permission access to the information held in the memory, they are strictly limited by the coding.

Electronics and computers are heavily used now in banking but electronic banking, at home or elsewhere, is still experimental. It will come in time and it will depend entirely on computers. Behind the scenes in banking, computers have imposed services to clients with the swift cheque clearing system and automatic adjustment of balances. Such changes are not as yet fundamental although a new system, CHAPS, allows for interbank computer contact, even on an international scale, on a computer-to-computer basis — not through people.

One related service which would not be in operation if it were not for computers is the credit card industry. A mere ten years ago credit cards were virtually unknown and when dimly discerned they belonged to affluent globe-trotting businessmen whose favourite game appeared to be to produce yards of plastic cards from their wallets. The use of credit cards is now very widespread and most large financial deposit-taking organizations issue them as well as chains of stores or department stores. As the spread of the cards has become wider so the chances of theft and fraud have grown, so that some level, albeit less than adequate, of safeguards have had to be introduced. The system works on the card number being recognized and billed almost instantly at the credit card headquarters. The number of transactions is such that if such a task were attempted manually the delays would be too great for the retailer or wholesaler to bear. It is now possible for the shop or garage owner to phone the headquarters of a credit card issuer and to check the status of the card, its credit level, and whether it has been *reported* stolen. As credit cards are still beloved of businessmen and they do tend to travel — although international teleconferences and communications should reduce this somewhat—the companies have to deal with all problems on a multicurrency basis. Without the computer, credit would have remained in the twin provinces of personal contacts and exclusivity to a small group of people—nowadays, even trade union officials are trusted to carry plastic cards.

Finance and financial transactions have played a large part in this chapter to date, not because I believe that they are of paramount importance but because the finance industries have been amongst the earliest and most intensive users of computer technology. There are, of course, many other elements of this genre which have nothing at all to do with television receivers or the money industry. One such area is help for the disabled, although in one respect at least there is one thing in common. The optical scanning equipment used by the banks and credit companies is similar to that used in reading machines for the blind. These machines go some way towards reducing the dependence of blind people on Braille productions or on people reading aloud to them. Yet again, this optical scanning system, let alone the voice production, could not exist without computer input.

Machines are based on character recognition and thus pattern recognition. The new machines are capable of reading any Roman style set typeface, which is a massive advance over those that could once only read special typefaces. One of the interesting facets of the machine is that it has an ability to learn—it is not programmed to read all possible type faces and whilst it does make mistakes, it improves progressively. Readers, especially those programmed for English, have to be delicately handled, pronunciation is anything but standard, punctuation, which can completely change the meaning of a phrase or sentence, has to be taken into consideration, and the grammar continually checked. It is an easy machine to use for non-sighted and non-computer people. The *Kurzweil* machine, named after Raymond Kurzweil, its inventor, has three drawbacks. The first is price: it is expensive to buy and can be expensive to run, and this cuts it off from many ordinary blind people. It cannot read newspaper print because the reverse side often shows through and it cannot read handwriting. Finally, its audio quality is poor, as one would expect. It is tinny, disjointed, and flat, and its ability to cope with punctuation is poor — the punctuation marks can be programmed to be actually spoken, e.g. 'He stood in the rain "comma" without a hat "full-stop".'

The disabled are people who, in general and in theory, should benefit greatly from computer technology. Across a range which covers artificial limbs with sensors and learning facilities, through hearing aids for those with no auditory nerves, to computer and chip-assisted vehicles, the disabled could live more fully. Even blind typists are catered for by special word processors and the aged and infirm by alarm fail-safe mechanisms built into their homes and telephone systems. All of these things and many more are possible, but without a price subsidy the generality of disabled people who are either without a job or in low paid jobs just cannot afford these items. Without long production runs the cost of the products will not fall, so there is a classic commercial Catch 22 operating. It would be sad in the extreme if computer technology did not benefit those in the most need, and this includes the disabled, the old, the poor, and the sick. Occasionally an experiment lifts the spirits, e.g. Tesco, the retail supermarket, and a local social services department used Prestel for home shopping for the housebound, but uplifts of this nature are too few.

Whilst many totally new horizons can be opened for the disabled through computers, the same can also be claimed for those who are sick. The development of organ transplant techniques is one that has needed computers for tissue typing and matching as well as criminology research. Machines that can analyse brain scans or electrocardiograms are now also computer analysed. The differences between old and new techniques are more in the realm of prevention than cure. A person can now have an ECG every month and have the minutest changes monitored. Changes can then be made to diet, lifestyle, stress, and other factors to avoid a heart attack or perhaps a stroke. It could also be, on a less positive note, the greatest boost to hypochondria yet invented. Transplant surgery could not exist without computer-aided tissue typing and matching whilst medical research, especially epidemiology and cancer research would be far behind its present position. Scanners, ultrasound, electromagnetic, and light wave technology all need computer analysis and preparation to work at all.

Research in general is a heavy user of computers, be they in social sciences, physics, or linguistics. Much research could not be undertaken if computers did not exist. One obvious line in this respect is the analysis of words in long works such as the Bible or Shakespeare; patterns found which can prove to some extent that a single writer did, or perhaps did not, write all of the works. Many other bits of research in completely disparate subjects which require the handling of considerable statistical data would be practically impossible without computers, although in theory they could be done, taking a very long time, perhaps even more than a single lifetime. Disciplines like econometrics or astrophysics come into this kind of category, although it must be admitted that neither of these subjects tends to have a direct impact on consumers. There are, however, some indirect effects. Indeed, econometrics is of vital importance to consumers in the centralized economies like the Soviet Union, where the allocation of goods and services is not left to the market and prices but to central or regional planning, and this requires a most sophisticated computer-based econometric model. Astrophysics has perhaps a slightly more tenuous direct effect on the average consumer, although satellites are starting to have some impact.

Satellite telecommunication systems tend to be used by governments and corporations rather than individuals. However, those people who do want to telephone their loved ones, or perhaps enemies, in the United States or Australia can now do so more cheaply and easily than when the older systems were in use. What is new is the ability to watch a sporting event as it happens some 12,000 miles away, or for a paper to be printed using control mechanisms and information channelled over by the satellite. Faster news and opinion (not necessarily more accurate) is making people better informed, at least in theory. In practice, there is a disturbing trend in communications, its censorship, and ownership and the power residing within the system.

Much, like satellite technology, space exploration, and so on, would be impossible at its current level of sophistication without computer technology. Yet again, its impact on consumers is as yet strictly marginal. There may be some psychological gains within a country that has just sponsored a 'first' or a space breakthrough, and there may be some spinoffs both in terms of technology and souvenir production. The United States certainly developed miniaturization and thus spawned the entire microelectronic revolution. Man would not have been on the moon nor space stations have docked with each other if it were not for computers, yet precisely what this has done for the average consumer is as yet unclear. It is, moreover, unclear whether outside of defence mechanisms any advantage will accrue to ordinary people.

Other than the financial industries and services the area which has had the greatest amount of investment in terms of money, people, and ingenuity, has been in the leisure industries. Computer and video games cannot exist without computers, by definition, and these are a growing addiction. The trail blazed by *Space Invaders* has been followed by *Pacman* and a host of other space and seek and destroy games, which rely on a high level of coordination and an ability to withstand boredom. Prices have fallen so that watches or pens with games incorporated can be bought for far less than the price of a pair of football boots or even a football. These, and the growth of amusement arcade chip games, even computer style pinball tables, and the development of video cartridge games played on domestic television sets, have provided an explosion in new leisure facilities. Not all, however, are for the manually dexterous. Computer chess or Mastermind are both cerebral games, as are the games for younger people which teach spelling or simple arithmetic. Interestingly, there is a difference in emphasis between games in arcades (coin-operated machines) and those played at home. Arcade owners want a fresh coin in the slot every minute and a half, whilst a home game, similar in every other characteristic, can last up to half an hour. In other words, the emphasis in arcades is on reflexes.

Whilst children both learn and play with these new machines some even design new games and make considerable fortunes. Young people seem particularly adept at thinking in computer style, rather like some young people master music or mathematics. Some American 11 and 12 year olds do not stop at games but actually produce other programmes, word processor systems, for example. Whilst money is said not to be the motive (rather the challenge of the programmes themselves), a considerable amount of money is there to be made. Annual royalties on a good selling computer game can be as high as £60,000. Computers are now playing a part in the more traditional toy market, too. Programmable vehicles and radio-controlled planes and cars are now a commonplace. Train sets and racing sets have computer control systems including chip technology in the engines themselves. Young people are growing up with computers, yet the danger is that they will neither realize that they are doing so, nor will they even realize that computers are involved in what they are doing. Only those encouraged to delve beneath the surface will really benefit in any longer-lasting manner.

Games are an extremely new facet of computerized leisure, videorecorders and videodiscs are another, and a third change in our entertainment system is in live entertainment. Without computers, the concept of the light show, using sequences of lasers and holographs would just not be possible and a totally new art form would not have emerged. This must not be confused with computer act, which is confined to either the printout of a Jayne Mansfield type of girl in profile or to some form of random paint distributor. The common 'discos' with patterns of flashing lights depend on basic integrated circuitry, sometimes in its most elementary form, at others in very complex arrangements: some pop groups are more electronic than musical. Clubs and discos compete on the basis of the most expensive computer-controlled light system. There are now live theatre productions, especially those which use closed circuit video to simultaneously transmit parts of the action onto screens for double or multiple images, which would have been unavailable some two or three years ago.

Whilst computers have painted, printed, and lit stages, they have also written poetry and prose, have sung and are being programmed to produce music, and, nowadays, synthesize sounds. The advent of electronic music with synthesizers of all shapes, sizes, and power effectively means that at times computers are creating new musical instruments or perhaps that computers themselves can be made to act either as musical instruments or part of one—much like the reed in a woodwind. This use is now widespread both in popular and more serious music.

Some mechanical gadgets are almost treated as toys by some adults, especially men, who are peculiarly susceptible to these things. 'These things' are remote control systems for television sets or such new gadgets on cars as automatic tyre pressure warning lights. It is possible for a man to indulge in play and work of this type at one and the same time. An instrument like the microwriter, which by the use of five buttons and one hand can effectively type, is an amazing 'come-on' for someone wishing to show off at his local club. It is also extremely useful and easy to use and may well be the forerunner of a series of typing machines without keyboards which will fill the gap for keyboard-shy men until voice-controlled computer and processors become a commercial reality.

In recent years the United Kingdom seems to have lost many things, some almost traditional, like brewery dray horses and telegram services. However, we seem to have replaced the latter with 'kissgrams' and 'suspendergrams' and services like aircall, where people can be paged by telephone calls. This can be done in cars, trains, indeed anywhere, however embarrassing this might prove; conversely, like the microwriter, the effect can be impressive in the extreme. Many of these systems, especially the large answering service system in San Francisco run by a Delta computer, rely on electronic computing power, although few are as yet in full operation or have reached anywhere near their full potential.

Nevertheless, new services run by national and international telecommunication agencies will follow on the use of microelectronic and conventional computer usage on an annually ever-heavier basis.

The computer is also opening the way forward for competitors to the national agencies to offer some of the more profitable services on a cheaper basis. Most of the services will aid business and commerce more than the individual, rather like satellite communication systems, but some may be used by individuals and some could be used by the aged if they are made available at the right price. These devices are basically telecommunication warning devices. Some of the new systems will be used in the home for home working (the modern electronic variation of 'outwork'), but skilled rather than the traditional unskilled assembly, or semi-skilled tailoring work. Some cynics believe that managers who claimed to work from home had to be treated with the contempt usually reserved for those who claimed that the 'business lunch' was hard work. In the future it is probable that such claims to working at home will not only be monitored through terminals but two-hourly progress reports and checks will be made. No longer will this excuse be a matter for suffering amongst secretaries and gossip in the executive toilet.

Politics and computers tend not to mix terribly well. It has always been possible to run a totalitarian regime, or any form of dictatorship without them; with them it is so much easier. Many of the issues involved in this area will be explored later in Chapter 8, but it is worth mentioning the use of computers by political parties to keep their records. Computers have such a mystique that the Social Democratic Party in the United Kingdom thought it worth while to announce publicly that they would be using a computer for their records and membership. Their grasp of public relations is somewhat different to that of the Labour Party who have had a computer sitting in their Head Office(s) basements doing next to nothing very quietly for at least fifteen years. The use of computers to analyse opinion polling and election results has also had important political repercussions. Strangely, most computer professionals do not like being reminded of this, nor, often, the other powers that reside in those who understand the machines. Most of these people feel that their machines are tools, that they merely 'follow orders', and that they themselves are politically agnostic or, at the most extreme, moderates.

Robots have yet to reach the home. It is only a matter of time before they will, although they are more likely to look like articulated giraffes or truncated tortoises than film and science fiction television humanoids. Cleaners, cookers, and maintenance robots could well, once the science of sensor technology improves, be cheap enough on a mass-produced basis to be viable (especially if the Japanese fifth-generation programme stays on course) well before the end of this century.

Science parks are the type of quasi-public places that will attract robotic exhibitions, and some theme parks, notably Disneyworld, already rely heavily on robots and computers. The concept of the science park is American, more precisely Californian, and it is now intended to open at least one in the United Kingdom. The concept is to have a selection of small high technology companies clustered around a university which specializes in science disciplines and can make its resources available to the firms. As an adjunct to this, public displays arranged between the university and the park companies are intended to attract the local population and stimulate the imagination of local young people.

In terms of what can exist without computers, a computer program designed to write computer programs is quite clearly getting near the ultimate. Several such programs exist and one, *The Last One*, is cheekily named, too. However, the most science fictional of the new procedures involving computers and computer technology involves the amalgamation of people, matter, cells, and biology.

The development of genetic engineering, i.e. the manipulation of cells and cell nuclei to create new living forms both animal and vegetable, would not have been possible without computer back-up. As a technology it attracts critisism of (with the overtones always associated with Dr Frankenstein) cloning and to some extent experiments with animals, none of which are totally fair but none of which can be totally dismissed out of hand. It is a frightening and potentially far-reaching technology, capable of increasing the nutritional yield of plants, curing diseases, even cleaning oil sludge from pipes, but also capable of misuse and prone to the accidental creation of an organism which could be hostile should it escape from its designated environment. However, a more direct use of computers is the start of the development of biological computers — microelectronics and biotechnology combined. *This is the start of bionic man.*

An American hopes to produce a 'biochip' in the next year or two. Protein chips are to be used rather than the standard semiconductor materials. Artificial proteins have electron beam etching and are then dipped in silver nitrate, the silver depositing from lines of about 4μm wide. A chip of this nature would have over a hundred thousand more switches per unit area than existing chips and operates at far greater speed. Whilst this is a purely theoretical exercise at present, the company has a grant to develop a chip based on protein to react with certain brain cells and act on the sight centres of some blind people. The bionics can be applied if and when these chips use DNA codes as programming agents. A computer built on this basis would be controlled by enzymes (perhaps hormones), be self-repairing, and have a vast memory. It would be awesome.

Mankind's inability to see into the future is one of the more appealing facts of life and by definition this includes the pattern of technology. Guesses can be made, some more inspired than others, but the one constant factor is that we do not know what will happen. Given this, quite what developments the computer will spawn, directly and indirectly, what fads and fashions will emerge, and what will last and change our lives and societies are as yet unknown. There may be no effects at all and the biochip may have to be consigned to the dustbin of technological 'may have beens' like the Brabazon, the Bacon Cell, and Zeta—all world-beaters on paper in their time. Computer developments will undoubtedly be littered with some of these, but the probability is for new and radical products and services over the next two decades, not of the faster/cheaper variety but totally new things that would not have existed without computers. The problem or the beauty for this book, commentators, analysts, politicians, indeed all of us, is that we may suspect these things but we can neither prove that they will be there nor prove what they will be. Indeed, it takes the perceptive science fiction writer to even guess what they will be or even look like.

The recent past may lead us to suspect the worst, however— that is, the heavy use of computer technology in war, depth, and arms rather than in life and life-sustaining and enhancing systems. Such a tragedy is to be avoided at all costs.

Chapter 7

Government's Use
of Computers

I F THERE WERE TO BE AN OPINION POLL TO FIND THE LEAST
popular body in any modern state, government, or at the
least some branches of it, would be at or very near the
top. This has been so throughout history. More often than
not a government has been identified with constraints,
repressions, interferences, and above all taxes. None of these
factors can be described as positive and all of them are easy
to caricature so as to give a picture of an all-embracing octopus
squeezing the freedoms out of individuals. Politicians
themselves are treated with more than a degree of scepticism
as to their motives and so are civil servants and other public
sector administrators, perjuratively described as bureaucrats,
faceless or otherwise.

Most people, however, will treat government as a necessary
evil to be tolerated or grumbled about, but ultimately obeyed
as and when necessary. The fact that all nations have found
it essential to have a system of government, albeit the types
have differed immensely, rather than choose anarchy, points
to this ultimate respect. No-one actually likes paying taxes,
but most of us do; few people agree with everything that a
government does or stands for and as a corollary to this there
can be no such thing as the national interest in practical terms.

Despite these drawbacks and despite an easily understood
anti-bureaucratic attitude prevalent in the industrialized world,
the concept of central government survives, indeed in practice
it is expanding. In short, government is one of the major
world-wide success stories of the late twentieth century.
Individual regimes may have foundered from time to time
but the concept as a whole has burgeoned.

Whatever the political system and however the government
came into power computers have played a large part in this
success story; indeed there are now some regimes which
depend on computer systems to remain in power, for their

defence, and for the smooth and efficient running of the state. It is very doubtful whether the clock can ever be turned back and these countries revert to their pre-computer mechanisms. As this applies to the majority of industrial states it follows that the computer has become an important part of the state infrastructure, like roads, electricity, or gas. Central government is not the only form and nor is it the sole governmental user of computer power. Within federal systems each province or state uses electronic systems, as do local authorities of various sizes and powers; they are becoming the ubiquitous administrative and executive tools.

There is no doubt that a country can be governed without the computer; several thousands of years and a large number of empires, dynasties, revolutions, wars, and political systems have proved this point. There is equally no doubt that it is easier to control and otherwise govern a country with the assistance of electronic computer systems; efficiency is enhanced alongside an ability to undertake new tasks. Both of these functions are important. A country which can collect all the taxes due to it and can trace those avoiding payments is obviously better off than one which cannot do so, if only because it can raise taxes in the expectation that a certain amount of revenue will inevitably accrue to the exchequer. A country which can provide services to its population over a wide spectrum, health, education, public hygiene, law and order, and security, will tend to be more politically and socially stable than one which cannot do so. This is not a political value judgement — the means of delivery of these services is irrelevant up to a point. Governments, however, have a duty to see that none can fall beneath socially accepted standards and to facilitate the means by which this is done. Computers are nowadays an integral part of these services and the expectations of the consumers are so high that the diminution of service standards which would follow if the computers were withdrawn would not be tolerated for long. Whether they like it or not governments are increasingly trapped into computer usage and there are times when they decidedly do not like it.

Government in a modern industrial state deals with a series of complex administrative problems requiring a mass of statistical data as well as political and philosophical direction. Furthermore, the number of decisions required tends to increase year by year as the duties and responsibilities of governments increase. It appears to be some rough measure of civilization to show compassion, especially on a collective scale, and many of the newer services and duties are devoted to this end. Even governments which have swept to power on a platform of reducing central government's involvement in almost everything have found it a remarkably difficult task to fulfil. People actually want other people to have jobs, want to see well-educated and fit children, want to see the older generation looked after well, and do not want to see hunger, disease, or cruelty. These matters require resources and money to achieve and because little if any profit can be made out of their mass provision it has become necessary for governments to provide them. Despite the fact that tax paying is not a popular past-time governments are forced to levy taxes and provide more and more services even when committed to do the precise opposite; the people who mandated them in the first place are the same people who force them to abandon the original policy. In a modern industrial state there is a deep and lasting need for governments to do somewhat more than merely administer the laws and constitution. Administration is, however, the forte of the computer, it being a repetitious task for the most part, and much of the capacity of government computers is taken up by routine data and programs.

There are two distinct forms of administration needed in government, be it central or local. The first is to ensure that all the statutory duties are being met properly and the second to ensure that the department itself is functioning efficiently and properly. Both of these prime functions are aided immensely by the use of computers; indeed, they were originally designed for such uses. Obviously internal matters such as payrolls, invoices, bills, and personnel are treated in the same way as in the private sector, possibly using the same programs. In some areas, especially the personnel one, there is the additional factor of state security, and computers are used here too, although to judge by recent spy trials in the United Kingdom the systems leave rather a lot of room for improvement.

Some government departments have an immense administrative task. Social security is one such as it needs to maintain records of all the people with a social security number, keep it up-to-date, and minimize the mistakes. In the United Kingdom the largest computer installation is that of the Department of Health and Social Security; the new proposed government centralized computer system is to use the DHSS data bank as its basis. Much of the routine administration and information is classified as secret, strange as that may seem. Defence information, whether it is concerned with numbers of people employed or of missiles stockpiled, cannot be obtained without special clearance. In an imperfect world such caution is understandable, if not always compatible with open government. It is when such restrictions are placed upon seemingly harmless data in other departments that fears start to be expressed. We shall look at this twin problem of obsessive secrecy allied with the potential misuse of data in Chapter 13.

Administration is of course the major role of local

government, indeed often it is said to be the only role. All the local services have to be provided according to statute and in a large urban area this can be a herculean task. Like central government local authorities were early users of data processing; indeed, they helped stimulate and fuel the early growth of the whole computer manufacturing sector. In recent years there has been a tendency to share computer facilities between councils so as to get economies of scale and to gain access to more powerful machines than any single authority could have afforded. As a result of this growth computer staffs and computer literate employees are increasing in number very rapidly in the public sector, with all of the additions to power and influence that this implies.

Running a country is a formidable task which gets more difficult as the years go by. This is partially due to the increase in the number of areas in which government intervention is now required but is also partly due to the increasing complexities within a modern state and also the deepening relationships between such states. Another degree of difficulty is added by the propensity for the media to check on and investigate decisions made by those in power so that the administration of a nation is open to constant scrutiny. Government itself tends to minimize the outflow of information in such circumstances, and nowhere has this art been better refined than in the United Kingdom; the United States, on the other hand, has a far wider ranging and investigative media (especially the press) and far more liberal libel laws. There is thus an increasing tendency in most industrialized countries to ensure that no errors are made, either of judgement or of fact, so reinforcing the use of computer installations. Whether or not such a tactic actually minimizes errors or whether it merely becomes easier to hide behind computer mistakes whilst at the same time making it more difficult to get at the truth at all is a matter for conjecture. Probably both scenarios have an element of plausibility.

Decisions have to be taken in the light of the available information; often a wrong decision turns out to be a correct one, but based on faulty or incomplete data. National governments have the duty of arranging for the collection, the maintenance, and the publication of the statistics relating to their country. Whilst standards vary widely and the collection methods and bases differ across international borders there is a pride taken in the accuracy of those services. Statistics are kept about almost everything; at least this seems to be the case. Businesses have forms to fill in concerning their staffs, their output, their products, their VAT and other taxes, their physical premises, and their intentions for the future. An individual has a similar cross to bear when just coping with the exigencies of everyday life — buying something on credit, renewing a driving license, applying for a passport or planning permissions. We fill in forms designed for computer use rather than for the convenience of the hard-pressed consumer, and this dichotomy itself results in poor information due to incorrectly filled in forms. If, however, we want efficient government we shall have to put up with the collection of such data; indeed, as the state becomes more complicated even more forms will have to be completed. It appears to be a small price for a high degree of civilization.

The data are needed for differing purposes. At one level it is disseminated widely to allow the population, and more especially the specialists within it, to know how the country is progressing. Economic statistics are a good example. They are used and manipulated by businesses, academics, and trade unions to argue with the government of the day (or more rarely to praise it) and to forecast or plan for the next year or two.

Such data are used in a very similar way to those supplied by the meteorological office, the only real difference being that of longer time spans with economic forecasting and statistics. Statistics on health or sickness, on house building and population densities, on strikes, on unemployment and hours worked, on class sizes in schools, on television viewing, and thousands more are the stock in trade of the government staticians. In turn this means that they are the bread and butter of the government's computer service. Without computers some of the statistical series would not have been collected and the physical and mental effort in doing so or the labour-intensive system that would have to have been set up could not have been supported. This applies at least as much to the manipulation of the data as to the raw material itself.

Other statistics are needed for other purposes. Governments themselves have to plan their objectives whether they are in economic or other fields. Birthrate and infant mortality figures are thus essential in arranging for education provision at all levels, whilst the growth or otherwise of railway freight services have an impact on the road building and repair programmes. In these instances the computer aids the efficient use of national resources, although in some instances the service itself could not have been developed without the advent of the computer. This is more clearly demonstrated in the uses of the data than in the collection or dissemination of the facts. Multiple regressions and other mathematical operations are now performed easily and, more importantly, swiftly by computer when some two decades ago a tedious and time-consuming calculation would have been needed; the odds are that this would not have been completed by the time a decision was required. Computers have thus brought into being a whole new dimension of planning in depth when swift responses are needed — a new and valuable tool for government.

General administration reaches down into the most unexpected corners, as does the use of data processing by governments. Planning, be it of roads, factories, or dwellings, often entails the use of esoteric environmental data bases involving the rarer insects and plants; civil servants maintain these stores of knowledge on state computer installations. In West Germany the Ministry of Agriculture has put information concerning such matters as the differing types and levels of soils, water supplies, hedgerows, and possible crops onto a data base. In keeping with the country that has seen the emergence of the Green Party, each area is classified as to its environmental importance and a form of data map is produced. An interesting use of this facility was when it was used to arbitrate in a dispute between state planners and environmentalists on the choice of route for a new road. The data map revealed a third route which met the objections from both sides. The computer used as an arbiter or judge is an interesting if slightly chilling thought, one perhaps that Kafka would have exploited, using its sinister undertones. It clearly, however, has a potential for great benefits, especially when competing interests need to be reconciled.

At all times in history all governments have needed money and, other than by conquest, taxation has been the most practical and tried and tested method of raising it. It is thus quite clear that computers are not necessary in the government revenue-raising process. It is, however, equally clear that in recent years many industrial countries have computerized their tax-collection methods and have thus made the exchequers dependent upon the goodwill of the computer staffs involved. Such a change runs deep, although in some places like the United Kingdom a combination of inertia and union disapproval has resulted in a very slow take-up of new equipment in the personal tax areas. Indeed, a new system has, at the time of writing, still not received final approval in all of its detail. From the point of view of the UK government this lack of progress is a mixed blessing. The cost of an all-computerized income tax system is high and moreover the cost of its breaking down is high too. There will obviously have to be a back-up system both for this and internal security reasons, adding to both capital and manpower costs. Income tax is, however, a prime example of a system which can be computerized to great effect. Long-term running costs can be cut and the speed of income reaching the exchequer increased markedly whilst the number of defaulters should be correspondingly reduced. But for one niggling but major doubt, that of personnel problems, governments would gain massively from electronic tax payment systems.

Value Added Tax (VAT) is a tax almost wholly dependent upon computer use: from its inception in the United Kingdom there has been a heavy machine involvement. The 1981 civil service strike demonstrated the vulnerability of a totally electronic system to a reduction in industrial relations harmony. A cheque mountain developed to deal with incoming or outgoing cheques manually, even if there had been workers willing to do so. It can be argued, and I shall do so in the second half of this book, that a small number of workers traditionally regarded as professional and thus non-militant can stop the entire country. There is no easy answer for any government which subscribes to the International Labour Organization Conventions on free association to form a trade union and the right to take industrial action, which most countries do. As it is more than likely that the use of computers by government will grow, especially in the tax field, this becomes a critical problem. A government which cannot pay its own wage bills, let alone its other creditors, cannot really govern beyond the time that the commercial credit lasts.

Whilst this point has never been reached, and commercial prudence, not to say necessity, makes it a difficult prospect to envisage, the authority of government could be at risk. In the last analysis a government can survive a dispute which attacks people, but when the machinery of government itself is impaired then a determined set of strikers could win. The 1981 civil service dispute demonstrates just how hard such a struggle is against an equally determined government.

Even today, in the United Kingdom, customs duties, local rates, corporation tax, the excise duties on alcohol and tobaccos, not to mention national insurance contributions and benefits, are all dependent on computer power. Not only would national and local governments be starved of cash were the system to 'go down' for one reason or another but, almost as damagingly, records would either be lost, destroyed, or both. This is the tax evaders dream but a government's nightmare. Tax evasion is one of the recurrent problems of government; in some countries it can be so prevalent as to be a national hobby, whilst in others it has reached epidemic proportions. A tax system like VAT reaches into the sinews of an economic system and can be used to check on income profits or turnover tax payments as each transaction is recorded in the process of adding the value. If this check were to be done manually the cost would probably outweigh the benefits in terms of the money reclaimed. Computers make such a strategy possible both financially and practically. Value added tax is thus, in every dimension, a computer tax.

The new computer systems now in operation at both airports and docks to help speed the collection of duties are wholly dependent upon computers. If these were to fail there are simply not enough skilled staffs to maintain a viable system and to allow a commercially viable passage of goods.

By and large it is easier to appreciate the extent of

government's dependence on computers in the general administrative fields by trying to find those places where computers are not used. It is an exhausting and daunting task. Some person-to-person services, especially in local government, some benefit advice, or indeed surveillance centres, and services like refuse disposal and street clearing are, and probably will continue to be, performed manually. Even in these sort of areas, however, computers are used to prepare the schedules and to allocate resources: the totally non-computer areas are now almost non-existent. Even where such gaps appear at present they are rapidly becoming filled by the newer technologies. The diplomatic service, for example, has been one of the last outposts of the amateur, even in such countries where professional civil servants rule, such as France and the United States. The advent of computer-based satellite communication systems has started to change this because the faster information requires ever-quicker analyis and action — professionals now are in the ascendancy.

A side product of this change is in the time honoured art of spying. Not only do modern spies have to be *au fait* with new listening and interception devices but they have to manage computer random codes and hopefully manage to break those of their adversaries. Spying is now a declining trade in terms of manpower, or, more accurately, bearing in mind Mata Hari, people. Satellites beam back ordinary X-ray, infrared, indeed all sorts of photographs, unhindered and untrammelled by humans; only human faults or passing meteroites pose a threat to uninterrupted spying. Regrettably, in this increasingly utilitarian world even the romantic fields of endeavour like espionage have become automated; the computer expert has become more valuable than Bond, Smiley, or any vamp and the world has become that much poorer. It is not as if their passing has made the world safer or stopped the practice—it has merely depersonalized, or perhaps the proper description is deindustrialized, an ancient service—and, moreover, one which most governments refuse to admit even exists. It has to be assumed that whenever one of the satellites, equipped with heat-sensitive cameras which has been submarine tracking or passing over land and monitoring all new buildings to the details of a pram shed, crashes to earth in the future it will be described as a weather balloon. The sophistication of both the new microelectronic or computer-based hardware and the analysis of diplomatic statements, data, or physical constants and variables—even the weather—has resulted in far more information for policy makers. The age of computerized foreign policy is with us; long live Talleyrand.

There is a tendency in the world to believe that information is a valuable commodity in itself and there are times when it seems that governments have become fully paid-up members of this sect. Prediction is, however, a critical part of the art of government and statistics can help move this technique away from the older tea-leaf based methods. However, the data cannot be used in a vacuum. A plan or model is used to simulate the economy in much the same way that the models of bridges are used in stress tests. The model is put onto the computer and various changes are made to the economic parameters, e.g. the rate of inflation may be increased and the changes in the other variables, perhaps output or the balance of payments, are noted. The problem which we shall examine in some depth in Chapter 9 is that the computer gives credence to what may be a totally spurious exercise. An economic model is only as good as its assumptions and these tend to reflect the prejudices of the model builders; whether they are political or strictly economic make little difference to the argument. Fads like the level of the money supply come to the fore for a few years only to be replaced by the next favourite, with the models being altered accordingly. It is not surprising that the record of accurate predictions is not terribly good, especially in the United Kingdom where the political control is too often exercised by civil servants who know little about economics and even less about computers; their motivation is political rather than technical. In Germany, France, and Japan this is not the case. The UK treasury model is now available publicly at a modest fee for those who would care to test their pet policies upon it. Nearly every group which does so changes the assumptions and occasionally the relationships in the model and this results in complete incompatibility between the different results and thus no real comparison can generally be made. We get a more erudite squabble—but little else.

One of the most emotive matters in government is law and order. Whilst very few people will condone crime, especially if violence is involved, there are distinct differences between those who feel there may be unacceptable costs in maintaining law and order and those who feel that no cost is too great. These sides tend to be labelled as either liberal or conservative, although there is no hard and fast split on political grounds. The computer is very much a part of this debate. Many police and security forces around the world are using computer data bases to maintain a check on the inhabitants of and visitors to their countries. It is the method of collection that leads to the disquiet as well as the fact that most people have no idea that data on them is being held, and even if they find out that it is they have no access to it. Errors or coincidences are thus perpetuated, if they existed in the first place. In the United Kingdom there is absolutely no check nor any redress in the case of such an error.

Police forces in the United Kingdom have kept computer records of people charged with offences, and these records stay in existence even if aquittals are made subsequently. However, police computers also store circumstantial evidence, perhaps uncorroborated, perhaps given by an individual with a personal grudge. There is a built-in possibility of a serious miscarriage of justice in the event of enquiries being made through these channels, according to those who oppose the use of computers for these purposes. On the other side, the supporters of the system claim that no such risks exist and that even if they did the benefits in combatting crime far outweigh these costs.

These arguments take on extra dimensions when central computer files are maintained and these are then linked to non-police and non-security force computers. A genuine case for worry arises from these new data linkages, as with the best will in the world the wider the spread of information the greater the chance of accidental leakages or misuse, let alone deliberate malicious acts. Computers are not a necessary component of these data collection systems but they have proved to be a very useful aide in them. Not only can information be retrieved very quickly, and speed is often the vital ingredient in catching criminals, but they can narrow down or even draw up a list of suspects. This is easily done, for example, by asking the computer for the names and addresses of all men 6 feet 3 inches and over, with brown hair, about 35 years old, and known to have been involved in armed robbery. Once the computer has disgorged its list it can be further refined by asking for a subsection who live in the Glasgow area, if of course the original list is not too long for this to be done by simple manual checking. The known accomplices can then be traced and perhaps crosschecked with other suspects or with other information or descriptions.

At one time it was thought that this form of computer detection signalled the end of the successful criminal, especially by the US authorities, and that police forces now had the upper hand. In hindsight such a claim had to be patent nonsense. To start with only the relatively unsuccessful criminal finds him- or herself in the computer bank at all; the successful ones have never even been suspects and certainly take great care not to be associated with known criminals. The computer also contains far too many names of people who are not really miscreants nor indeed deserve to be on the computer, but who have been the subject of misinformation or an accident, e.g. parking in the vicinity of a crime. This last instance is far more prevalent than one may believe. The plethora of choices not only slows the entire process but also results in the following of paths into blind alleys and even further delays, let alone embarrassment. To cap it all the information may act as the trigger for the investigation initially. If either or both of these pieces of information are wrong then the investigation will go wrong too. An example of how computers cannot guarantee success is that of the delay in arresting the 'Yorkshire Ripper'. According to press reports, the man who was subsequently arrested and found guilty of the murders was selected for interview several times and part of the selection procedure involved the use of a computer to trace his car number which had been taken near the scene of some of the murders in Leeds. In this instance the computer did its job, albeit probably naming very many more suspects, but human fallibility spoilt the process.

Human judgement must be an integral part of the police investigative procedures and this will always mean that such errors can take place. A second unfortunate event was the result of the police receiving a taperecording of the person they believed to be the genuine 'Ripper'. This resulted in a computer trawl for a person who came from a part of Britain suggested by the accent on the tape-recording. In the event the area was the wrong one; the tape had been a hoax. The computer had been sidetracked by false inputs. As information received by the police is vital to the start of many such investigations it follows that for the computer detection systems to work the information must be accurate. The computer has the effect of compounding the original mistake in a way that manual detection cannot do, basically because people are less efficient than computers. The broad lesson is that this efficiency is brought into play *irrespective as to whether the original premise is right or wrong* — computers cannot distinguish between these positions; they merely process on, following orders.

Police purchases of computer handware and software has been described recently as explosive; it is as though police forces have just discovered the holy grail. This is partly due to the movement by the police into what has become known as 'civilian control'. Some of this concerns the monitoring of rush hour traffic or football crowds, but other facets include riot control, both before and during the event. Some senior policemen believe that they have a duty to spot those who they consider to be subversives and keep them under some form of surveillance. In other countries, especially the Communist ones, we tend to look upon such behaviour as symbolizing a 'police state', yet democratic countries like the United Kingdom, Germany, and the United States practise this observation quite unashamedly. Some of the computer installations are huge: the London Metropolitan police arrangement will have over 600 terminals. The growth in police computer use is stimulating the linking of computers of different forces to form the Police National Computer and, quite often, the local authority computers as well as other outside installations like the vehicle registration centre. The same sort of activity takes place in Europe or the United States. New police computers not only interact in this way but can log emergency calls, pinpoint and analyse incidents, perform personnel and logistical functions, and deal with telephone enquiries.

The role of the police in national security operations inevitably brings the forces and individual officers into the arena of political value judgements. For a computer to operate in this field in a sophisticated way, rather than just tagging a person as potentially dangerous and no more, the system has to deal with hearsay and other intelligence data, and this generally requires free text systems. This is one of the fastest expanding areas within police force computing. That every state has the right to protect itself, indeed a duty to do so, is almost universally accepted and computers are playing an increasing part in this process. There is a danger, however, that in attempting to defend the values of the state methods are used which are diametrically opposed to those which are being preserved. This paradox, which faces those in control in all democratic states, is certain to grow in intensity as the capacity to collect and process data on populations grows with the advent of new, better, faster and cheaper computers. Internal security is only one facet of protection however; defence against external attack is even more heavily computer and electronic oriented.

Defence is the second universal function of all governments, the raising of taxes to pay for it being the first, and in many industrialized countries a substantial proportion of government revenues are channelled into this direction. In truth most of the money is spent on items which everyone hopes will become obsolete without every being used, and entire weapons or defence systems are premised on this basis. This is of course the stuff of governments;

private wars, though theoretically possible, have dropped out of fashion.

Computer involvement in defence is extensive. The early warning and surveillance systems, both satellite and terrestrially based, the communication systems, and the weapons and their delivery and guidance systems are all heavily computer dependent. It is probably true to say that all modern defence or indeed offence strategies rely upon the proper functioning of computer technology. Taken a stage further, this means that the deterrent theory or, as it is sometimes known, the balance of terror is a computer-based state of equilibrium—not perhaps the most reassuring of thoughts given the fallibility shown by computers in the last few years. It is one thing to get a faulty electricity bill, quite another to start a nuclear war by mistake.

The scares in 1981 and 1982 caused by computer malfunctions in American tracking equipment made the world sit up and realize that the technology which underpins world security is by no means infallible. In the long run this is no bad thing; awareness of potential problems is preferable to a spurious security based on blissful ignorance. Some experts have argued that the fact that no harm came from the errors shows that the fail-safe procedures are effective and that we have nothing to worry about, but somehow the possibility of such lethal consequences of these mishaps make this a less than convincing argument.

Radar, when used to provide blanket screening and warning systems, has to be computer controlled whilst data processing analysis and recognition and identification techniques are standard in military observation posts. The communications methods which link together the early warning facilities to politicians and service personnel are totally electronic, often using satellites as part of the process. They are coded by computer and only capable of being deciphered by a computer. The modern world is a place of listening, tracking, and communications stations facing what the nuclear powers believe to be their potential enemies, the whole girdled by satellites performing similar functions. Computers make these pieces of equipment work and enable them to communicate with each other. The theory of deterrence not only means that the opposition must know what threat you hold over them but must also believe that you are making strenuous efforts to find out their strengths and weaknesses. If these conditions do not hold then one or both sides may believe that the other is not taking the deterrent seriously and the delicate balance breaks down. *The conspicuous use of computers is thus a vital component in the search for global stability.* The UK government makes but token protests when so-called secret communication centres are exposed to the public gaze, providing not too many details are made known. The approach of other governments is little different in the West and the East uses different methods to display its interests.

If it is important for any single nation to believe that the others are doing their utmost to find out what that country is doing and taking steps to ensure that they are at least one step ahead all of the time, then it is as important to note the obsession with secrecy which pervades the rest of the defence establishment. In truth even in the area of early warning and detection systems, governments still have to maintain some sense of outrage when exposures take place. The only complete exception to secrecy is when the government needs to reassure its own population that it is doing all in its power to protect them and to convince its enemies that they cannot succeed. The early warning establishment at Fylingdales on the Yorkshire Moors is a classic example of this approach — it was opened in a blaze of publicity. Military and diplomatic communications are not treated with the same openness.

Communications and logistics have been instrumental in winning more wars and battles throughout history than inspired strategic leadership, and their importance has increased rather than waned in recent times. The newer communication systems are all electronic and digitally based. Whether these messages are applied to the tactical battlefield or whether they are vectors in the cold war, the speed at which they travel, the accuracy of the message itself, as well as the accuracy of aim to the delivery point is most important. The amount of expenditure in military electronics is not only immense in itself but also makes up a disproportionally high percentage of all scientific research and development in countries such as the United Kingdom, the United States, and France. Not only is money diverted in this manner but the scarce resource of skilled labour is preempted too; this has repercussions in the wider economy at times of full employment.

The principles underpinning the new communications are the same as those which are driving the new guidance techniques: very high or extremely low frequency radio, digitalized messages along fibre-optic cabling, computer banks linked to heat sensors or maps, and the additional use of lasers. Computers have become familiar tools in such systems. A new warplane will have at least four computers on board and have all of its guidance equipment machine controlled. The pilot, although still essential, is becoming expendable on certain types of missions. Missiles are now the favourite form of carrier for the delivery of explosives, and these often entail aerial launchings. The battle for the Falkland Islands demonstrated the power of the missile as well as its accuracy; without computer-type electronics such missiles would be no more effective than the old-fashioned torpedo. Other bomb or shell guidance procedures using laser beams are now in everyday use amongst modern armies. Overall the improved capacity to wage war now comes from the accuracy with which targets can be found and hit rather than the improvement in warships, tanks, or the flying capability of planes. Clearly nuclear warheads on missiles, shells, bombs, or rockets have added the extra horror to modern warfare, but they do have to be accurately and reliably delivered. Computers have made the nuclear threat that much more real, and horrific.

The computer 'avionics' in the modern warplane in what turns it into a lethal machine; the recognition ability of new radar which enables it to distinguish between a friendly and a hostile missile is what makes it so valuable in defence. This latter ability is, however, not as clear-cut as it may seem to be. Someone has to programme the computer so as to distinguish between different forms of incoming objects, and human error may creep in. If a country is at war with another and one of the countries uses a missile purchased from an ally of the other one the computer controlling the radar may not be informed of this change of status. It may be that the missile was bought secretly so that it would not have dawned upon anyone that a change was necessary. In either event the defence system will usher the weapon through. This apparently happened early in the Falklands War when the first few Exocet missiles struck British ships; the missile was, of course, purchased from an ally, France. Yet again computers are only as good as their programs — and thus human beings.

Guidance systems are now the key to military superiority. The Cruise missile over which there has been such intense European discussion is really only an almost obsolete rocket carrying a standard nuclear warhead (if such a thing exists) but capable of travelling beneath radar screens. In theory, and perhaps in practice, this makes it undetectable. The guidance system works on contour maps fed into an on-board computer and its accuracy is credited with being remarkable. It is not its power nor its range that makes it such a threat to the Soviet Union but its ability to actually get its explosive warhead precisely on target. As the Soviet Union lags well behind the United States in such technology they have an additional reason to feel threatened, as they cannot retaliate in kind.

Warfare has become more deadly and more civilians have become at risk. Even the new, sophisticated computer languages like ADA are being nominated as potential villains of the piece because their complexity may lead to errors. ADA, like many other electronic and computer advances, has been nurtured by a government expenditure, often as a side effect of military developments. It is almost a subtle joke that those governments which dislike government intervention in industry the most are those that generally spend the most on defence and thus on the computer industries.

If H. G. Wells and other historians are right then war will always be with us; thus military expenditure and computer development and procurement will stay with us. Other historians have noted the propensity of governments to intervene more in the running of society and it is quite clear that this involves a greater need for the use of computers. That governments will, from time to time, attempt to use the prodigious capabilities of computers in not entirely ethical ways is no more than a comment on the lack of perfect in humans. We have all, except for the very young and naive, come to expect governments to try to gain an advantage for themselves; cynicism has pervaded our approach to this form of human endeavour.

Governments of all types and persuasions will find more

and more uses for computers as the drive for efficiency and expansion proceeds. Few of the effects, or indeed the installations themselves, will be visible to the public. Whether the effects are good or bad will depend upon the prevailing value judgements and ethics of the time and the judgements made will determine the viability of the government or indeed the political system itself.

The worst possible case is far worse of course. The judgement will not be made by the generation taking the original decisions but by their descendants, should any survive. Nuclear war is unthinkable yet lurks in the background like a recurrent nightmare at international gatherings or in the corridors of government. The hope must be that there will be people left to pass judgement on our ability to control governments and their use of computers.

PART II
The Effects

Chapter 8

The Less Tangible Effects

I T IS PARADOXICAL THAT THE TECHNOLOGY WHICH IS developing as so potent a tool for assisting the devolution of power and decision making has been responsible for stimulating the centralization of these functions. What is more a technology that is getting smaller by the day, cheaper by the hour, and easier to use by the minute has inadvertently proved to be the ideal tool for increasing the size of all kinds of bodies and institutions. Neither of these effects will find many defenders (at least in public) because the prevailing ethic at the moment is quite the reverse. Small, if not beautiful, is certainly handsome and devolved decision making is the buzz-word of the 'liberal' wing in most parliamentary democracies. This trend to central and big was explicable in terms of the early computers which were not only large cumbersome machines but tended to function at a head office level with few if any terminals for outsiders and using a very specialized staff. The relatively unchanged attitudes are less easy to understand or indeed condone, given that the technological means now exist to alter the situation.

Whilst it has always been a rarity to find a person who would claim that 'big' was good there have been many euphemisms for precisely this thought. Economies of scale, or in more upmarket terms, industrial synergy, is one of the most commonly used of these, generally but by no means exclusively, in respect of the manufacturing sector. Another way of justifying increasing size is to explain that the existing size is too small to either have a good base for exports or to have a broad enough product range or even to employ enough people. This is the negative argument; it is not that big is good but rather that small is not efficient enough for one reason or another. Whilst big companies, big countries, and other big organizations and departments have always existed the computer gave their formation and their viability an extra impetus.

219

Some computer effects are highly visible; others are rarely talked about or noticed but are no less important for that. Computers differ little in this respect from other tools or mechanisms; the most effective cures in medicine are often the least spectacular, the best pills often coloured white. The use of computers to facilitate the increased size of various bodies is one of these almost hidden side effects, but an extremely important one. It has been argued that this effect gives almost the only tangible evidence that computers have existed at all. Whilst this may be a cynically jaundiced view it does contain more than a germ of truth. As yet no other major basic changes have been laid at the door of the computer room; centrally, bigger, and faster have been the legacies to date.

It was a logical progression for development to proceed into large and just as importantly transnational companies, which accelerated through the 1960s alongside the growth of corporate computer use. The one followed the other and soon became mutually reinforcing. Many of the large companies grew by mergers and take-overs rather than sheer expansion. Many of these mergers could not have taken place without a computer analysis of the accounts, the product ranges, and potential markets of both of the partners. These analyses showed whether or not the two organizations were compatible. In terms of organizational requirements large firms, especially those with interests in several countries, need constant checking and advice. A large decentralized company has to ensure that the profit or market share or revenue centre is performing according to the global strategy. This may entail the daily checking of cash flows, sales, or whatever criteria the parent company has laid down for the subsidiary. Daily, even weekly, checks of this nature cannot be made without computer technology intervening both on the telecommunications side and the accountancy and analysis functions.

Large centralized companies have different problems and thus different uses for data processing facilities, most of them stemming from the proposition that a centrally controlled company is also more likely to be a single or related product company. Motor manufacturing companies fall into this category. The larger companies in the particular industry are all busily manufacturing 'world cars', which are merely cars which have been designed to meet the demands of markets all around the world, from the United States to Nigeria and from Japan to Iceland. This development means that the same basic model car is made in different parts of the world simultaneously; the computers are needed to work out the production schedules in order to ensure that there is no overproduction on one continent and a shortage of vehicles in another. The running of such a company becomes even more complicated when partially assembled bits of cars are traded between the different parts of the same company. Thus an engine made in Belgium may be assembled into a finished vehicle in Brazil after meeting its drive train which was made in Germany. Not only do computers have a planning and component scheduling function but they have to deal with the customs and excise of different countries and different currency and taxation systems.

A large transnational corporation can, when run efficiently, give its owners, most often holders of publicly quoted shares, an extremely high and safe return to their capital. Alternatively, it can maximize its sales or market share and minimize its tax liabilities whilst ensuring that it maintains a healthy cash flow. An optional extra in these cases would appear to be the 'salting away' of spare cash in tax havens, often for disposal by senior executives. For a company operating in, say, thirty countries the options can be bewilderingly large, and computers are used to chart the optimum path through or around any obstacles. Transfer pricing is an additional and time-hallowed custom which complicates the arrangements. The advantage that transnational companies have over domestically based companies is that, in theory, and indeed in practice, they can arrange for their profits to be made at the right time of year and in the right country so as to reduce their total tax liability. They are enabled to do this because different countries have different tax rates and regulations, some of them having virtually no company taxation at all. By means of selling their own products to their own subsidiaries in different countries at 'micky mouse money' prices a branch of a transnational company can make a loss or a profit wherever it chooses. It will try to make losses in high tax countries and take the profits in low tax countries, given of course that capital grants may be obtainable in some places and that the exchange controls allow the movement of currency out of the favoured country. As transfer pricing is illegal, all trade is supposed to be conducted at 'arms length' prices; this is a difficult practice to stop in that companies have to deny that it exists at all. The fact that mislabelling of goods to confuse customs officials goes on is hardly in doubt and that these goods are often on a sort of world tour, stopping off at various countries for a day or two before being shipped on, is a matter of record. What is not, and because of the nature of the practise cannot be, publicly admitted is that these 'corporate wrinkles' are often worked out and coordinated on the company's computer at its head office.

The trend to bigness not only affects companies but government too. The 1960s and 1970s ushered in the age of the megaministry in the United Kingdom. Separate

Departments of State were merged to form giant ministries like Education and Science or Industry and Trade. These were partly as a result of a new philosophy of the art of governance but also partly because the confidence released by the computers' arrival on the scene gave both politicians and civil servants a false sense of omnipotence. This was after all the age of the 'white heat of technology' when the Prime Minister pinned his hopes, and the governments policy and reputation, on the success of science and its exponents and technologists; computers were an integral part of this misplaced faith. The late 1950s through to the early 1970s were years of unprecedented growth and unbounded optimism in the ability of science of solve the outstanding problems of the day. That nuclear power would solve all of our energy problems and the 'green revolution' solve the misery caused by starvation in the Third World were never in doubt; they were amongst the leading articles of the faith. Computers would solve the clever questions and get rid of all the drudgery in office jobs. In fact the world drifted off into another direction with organizations becoming increasingly centrally controlled as well as larger.

Not unnaturally these moves upset established patterns of behaviour and power relationships between people and groups of people. The latent abilities of the computer were just being recognized and exploited. These were not the electronic skills that the inventors of the system had envisaged as being the sole use of their brain-children but the power-enhancing effect that control over the installation could bring. It was never vital to understand how the machines worked, let alone be able to make them work; rather it was and remains necessary to recognize power and how to achieve it and then retain it. Computers are an asset in this field of endeavour, especially to the people who control the disposition and the output of the installations.

Information is power; this is the current 'wisdom' and pervades the thinking of managements and unions alike as well as the media and academics. If it is the truth then it follows that those who control the content and dissemination of the information also have the power. Thus the managers, the administrators, or the media people who decide what information is received by whom are the persons who ultimately determine the attitudes and responses in a society. It may be that the original premise is wrong and that information is now more than a luxury to most people; it only represents power to those who deal in information and such people are trying to 'hype' their own abilities. In any event it matters little which of the opinions represents the truth; the dissemination of information is most important even if it is not vital.

The 1960s heralded the start of information rationing by machine. Managers or other senior personnel, once accustomed to receiving almost unlimited information from their organizations, were treated to small portions of it instead, portions which were administered by computer programs rather than overtly by the whim of other senior employees. Some departments, divisions, or companies were thus relegated from the mainstream of the organization. The whole tendency was to remove power or discretion from certain individuals or departments, and rather than allow the power to rest in yet another peripheral area it moved inexorably to the centre. A form of industrial commercial and governmental centripetal force was at work in this period.

Modern technology has made it possible to reverse this movement and to give an added viability, even an added dimension, to smaller and more decentralized units. Existing habits obviously die hard, however, and those people who have power and influence are loth to let it go; the result is that the newer systems have all sorts of brakes and checks to ensure that only residual information and discretion is received by or can be exercised from the periphery. All the disseminated data processing techniques, the intelligent terminals, the 'on-line realtime' (or in English, VDU's linked into the main computer which carry updated information as the messages into the computer systems change) are, for the most part, used to carry out simple clerical operations. The ability of individual managers or administrators to retrieve any information that they wish from the computer is constrained by the 'need for security and privacy'. This is a semantic device behind which senior management hides: a conservative centralist philosophy is the key to the unchanging use of computers, not something inherent in computer technology itself.

Government of all descriptions grew in the period under discussion. Local government was reorganized and as a result some extremely large local authorities were formed in Great Britain. In conventional terms, especially given their vast responsibilities, they would have been inoperable without computers or an immense staff increase to perform the routine tasks—the rate and rent collections, for example, or the administration of housing estates. Computers were not, indeed are not, essential for the running of these new large bodies but without their existence it is highly unlikely that the notion of giant councils would have been accepted. The very existence of a machine which could solve problems, combined with the fashion of the time favouring the 'efficiencies' of bigness, proved irresistable to the policy makers. Probably the greatest success of this era amongst those who were proselytizing for 'big' was the formation of the European Economic Community (EEC), a supranational government.

Most people in government or any other large organization will claim that their greatest difficulty is to communicate with other people within the same organization. A government system, moreover one which has a singular penchant for the use of bureaucrats where one would expect to find politicians in normal government of the size and complexity of the EEC, must be a heavy user of electronics, if only to communicate properly. There can be no doubt, however, that the political forces behind the formation of the EEC would not have been halted had the computer not been invented, but the organization would have had to start and then develop in a very different way, both politically and in structural terms.

Large and central must be linked with fast to give the full flavour of the computer's impact to date. Almost everything that can be done by computers can be done by humans, although in almost every instance more slowly. Administrative and clerical work, arithmetical computers, graphics, instructions, and reading are just examples. In general computers or computer-driven machines are faster and often more reliable than other machines. On occasions these abilities can save lives, can win contracts, can increase profits, or can even win elections. The value of computers in this limited non-specific sphere should not be underestimated; they have aided many people and many organizations over recent years. This less than holy trinity has been the major contribution of computers to the present time. If this sounds negative just consider the difference in emphasis between the new and fundamental changes and products and the far greater number of amended rather than totally new products and services.

It could be argued that the computer is but a tool in the truly conservative mould; it has produced little in the way of innovative changes but has stimulated a large number of increases in productivity and efficiency. In broad terms it has bolstered the prevailing ethics rather than challenged them by making the existing systems work far more efficiently. Whilst this scarcely seems to be the product of the machines of the future it does not, indeed must not, represent their ultimate potential; it is rather the results of the limited ambition of those who have had charge of them. It is as though the first people to discover the wheel used it only to move stones from one place to another and ignored the possibility of moving food or themselves, let alone pulleys and the range of simple engineering devices which need it.

An unfortunate side effect of the way that computers operate, combined with the sort of tasks that they have been set to do, is that a marked standardization process has taken place. The data that are fed into a machine have to be put into a standard form. In turn this means that data collection systems have to be standardized and the forms or whatever systems are used to collect the 'raw material' resemble each other ever more closely. Idiosyncracies, whether personal or corporate, become less of an amusing talking point and more of a nuisance; indeed, they generally have to be eliminated for the efficient running of the installation. As the computer now controls the data flows this really means that individual foibles can be tolerated only within narrow margins in most organizations. Regrettably this has even greater secondary effects than the sad decline of the individualist or perhaps eccentric.

People are now being hired in the larger organizations because they will fit into the existing structures and accept the constraints that these structures impose. In practice this has resulted in the employment of bureaucratically oriented people instead of those who may have had greater imagination or vision. Whilst the two attributes may not be mutually exclusive the personnel policies and the interview techniques used to fulfil them have conspired to freeze out those applicants with suspected unconformist traits. As far as the United Kingdom is concerned, this is very nearly a disaster. The lack of risk-taking management or as Keynes put it 'animal spirit' in industry, especially the manufacturing sector, has contributed in no small measure to its decline over the past three decades. This spirit and the flair which goes with it is hardly likely to survive the computer-related interview techniques or the drift towards hiring steady, sober, safe staffs. It may be suitable in other countries where there is a steady supply of entrepreneurs and engineers with a head and desire for business practices. Standardization is precisely what the United Kingdom does not need, yet it is precisely what it is getting.

In work terms a standard output can be continuously monitored by computer; typing and other clerical and computer work are classic examples. People who, for one reason or another, do not conform to the norm can be questioned, cautioned, disciplined, or, at worst, fired. Trips to the toilet and the length of time spent there can be checked against the norm and not unnaturally workers tend to resent these intrusions. Allowances for health reasons can only be made if the illness or condition is made known and there are times when the employee is embarrassed or does not want the facts to be public knowledge. Adhering to such standards, unthinkingly and unwaveringly, can result in considerable unhappiness.

Computers encourage the setting of standards and their subsequent monitoring, but it must not be thought that computers inspired standardization — they only made it more practicable. Some standardization is good, however. Computer-driven measurement equipment and testing rigs have raised quality control overall and have therefore given the consumer a consistently better and often safer product. The standard of standardization quality has risen! Other goods, especially spare parts and components, have been designed to give the consumer the benefit of interchangeability and thus flexibility, and computer-aided design techniques were a key element in this advance. The same argument applies to the ability to link together the telecommunication systems of different countries. It is ironic in the extreme that the computer, which has played such a large part in the harmonization, standardization, and compatability movement has, when taken as an industry itself, been the most resistant of all to adapt to standardize its equipment.

There are now areas where computers have made it possible to measure dynamic elements (perhaps a hire purchase repayment) against standard rates or responses and to highlight the aberrant ones. This can be fraught with dangers. It relies upon the computer obtaining accurate information in the first instance and also on the premise that no unusual circumstances have supervened. The early repayment of a mortgage on a property may not be accepted by the computer as it is so unusual, indeed in current tax circumstances it is generally an irrational act; the fact that mortgage payments are not being made can well lead to a presumption that the person is in arrears. In turn this can have repercussions on the creditworthiness of this person, who because of too easily obtainable computer data of this nature may then find it difficult, if not impossible, to get another loan. The norm or average is, if taken literally, not a practical or useful concept. It requires commonsense and sensitivity to interpret it and unfortunately no computer has *yet* been programmed with such characteristics. The fifth generation will, however, if it lives up to its pre-production publicity, start to fill the gap. The state of the art is such that the opposite is true now in that in commonsense terms computers rate well below earth-worms — they are good at doing what they have been told, but not to pass judgements or to vary their instructions. If you do not feel that this is an important matter and that the concept of the norm or average is not misleading then consider legs. The probability is that at most small meetings or gatherings of people there are a higher than average number of legs. This is obviously because whilst some people have one or no legs the number of people who have more than two legs is zero. Thus the average number of legs per head of population is less than two and therefore no-one fulfills the average. The problem arises in persuading the computer programmers of the equivalent absurdities in financial or behavioural matters.

One of the least publicized effects of computer usage is the growth of computer crime or fraud. Because the fear of copycat crimes prevents much of the detected crime coming to court at all, let alone receive publicity, and the successful crime is never detected or the culprits have long since disappeared, it is likely that the law breaking that comes to the public's attention is only the tip of the iceberg. This is despite a legal requirement in the United States to report any computer fraud in financial institutions. It is estimated that in the United States each computer fraud averages a net haul of between four hundred thousand and half a million dollars whilst the more modest criminals in the United Kingdom and Europe netted on average only fifty thousand dollars per swindle.

Neither figure tells us overmuch in that there could be one massive fraud and thousands of small ones or no large ones at all but hundreds of medium size. Whichever is the truth there is no doubt in anyone's mind that illegalities of various kinds are on the increase; indeed, like the informal economy of which they are a part, they are a growth industry. So prevalent has it become that several studies have been made and agencies whose only functions are to stop computer crime and to secure the computer operations have mushroomed in the past few years. White collar crime is now big business.

Few detailed descriptions of the methods emerge for security reasons but computer crime is slowly being classified and some news does leak out. The perfect computer fraud penetrates the system, extracts large amounts of money or credit, and then removes all traces of the penetration. There are different methods of getting into a system; most experts believe that systems are now more vulnerable than the computer itself. The 'trapdoor method' is used by real or bogus service engineers or other non-regular personnel, or through an insecure software system. 'Trojan horses' is another method entirely and depends on the knowledge of secret codes or entry passwords. Additional instructions can be written into programs and telecommunication lines can be interferred with or trapped. The most quaintly named of the methods is 'superzapping'; 'superzap' is a programme that is used in emergencies to get access to all of the contents of a computer, and as it by-passes all the normal controls the implications of this are obvious.

Banks and other financial institutions are obviously favourite targets for white collar criminals. Fictitious accounts and dormant and nominee accounts are the most popular devices. If the 'salami' method is used, i.e. by removing small amounts a slice at a time, it may be up to a year before the loss is noted; fractions of a penny interest on deposit accounts have been a fruitful source here. Other time-tested methods have been fictitious employees or fictitious deductions from salaries and the retention of dead employees on the payroll. Special accounts nearly always have to be arranged. In October 1978 a data processing consultant transferred ten million dollars from the United States to a Swiss bank account and was only arrested when a subsequent transaction on diamonds went wrong. *His employers had no idea of their loss until after his arrest.* The top 7 per cent. of computer crime is estimated to account for a very high percentage of total losses and is performed for the most part by senior employees with a high degree of freedom within the organization.

Whilst most of the fraud has money as the motive some people, especially highly skilled computer workers, try to beat the system because it is there—it acts as a challenge. Bored or disgruntled employees are supposed to be more likely to attempt to break a security system and one pessimistic study asserted that only 25 per cent. of employees will be honest all of the time whilst 50 per cent. will be as honest or crooked as the system allows them to be. To put computer crime into perspective, Interpol have publicly suggested that white collar crime accounts for 2.5 per cent. of the GNP of industrialized countries—a massive figure comparable to the amount spent on primary education. A reputable consultant in this field does not believe that the figure is anything like as high as this estimate, but does believe, however, that by the middle to late 1980s it will be so high as to cause 'economic chaos'. The FBI had to admit that unauthorized persons had obtained access to their own internal files; there is little that can be added to that statement in terms of crime, its potential, and its success.

There are two further facets of computer crime. The first is that the definition of crime does not include many computer specific practices. At its simplest the stealing of time on someone else's computer is a difficult area in which to get a successful prosecution. Stealing time has not yet become an offence whilst trespass or interference with the telecommunication system may be unprovable or inappropriate.

Computers may also play their part in crime. Companies have been set up specifically to get a good credit rating by paying for goods and repaying loans on the nail. Computers make the dissemination of that rating somewhat faster and wider so that in a relatively short period the firm can build up a mountain of free stock and unpaid bills only to disappear or go bankrupt. In the same vein companies have been set up in order to fraudulently claim VAT input refunds; although not trading at all, the computer printouts give the enterprises the correct air of efficiency and authority.

Politicians have cause, though not too many know it, to fear computers. Opinion polling has become a latter-day spectator blood sport; the media finds the statistic closest to its heart and generally most embarrassing to its political adversaries and gives it a high degree of prominence. Whilst most politicians have a fixed smile as they say it, the often repeated slogan is that opinion polls do not matter and mean nothing. The trouble is that they do, both to the morale of individual politicians and political parties, and in practical opinion-forming terms, as the 1983 UK general election demonstrated quite efficiently.

Although experts differ as to the precise effects of polls on opinions after they have been published, the fact that it is known that 60 per cent. of the population think Margaret Thatcher is doing a good job must have an influence both on the other 40 per cent. and on the strength of convictions of the 60 per cent. themselves. Polling is not, however, a matter of discovering opinions on simple matters. For many years now the political parties have been commissioning major surveys of public attitudes to policies, to events, to people, and to concepts. The results are broken down by social class, sex, area, job, age, and income, and perhaps into even smaller subgroups.

Analysis of these surveys can be done manually but speed, especially near to an election, is vital and the sheer volume of calculations is formidable in the extreme. During the EEC referendum in the United Kingdom the European Movement YES side, being flush with money, commissioned a daily poll and found that whilst people knew that food would cost more than before, other matters took precedence. Peace and security in partnership were examples and the campaign was adjusted accordingly. At a general election the major parties do roughly the same thing and although it is almost impossible to introduce new policies, some can be highlighted and others quietly forgotten, although this latter tactic only works if the other parties allow it to. For example the survey may suggest that the campaign is targetted wrongly so at a moment's notice young people may have to be drafted in to front a party political broadcast. Obviously the United States are the heaviest users of this form of political engineering but France, Germany, Spain, and the United Kingdom are catching up fast. The Social Democratic Party (SDP) in the United Kingdom relaunched itself in January 1983, with the help of a massive attitudes survey, after dropping over half of its polled support. This instance of a party looking for policies, though common in the United States, is unique in the United Kingdom. Another SDP initiative was to put its membership onto a computer and claim that it was a technologically oriented party because of this action.

Political parties or individual politicians can, in essence, now sell themselves like packets of detergent. It is arguable that television, being such a powerful and instant medium, is equally responsible with computers for this drift into a combination of slickness and 'hype'. The selling of policies or people is one of the more distasteful effects of the newer technologies as it seems to imply that there is a lack of fundamental belief amongst politicians and furthermore that the moral and leadership elements of politics and the policy formation roles are being abdicated in favour of a populist approach. It may be a salutary thought for politicians to dwell upon the apogee of populism, the Roman mob, and the toll that this took of the politicians of the day. It may look as though it is the easy option, but it is a short-term approach and uncontrollable. In the United States, where political advertising is allowed and consequently money is a most important electoral asset, there have been a series of books on the making of various presidents. In all of them it is only too clear that the marketing people, using sophisticated computer analysis, had a more important effect on policies and the direction of the campaign than the political advisers, who had themselves been influenced by the market surveyors anyway.

The United States is the home of another computer effect on politics. At presidential election time the major broadcasting networks take a sample of key electoral wards per state. These are adjusted for their representation and predictions are made by two means. People are polled as they leave the voting stations and/on the early counting area results are fed into the computer. The programs, which are simple in concept but detailed and tedious to set up, then roll in order to predict the likely outcome and the margin. There has been a noticeable improvement election by election in the quality of the predictions and of the computer presentation; accuracy is now almost assured. In addition computer graphics now make the results attractive and intelligible and promote good understanding. The British television channels have the same sort of coverage but there is one major difference. When the polls close in Britain all the constituencies close together; in the United States there can be a lag of four hours to the West coast states because the sheer size of the country means that it straddles time zones. As the early predictions came through based on closed polls in New York before the end of polling in, say, California there has been a suspicion that these computer techniques can change the outcome of elections. It is difficult to determine authoritatively in which direction the vote was affected. It may be that people decided to vote with what appeared to be the winning side; it may be that there was an overwhelming desire to bolster a losing candidate in a type of sympathy vote. There is also evidence that there was no effect whatsoever, which means either that no notice was taken of the predictions or that the effects tended to cancel each other out. Risks must remain, however, in these circumstances that the normal democratic proceedings could be upset and perverted. Putting crime and this media grouping together, what could stop a determined attempt to amend the computer program in order to falsify the predictions and perhaps the outcome. Indeed, it may be easier to get voters to give a deliberately wrong answer to the after voting poll or to make an error in the ward election return. Not only politicians could benefit from this malpractice; gamblers and organized crime could make a vast amount of money.

A final use for computers in the electoral process is in the voting machine itself. It is this machine that enables the early returns to be made in some parts of the United States. Whilst some are mechanical, others now have electronic mechanisms. In some states the list of questions, propositions, candidates, or referenda is so long that the machine has to keep running totals. In essence this is all a voting machine does. It may be that the extensive ballot paper would not have come into operation if the voting machine had not been available to count the votes; whether or not this is correct it is obvious that the machines are now essential. Safeguards against tampering in any way are in force yet suspicions remain; allegations are made after each election which are always subsequently disproved. The subtleties of the political process are such that the effects of computers are not noticed at all, changing nuances being put down to the inevitable shifts in the structures of societies. The delusion that we take our political decisions in the same way as did our grandparents is dangerous in that we refuse to recognize the new forms of manipulation involved. This means that, should the need ever arise, we are less well prepared to resist the blandishments of a potential dictator.

Market and consumer research have been with us for many years and have had a profound impact on the way that we live in modern societies. Computers have, however, added a new and extra dimension to their influence; indeed, computers could well have been invented to suit their purposes. Wider surveys, in-depth questionnaires, better analysis, much faster tools, an ability to handle more variables simultaneously and to refine the target groups, and ever more precise areas have conspired to move this form of research onto a new plane. Computer-based interview sessions or computer-designed group sessions have also added to the market researcher's armoury and given their product an added reliability. As we shall see in Chapter 10, these new gifts have a very important effect on consumer's choices, both in the range of products available and the places where they can be found.

The stocking of supermarket shelves is now an art form with the producers and wholesalers of products falling over backwards to get their goods displayed in the most favourable positions. Computer and hidden camera-based market research now determines the placing and packaging strategies of many consumer goods and even the actual colour of the product. Packaging is becoming almost as important as the product itself; in some instances, like the cosmetic and perfume industries, it sometimes appears to be the most important factor. This better knowledge of how a consumer will respond to various factors as well as a better monitoring and follow-up system has been used to reduce the element or risk in the new product launches. It additionally leaves the consumer open to more persuasion than previously, as the extra knowledge of consumers' behaviour is unmatched by a corresponding increase in knowledge of the products by the consumer.

If computers were right all of the time then a great deal of human worry would be removed from the world. The computer errors that are publicized are generally spectacular in the extreme — the gas bill for £500 when the house is not even using gas at all is the bread and butter of journalistic stringers. Most of this variety are easily dealt with, however, as the absurdity persuades officials to override the bill or perhaps cancel the previously unstoppable journal. Other errors are not so easily brushed aside and nor are they capable of being resolved quite so easily. Modern societies are having to learn to live with the consequences of computerization and an important chunk of these are the mistakes. The consequences can be horrific in personal terms and in aggregate they represent a form of cost to the community that has to be offset against the benefits. There is a tendency to try to write off these mistakes as aberrations, and trivial ones at that, which do not warrant concern, but this attitude takes no account of the misery which accrues through no fault of those affected.

Probably the most serious of the errors affecting everyday life comes into the financial category, generally affecting credit ratings. A false inclusion of a default or a court summons without showing that it was subsequently withdrawn can lead to the refusal of credit to that person and what is worse is that in general no reason is given. This leaves the victim totally mystified as to why he or she has suddenly become a financial pariah. Given that the reason is not known, it becomes much more difficult to reestablish a credit rating because the person cannot possibly know how to remedy the situation. It takes a very determined person to pressure the agencies which do these investigations (and often collect debts too) sufficiently for them to admit the error. These difficulties may be compounded because too often the information has been obtained in an improper manner so that the agency will not divulge its sources and put them at risk. It is the innocent consumer that suffers.

Errors in personnel records can have unfortunate repercussions too. References can be totally wrong, skills or qualifications can be transposed with those of other people with unfortunate results for both the people concerned and the employer, especially in instances of job changes or promotions. Criminal records are another field of potential disaster and because secrecy surrounds the holding of them mistakes are as difficult to investigate and remedy as are the credit rating errors. The ill effects might be far worse, however. From being unwarrantedly suspected of a crime through to having an unjustly high sentence passed via being refused a job because 'investigations' showed the existence of a criminal record, the outcome of mistakes is serious. The other side of the coin must be presented, however, and that is that there are almost certainly cases of omissions from criminal records; indeed, if one person is credited with crimes that he or she did not commit it is reasonably certain that the person who did commit them has 'lost' that bit of record. Not unnaturally such stories are rarely made public, those in whose favour the mistake has redounded will not be keen to publicize the fact whilst those in charge of the records are unlikely to make themselves appear incompetent gratuitously.

Looked at dispassionately all records whether held on a computer or otherwise are subject to errors. The computer, however, magnifies the error in two distinct ways. The mere fact that the information emanates from a computer immediately gives it a cachet, a significance, that manually stored and retrieved data cannot command. A second and more specific reason is that the information is often held in more than one installation and this means that a change in one data bank entails other changes though not necessarily the identical ones in other data bases. This can result in an escalating error-based profile of something or someone, or what is even worse a widening incompatibility between files. Medical records are one of the most vital aspects of modern medical treatment. Mistakes in drug sensitivities or physical signs, symptoms, and diagnoses, even if they be of omission rather than commission, can literally be deadly. Other sorts of errors, like the one which, in the 1970s, meant that the balance of payments as recorded by the Department of Trade was increasingly in error and was caused by the inclusion of data from a testing program, really had no long-term ill effects at all.

Computers are an integral part of what the phrase makers have dubbed 'the information revolution'. That this entails more and faster information is taken for granted and that both of these effects are good is also taken as read. It should not be. Information *per se* is really the prerogative of the erudite academic — most of us need information as a means to an end. In theory more information should mean better decision making; in practice this relationship may actually prove to be the opposite. There is a limit to the amount of facts that can be taken into account in a decision-making process before diminishing returns set in. What has always seemed to be an uncluttered path may suddenly be strewn with all sorts of extraneous bits and pieces which serve only to confuse the issue. The more information is made available, and we must assume that the vital information was already available as decisions were already being taken, the more likely it is that the wood starts to be obscured by the trees. As a society we run the risk of becoming chronically overinformed and moreover with progressively more trivial or more esoteric pieces. If more information does not necessarily do us good then faster information has potential disadvantages too.

The problem with instant information is that people start to expect instant analysis and instant decision making, neither of which inevitably lead to the better enlightenment or better government of people, countries, or organizations. There is a confusion in the industrialized world between fast and good with a significant number of people, many of whom should know better, behaving as though the two were synonymous. The speed of the decision making may be enhanced, the analysis that follows the information may be faster, but the quality of both may remain the same or indeed be impaired. For the quality to be better we have to assume that the original methods of dealing with information led to poor discusions on the grounds that delays affected the quality of the information itself. There are probably cases of this type where the new computerized systems have been an unmitigated blessing; there are many more where the extra speed has added some convenience, some profits, or both but little else. Providing that we realize that the information technology revolution has these effects then there should be little in the way of future hostages to fortune. When we start to suggest that the new office or home information systems have become decision makers themselves or even that they have become *the* vital part of this process, we must stand back and think what it is that we are saying.

Computers and systems are only as good as their programs and that means systems designers, analysts, and programmers. People make computers worth while, and indeed make computers. We must not fall into the trap of attributing inherent intelligence to systems which get their instructions from people and function at their behest. To do this is to build up fears and expectations in equal measure, neither of which is likely to be fulfilled. This side of the problem is only part of a wider difficulty in the perception of the computer by ordinary people. 'Efficiency' is the keyword in systems, not 'better'. Even if we all believe that computers are machines their use does not automatically mean that the job is performed in a better way or that there is any qualitative difference in the services provided. Customers, whether of goods or of services, have developed ever-increasing expectations, and the fact that a robot or other computer-driven systems play a part in the process can be used as an advertising ploy to show that the product, be it a car or a holiday, is better than it would have been. Regretably even the 'best' advertising is not always correct! Misconceptions of this type do not help the image of computers or robots when ultimately people's experience shows that the products are so similar as to make no difference.

The instant reaction of television pundits is now another area where change has taken place. Instead of a calm thoughtful reaction politicians and commentators have to provide instant, hard-hitting statements. No politician would dream of saying that there needs to be time for reflection and thought and that no statement will be issued, yet this is precisely what may be needed. Immediacy in news and opinion is now often the most valued feature of current affairs programmes.

Subtle changes have been the subject of this chapter, changes which have crept in almost unnoticed and which on first glance one may not have attributed to the computer. Many of these have affected attitudes and the way that we tolerate things. Has the computer the responsibility for dulling our sense of injustice and fair play? Mistakes are now remote controlled and an individual consequently more difficult to blame. The sense of witch hunt or vengeance has been subverted technologically and computer smashing appeals to Luddites but few others. As a result people take computer mistakes for granted, are amused by them, perhaps even shocked by them, but are never made angry enough to follow the incidents through to their logical conclusions. Subtleness is by definition not an immediately noticeable quality. Adaptation rather than conflict or revolution comes as a result of these changes and, as with the example of tolerance, so other attitudes have changed. Speed and flair rather than steadfastness and gravitas are two changes which have become apparent in the last decade; efficiency has come to the fore and the acceptance of change has eased marginally. The use of computers has had an effect on these attitudes if only because, at the very least, they are there, they are used, and they have changed the way we do things.

More than a few of the less tangible effects are negative. The crime and fraud, the insensitivity, the errors, and the openings for new potential abuses must be adjudged negative in everyone's book. The stimulation of large size organizations is a grey area if only because the case against is neither proven nor at times substantial. Many of the effects are excellent. The rising expectations, in health and education, as well as in nutrition and consumer goods, stem largely from computer-based systems and research. In total these effects are very much a mixed bag.

Misconceptions cloud this vast area, and it is time that the light was allowed to shine through; 'computers are merely machines' has to be the watch phrase. Powerful—yes, at times frightening—yes, omnipotent—no, reasoning—no, self-motivating—no. Many of the less publicized effects are a result of an adjustment period as computers take over roles and responsibilities which neither those operating them nor those on the receiving end have analyzed, and so there have been few steps taken to prevent or ameliorate the more undesirable side effects. These negative effects will disappear over time. What is infinitely more worrying is that few people directly or indirectly involved have given thought as to what the benefits of computerization should be outside of a single installation. The assumption that the benefits from all of these single operations, if they exist at all, will add up to a large benefit for society is totally fallacious. Society could as easily suffer as benefit. It is a subject deserving of thought, study, and above all wisdom—yet too few people have applied themselves to it, especially in the United Kingdom.

Chapter 9

Who Controls
Them?

POWER IS, AND ALWAYS HAS BEEN, ONE OF THE MOST coveted of prizes. Some people have wanted it for the most honorable of motives, others for its own sake. Some, like Henry Kissinger, when he attributed aphrodisiac powers to it, have seen it as a means to a totally different end. Power has stimulated more aphorisms, more works of fiction, and more real life drama than any other force or emotion, save perhaps love. Politicians, statesmen, generals, and the very rich wield power with varying degrees of probity and success and it is accepted in some form of public judgement that they should. Politicians are elected. They are thus entrusted with power because they can be recalled by the electorate that handed them the power in the first instance. Generals and other military top people only really have an opportunity to exercise power when their country is at war and at this point in time the people are glad to delegate it. The power of the rich is the power of the owner in any capitalist economy, and as such is eminently respectable providing that it is exercised quietly, although this stricture tends to apply more to the United Kingdom than other countries. These forms of power are all acknowledged and accepted; other forms do not have quite the same social approval, however.

The power of a trade union at the workplace is an example of a collective response which generally attracts almost universal opprobrium. Trade unions are also widely thought to have power where in fact none exists and what is more they are often then accused of abusing this non-existent power. The power of the criminal, drug peddler, thug, or indeed gun is not accepted as legitimate in most modern states even though many of these states and the long established families in them have depended heavily on these outlaws in the past. Most people also feel more comfortable if they believe that they know

247

who wields power; the power behind the throne or the *éminence grise* are not figures of splendour in history, even though they may have been responsible for the most glorious of days. Shadowy is the soubriquet most often given to these characters and shadowy figures tend to invite mistrust; the financier and the trade unionist have the same effect on public conciousness at the end, although for different reasons. Financiers work in the background; those to whom they provide the money — the entrepreneurs, the captains of industry — are the people to whom power is allowed because they are highly visible.

Computers work behind the scenes and form part of the social, commercial, and political infrastructures in industrialized countries. The people who design the systems and the machines as well as the people who operate them must also work out of sight of the public. There are not many of these people in any one country; the skills needed in data processing are in short supply universally. It still remains a small tightly knit group who are bound together by the cords of jargon and a shared knowledge in precisely the same way as the early priests. With the mass of ordinary people excluded from the knowledge and the rituals there will always be a tendancy to treat computer personnel with suspicion. If the conception of how much power resided in so few people gained a wider audience then the suspicion could well turn into an emotion more akin to jealousy. It is only too easy to whip up popular feeling against groups of people who do not conform to the 'norm', whether because of their colour, their race, their religion, or because they are part of a secret group like the masons. Even if these people or groups are at the bottom of the socioeconomic heap it is essential to 'loan' them some form of power so that they constitute a threat to the population. Whether this is power over all women, or the power or life or death, or the power to help the few at the expense of the many, these powers have to be believed in. Computer people are in a slightly different position in that they truly have power and very few people realize it.

The other side of power is responsibility. One of the major reasons for the mistrust that surrounds those whose work is the background is that there is no method of either bringing them to account or of checking to see whether they are acting responsibly. Kipling's famous quotation 'power without responsibility — the prerogative of the harlot throughout the ages' may be considered to be sexist in modern days but it encapsulates the general feeling about this phenomenon brilliantly. Less elegant slogans concerning a football referee's abuse of power rise from the terraces every Saturday. One of the problems associated with computers is that to exercise a control over those that work with them it is ultimately necessary to understand them. Few people in a position to control computer systems know much about computers at present. Perhaps ten Members of Parliament in the United Kingdom have a good working knowledge of computers and there are not many more senior civil servants. Both of these groups will have to rely on advice from amongst computer people. In industry and commerce the problem is the same, with the notable exception of course of the computer industry itself. It is also a problem that should disappear over time as computers become more familiar to young people and they start to occupy positions of power and influence themselves. This is, however, a long-term comfort; the interim generation has to be accommodated, hopefully without serious mishaps.

There is an old and invariably fulfilled assumption in the civil service that the person who drafts the agenda controls the meeting. They might also have mentioned that those who interpret the meeting and write the minutes control the next meeting and much more besides. Within the computer world the programmers and the analysts together write the programs and systems and thus the agendas and minutes. However, the computer itself and the peripheral equipment attached to it also have an important role in determining what actually happens. In other words, the designers of the hardware as well as the systems have both responsibility and power in the overall philosophy concerning the effects of computer use. An apt comparison may be that of the concert hall whose designer and builders have had such a strong influence as to whether a concert is enjoyable that it is at times equal to that of the orchestra and soloists. The question of control and of power that is to be controlled must thus be addressed, at least partly, to those who design the computers themselves.

Computer manufacturers have tended to give the user what they believed the user wanted not what the user really wanted, often on the grounds that the user did not know anyway. This has resulted in a multiplicity of complaints, the formation of user associations, and the proliferation of consultancies to help the afflicted. As the machines have become smaller and become more of an accepted part of office architecture so the manufacturers have started to take notice of the consumers' wishes. It is no coincidence that the initiators of the small business computer have been new companies, not the first- or second-generation mainframe producers. This new approach, combined with imaginative advertising, has started to change the image of the computer and what is more important has started to change both the image and the self-perception of computer users. The greatest step forward in this direction has come from the use of the 'mouse' rather than the traditional keyboard and the clever office layout display, both started by Apple. This movement towards the ordinary mortal must have the effect of demystifying the technology and the closing of the gap, albeit only slightly, between those who know and the overwhelming majority of us who do not.

Control of computers is obviously in the hands of those who are technically capable of controlling them, but only on a day-to-day or even hour-by-hour basis. Whilst this can be a most important sphere it is a limited one, a tactical rather than strategic advantage. Clearly there could be potential problems if the staff operating the machine are not totally trusted. In such circumstances there will always be a temptation for management to intervene or to institute safeguards or checks, both of which will be resented unless the staff under suspicion are consulted or forewarned. Many computer people see interference of this nature as a reflection on their professional skills and moreover one made by managers who are computer illiterate and, not unnaturally, this compounds the difficulties. These problems are difficult to articulate with the result that battles are fought between participants whose war cries are mute. They are introverted, internal battles.

With the best will in the world it is difficult for senior management to be at ease with the staff of a computer installation as they have little or no idea as to what they do and nor do they know what the machines do or are capable of doing. As they know that they do not know they become suspicious that someone has moved into that dark area and is doing something, goodness knows what, which is not in the organization's or manager's interests. Each and every day the computer staff have sole control of the installation, its output, and its well-being. The general management have to accept that their instructions are being carried out as far as is practicable and to the greatest extent possible. They also have to assume that fraud is not taking place, that their audits are adequate, that security is intact, and that the machinery being used is the best available for the jobs that need to be done.

Trust is thus an inevitable prerequisite in the relationship between the computer experts and the generality of decision makers, but it is a difficult relationship to maintain, not to mention foster.

Good relations are not helped by another dichotomy. The strategic control of computers is undertaken by general management. Their responsibilities include the allocation of resources within an enterprise, the information systems used, the capital available for expenditure, and the hiring and firing of staff. They also have to take decisions on product mix if there are products, sales if there are sales, and also customer or client relations. In short, general management allocates the computer staff their tasks with reference to the needs of the organization overall, not with reference to either the installation or its people. From a senior manager's point of view the computer is on a par with a sophisticated lathe or a new switchboard; it is a tool which can perform certain functions very well and efficiently. The difficulties that may result from an instruction cannot be appreciated by ordinary management nor indeed can the realism or otherwise of some of their own proposals. Only the computer professionals have the expertise to evaluate difficulties or new ideas, yet they are very rarely allowed to initiate the ideas in their own place of work, unless these are of the purely technical variety.

Both senior managers and computer people consist of small groups in any one establishment, indeed in aggregate in the United Kingdom. This makes the question of who controls computers even more important in two senses. Small groups readily lend themselves to the mutual reinforcement of ideas and philosophies as well as allowing for an easier interchange of these ideas. This results in strong attitudes and moreover ones which command almost universal support within the group; as this factor applies to both groups simultaneously any conflict between them is correspondingly hardened. Who controls the computer ceases to be an academic point in these circumstances; it is a real bone of contention which is fought over in thousands of small and different ways every year. No-one actually sits down and asks the direct question and starts a grand debate. Indeed, in some installations the debate never starts, in others it is constant. Rather the battles are over the day-to-day mundane running decisions that have to be made: whether to give priority to certain competing tasks or to maintain the normal service program schedule or whether direct access should be encouraged and if so to which people? These are the battle grounds.

The fight can also be between different groups of computer professionals. ADA, the new high-level language, is also a production line language in that it removes the initiative from individual programmers. About twenty people work on the program, each doing their own bit and using a manual to resolve all problems. This de-skilling removes any element of control from programmers and passes it onto managers. It also makes an entire program that much more difficult to check and as we shall see later in the book this has led to errors and to a keen debate about the uses of ADA overall.

The fight is continued in other, more fundamental ways too. Strategists see the world in the round, as it were, and computers represent a little understood but obviously powerful tool in the battle to outwit others in the world. The computer workers tend to see the computer installation as the world itself; they fight their battles in that environment alone. Managers, with their far wider interests, treat computer staffs much as they would any other and this does not go down too well with people who believe that they have a special expertise and therefore position. Those who have strategic obligations, senior managers or other senior people, see the computer as one tool amongst many and also probably have less knowledge about it than any of the other tools which they deploy. The impossible is not only requested but frequently performed as most computer professionals will boast. How an instruction is carried out is of no concern to the strategist; only the fact that it is carried out is important. The computer specialist, the tactician, is in a somewhat different position. In addition to knowing about the computer he or she is also capable of having an informed opinion on the strategy. Indeed, the computer worker is far more likely to understand the strategy than the manager is to understand the tactics. If this gives the tactician a sense of superiority it is not one that can be indulged in practice; seniority and muscle works in the other direction — the higher in the pyramid a person stands the less that can be dropped on him or her.

The second sense in which the small group is important is that because the battleground contains so few people and the ammunition can be so technical the number of people who understand that there is a problem at all is tiny. For so vital a point in the context of a modern society it is strange that conflicts and violent disagreements can occur with so few people involved or knowing about them. The general public is disbarred from taking part in the debate in these circumstances — indeed, by its very nature they cannot have the expertise to take part — and as long as most know little of the subjects in question this is an unhealthy state of affairs. The choices that have to be made affect ordinary people yet, as with other high technological areas, the people have no input into the decision-making process. As we shall see in subsequent chapters this can have wide-ranging effects on matters as diverse as supermarket shopping, defence procurement, the levying of taxes, employment in general, and job control and satisfaction.

These differences may well recede over time. More

commercial organizations than ever are compelling their managers to become what is becoming known as computer literate. As an increasing number of trainee managers and business school graduates now have a more than rudimentary knowledge of computing their control over computer professionals will be that much more complete. At a purely practical level the divisions are unhelpful. Whilst Adam Smith's division of labour and the Taylorist adaptation of it to mass production have worked in repetitive tasks the potential gaps that are left when non-manual work is done in this way can lead to disasters. When a new system is to be implemented a triumvirate of systems designer, manager, and programmer are involved, and this of course is very much a minimum position; at times there can be as many as fifty persons making their opinions known and insisting that the others take notice of them. The communication gaps left by this plethora of responsibilities are too often filled by the 'send reinforcements we're going to advance — send three and fourpence we're going to a dance' type of misunderstanding. The clever method of solving this problem is for the manager to learn programming, or so the classic consultancy judgement will dictate. Why not, however, also train programmers and analysts to become mainstream managers? In either instance the additional difficulties of initial bugs in the system, the changes to job roles initially plus the system itself and job roles subsequently, would be coped with more easily. The spread of the mini- and microcomputers can do nothing but hasten this move. It may be the most significant of all in the work environment in that managers will then be more attuned to data processing in technical terms and will thus be more ready to use computer services of all types in greater profusion than at present. It would in fact be the greatest spur to office automation yet seen.

The corollary of this is that managers at present act as a bar to technological change, especially in their own environments. There is evidence to support this contention, despite the fact that in Britain it is regarded as a heresy: the prevailing wisdom is to regard the trade unions as the major block to progress. Studies comparing attitudes in West Germany and the United Kingdom on the acceptance of both numerically controlled machinery and the newer office technologies showed that whilst both sets of managements showed an initial reluctance this was overcome more readily in Germany. In neither country was the attitude of the workforce or the unions an obstructive one. This does not mean that unions have no power when it comes to an industrial showdown, but it does suggest that unions have either not sought or have lost their battle for control over the new computer-based technologies.

Unions, acting as they do collectively, have the potential to halve or amend any computer system, and indeed have done so in the past. The best documented of these disputes has been in the United Kingdom, although the French unions have shown that a very small number of key computer workers can, by withdrawing their labour, cause substantial chaos in both the government and the banking sectors. 1979 saw two very important strikes in the public sector in Britain: the post office and the civil service. The post office strike was over pay and as a result operators in the installations dealing with customers accounts walked out and stayed out for nineteen weeks. The backlog of uncollected bills lasted well over nine months and was so large that the government was forced to admit that the Public Sector Borrowing Requirement (PSBR) was aberrant for some months — the backlog ran into billions of pounds. The civil service dispute affected defence and taxation establishments. It did not need to last long and the government backed down before much damage was done to the public financial markets or to defence or security arrangements.

In 1981 the civil service unions struck against using computer workers as the shock troops of the campaign. This time the level of pay was only one factor in the dispute as the methods of negotiating and of setting wage levels were at least as important. The strike lasted for five months. It affected the ability of the government to collect income taxes and value added tax, impaired the accuracy of social security payments so that overpayments were made, often never to be recovered, and severely curtailed the security and defence processes. Two years after the event it is still impossible to determine accurately how much money was 'lost' in the course of the dispute. The current estimate is that around £2 billion has been 'spent' in extra interest charges, irrevocably lost taxes, overpayments in some areas, extra staff, and overtime payments. In classic industrial relations terms the strike was a brilliant success — in actual fact it was a defeat for the unions and it is most instructive to ask why this should have been.

Power or control depends upon the ability of a person or a group of people to determine the course of events in any given set of circumstances. It is quite clear that the UK government had both power and control over the civil service workforce during the 1981 dispute. A strike or indeed any other withdrawal of labour depends upon the effects that it has on the general public, either directly or indirectly, through second, third, or even fourth parties for its success. The 1981 civil service strike affected few people directly in an adverse manner. It did, however, affect a substantial number of people in an indirect way. From an uncommitted point of view this meant that the public actually benefited; fewer tax payments meant a more general feeling of well-being. Given the fact that the entire dispute received but small media coverage and that this tended to dwell upon the negative aspects of the strike rather than the fact that the amount of taxes being paid was diminishing, it is not surprising that the public wanted to see the end of the dispute as soon as possible if they had a view at all.

This then brings into play the role of the media in disputes, especially those against the government of the day and especially a Conservative government. None of the mass media suggested that the strike was creating an embarrassment to the government, financial or otherwise. The problems of tax revenue and social security payments were forgotten, or totally discounted. There was absolutely no question that the defence capability of the United Kingdom was affected or that the internal, or indeed the external, security systems were impaired; both questions were treated with profound silence. More to the point the government took the decision that they would not be beaten, whatever the cost. A private sector firm cannot do this; an agency which depends upon a fixed cash flow cannot take this point of view either. A government which can issue additional government (or gilt-edged) stock at its own whim or can borrow internally in other ways can weather almost any financial storm. This is precisely what happened in 1981.

A private sector employer or indeed a more responsive government would have bargained in a traditional manner, but this did not happen. The losses were sufficient to make any rational employer concede, but from a traditional point of view the last thing that the government could have been labelled was conventional. It is now quite clear that any government with a strong political will can outlast a strike by its own employees, no matter how serious its effects, providing that neither the basic standard of living nor the security of the population is unduly affected or that people think they are unaffected. Given that the time lags are sufficient to outlast the action in terms of their effects and that as a result it is difficult to link conceptually cause and effect, a government has only to sit tight, pretend that the strike is only having the most marginal of effects, and it can outlast any short-term opprobrium. Such a policy depends upon two factors for its success. The first is the suppression of the real effects of the strike, especially in national security terms. The second is to publicize the most damaging effects of the strike, especially any which will affect ordinary people like the strikers themselves. A final alternative is to ignore the effects of the strike altogether.

That there were serious constraints placed upon military and civil communications, especially transatlantic ones, is no longer denied, even though such effects were hushed up during the dispute itself. The military and logistical implications were so great that one observer of this scene has stated that if the Falklands campaign had been needed during the strike there would have been no campaign—indeed, *could not* would be more accurate. That the costs of the strike were probably the highest in British industrial relations history is also now a matter of record, yet despite the costs the strike was lost.

It is quite clear that unions have the power to impose severe disruptions on the users of computers but it is now also abundantly clear that an employer who is in a position to ignore the dispute (and this is less likely in the commercial sector) can outlast the unions. In real terms the unions had their bluff called. One of the great nightmares has thus been defused—that of a small number of computer personnel holding the entire country to ransom. To realize how far the fear reached one has only to read the Wilding Report on the use of computers in the administrative civil service which was prepared in the wake of the 1979 strikes.

It states quite baldly that 'at the core of most of government's major administrative operations there is now a computer'; this trend was noted in Chapter 7. The report goes on to point out that 'another possible threat is that our own key computer operating staff, who could cause disruption disproportionate to their relatively small numbers, may withdraw their labour, this possibility makes computers attractive targets for selective industrial action in furtherance of a national dispute . . .'. After then stating that alternative procedures must be on standby the section ends with a sober thought. 'But we note with concern the limits to what can be achieved in this way: and the issue of vulnerability must be borne in mind when considering new applications.' As we shall see in Chapter 14 the mood has now changed and apart from the euphoria produced by the employers' victory senior civil servants believe that the newer distributed systems will make another 1981 very unlikely if not downright impossible. There may be a rather large element of wishful thinking and self-delusion in this argument.

The Swedish government, too, produced a report on computer security compiled interestingly enough by the Ministry of Defence and entitled *The Vulnerability of the Computerised Society*. The study, which took over two years to compile, looked at two distinct areas: acts of war or terrorism and the concentration of operations, and dependence on staff and the need for assistance from abroad. The report noted the increasing vulnerability of operations to criminal ventures, especially the Italian terrorist attacks on computer installations, which it cited as an example of not only what can happen in one country but also the difficulty of maintaining security along international data and communication systems. The report noted, for the first time publicly that 'Infiltration amongst persons with vital functions in important data processing systems may be a way of assisting sabotage, espionage, and the creation of confusion amongst the public.' Concentration was looked at, and frowned upon from a security point of view and in addition the report came to the conclusion that emergency planning is not all it should be. Staff control is called for especially in regard to disgruntled staff practising a form of sabotage like the destruction of the information in registers. This not being the United Kingdom preoccupation with industrial disputes is singularly absent.

The power of unions to disrupt is not a function of computerization; computers however concentrate this power in the hands of relatively few people. There are times when the very strength of a union is its weakness. In electrical power generation the consequences of a withdrawal of labour by engineers or computer switching operatives are so horrendous that neither group are likely to allow it to happen. The same limitations cannot be said to apply however to banks or insurance companies, the bank clearing system, local government or company head offices all of which depend heavily on computers and are still vulnerable. Employers take the threat seriously. The fingerprint department at Scotland Yard is now computerized and the staff manning that computer are hand picked and all non-union. The Civil Contingencies Unit which draws up plans to cope with large national or key strikes has to rely on military personnel in its planning but it cannot do so with computer strikes, there are just not enough suitably qualified military computer staff in existence.

Employers not only regard their staff in defensive terms but also now have back-up systems to take over from any system which 'goes down'. Whilst this is merely commercial prudence, the locating of these standbys outside of the country in which the main installation is based is an indication that strikes or civil disturbances are uppermost in managements 'minds'. The potential losses caused by a strike of computer workers is obviously thought to be high enough to justify the expense of overseas installations. Whether it is because of a lack of suitably qualified strike breakers or whether it is the potentially high costs involved, the private sector is still cautious about the possibility of trouble. Computer staffs are, however, unlikely to strike on behalf of colleagues unless they too would be direct beneficiaries of the action, as was the case in the 1981 civil service dispute. It is fascinating to note that the government awarded an increase of 18 per cent. to administrative computer staffs in 1982, at a time when other civil servants were having to make do with 5 per cent. It becomes even more fascinating when it is realized that the unions did not claim this amount; the government awarded it of its own volition, presumably to ensure a trouble-free year in the event of other civil servants being disgruntled. The shock troops would have been disarmed. For a government which believes in the evils of a large civil service and has attempted to cut manning levels as well as keep wage increases low, such an action is a clear indication that it believed that unionized computer staff have immense power — even after their 1981 defeat.

Power, however, does not equal control. Unions, indeed workers in general, have only a small measure of control when it came to either installing a computer or the design of the system and its impact on job content and satisfaction. Whilst in some countries these subjects may be discussed between managements and unions, especially those countries where industrial democracy provisions are in force, there is rarely bargaining on the issues. The control is almost exclusively vested in the two sets of managers, general and data processing, and computer professionals. Control implies a full or partial veto over proposed actions and within the United Kingdom this has never been achieved in these areas — only in the informal shopfloor arrangements of matters such as the shop stewards' control of track speeds has this ever existed.

In Norway a national agreement exists between the union centre and the employers' federation called the data processing agreement. This agreement lays down the steps that an employer has to take when implementing a new system or amending an existing system. This includes compulsory negotiations with the unions concerned and their agreement. In essence this gives a right of veto to the union although it is very rarely used, and thus an ability to control events. In the United Kingdom some unions have been negotiating 'technology agreements' with individual employers in an attempt to get the same degree of control, but to date the results have been firmly weighted in the employers' favour. Most of the agreements commit the union to agreeing to the introduction of the technology without any real *quid pro quo* in the shape of a clause-specifying agreement or even one which agrees to the *status quo* obtaining until the procedure has been exhausted. The TUC attempted to negotiate a symbolic national level agreement but the CBI, unimpressed by such symbolism, said 'no'. Other countries employ different methods. In Sweden the codetermination laws allow unions, and compel employers if the unions so wish, to bargain about subjects such as computers or other forms of capital investment. The Swedish LO state that 'union policy should not be to prevent but to exercise rigorous control over technological change'.

For the most part, however, control is either not on the workforce's agenda or has been denied to them; in either event it is the employer who holds most of the better cards. There is a public perception problem in that many people feel that unions can and do exercise a veto over the introduction of computer technologies whilst in the real world this is patently not the case. This misconception arises partly from the unions themselves which have habitually overstated the effects of their influence and power. It arises too from generalizations about the few disputes that have taken place over newer technologies or computers such as *The Times* dispute in 1979. The unions appeared to have forced Times Newspapers into suspending their new computerized proposals in full and to sit down and discuss manning levels, training, and related matters. Within twelve months, however, the technologies were being introduced and the new owners made it abundantly clear that without them they would shut the newspaper. Times Newspapers had won, although not convincingly, and the lesson that should have been learned generally (but was not) is that the introduction of computers is best done by consent rather than imposition. The lesson that seems to have stuck in the mind of the public, however, is that unions are 'Luddites' which is both an incorrect use of the description as well as being wrong in fact.

Control over computers and systems can also be exercised by less than gentlemanly means. It is possible to sabotage a computer or one, indeed some, of its programs. The use of a sledgehammer or hatchet is not the method in question; rather it is the perversion of the normal running systems themselves. Where the intention of computer fraud is to enter the system and then leave it undetected the intention of modern sabotage is to either damage the memory or programs perhaps by even wiping them out of existence or by subtly changing a program so that the error induced builds up over time. An inadvertent error of this nature gave progressively and increasingly wrong figures for the United Kingdom balance of payments in 1972 and was only discovered by accident after six months. It is possible to change banking programs, to amend financial statements, or to change the programs controlling the process in a continuous process plant for example. Groups of skilled computer people, programmers, analysts, and designers are discussing these matters as an alternative to conventional industrial actions. Certainly groups of schoolboys have shown recently that it is relatively simple to enter a system and cause a modicum of havoc using everyday technologies and a knowledge of computing. How much more successful a group of professionals could be.

Designers have an oversight of the entire control process. The specifications of the machine and the way that it is put together will go much of the way to determining how and by whom it is used, and this applies equally as much to the software and systems designers. Designs can sometimes go horridly wrong, although as in the case of the Convair aeroplane which had both of its wings fall off the faults are discovered most often at the testing and proving stages. Sometimes they do slip past, however. A worker at the Kawasaki plant near Osaka was killed by a robot when repairing a machine nearby and although the man should not have been in the area an investigation found that the design was faulty otherwise he would not have been able to get access so easily. This is probably the first recorded death by a robot and it passed off very quietly in media terms; one might have supposed that television would have been interested. As the population of robots increases so the chances of accidents, even fatal ones, increases too, and with a wider range of functions and extra robotic mobility these chances increase geometrically, unless design and production engineers take greater care. Regrettably the day when man injures a robot is news but the converse is not worth a mention may not be far away.

GIGO is probably the best known acronym for an aphorism (non-computer jargon) in the computing world, standing as it does for garbage in — garbage out. In practical terms this is a decidedly inelegant way of explaining that computers are merely as good as the people looking after them. Computers are thus vulnerable to human error. This is neither a new concept nor a startling one but it is not yet accepted by the public in general for whom computer infallability has become a watchword or by advertising agencies to whom it has become a selling point. In terms of control and who exercises it this is an important point. The public have allowed the control of computers to be exercised by others primarily because they believe that there is little or no choice in the matter; computers are not only mysterious but also infallible. In Chapter 11 the question of who adapts is raised; if control is allowed to be concentrated in expert hands the computer professionals' position is made that much stronger. It is this strength, almost amounting to impregnability, that is such a worrying feature, especially given the professionals' own recognition of the GIGO fallability.

Control becomes concentrated even more readily when the combination of obsolete skills and workers actually planning themselves out of jobs makes the long-stay employee in any one establishment an increasingly rare occurrence. Those who stay, who survive, tend to be, though not exclusively so, the career managers, and in this catch-all description is included data processing staffs. Overall this means that only a small number of people have a deep enough knowledge of the system to coax and massage it, and if necessary to challenge it. Obsolete skills have been a problem ever since skills were developed because there has never been a period when the crafts, arts, sciences, or technologies stood completely still — if the time period under consideration is taken to be long enough. Skills become redundant at the same rate as the technology itself changes and as the new electronics are not only changing rapidly but also becoming cheaper, and thus actually being used rather than remaining clever laboratory toys, skill obsolescence is approaching more rapidly. The range as well as the speed is increasing. Skills and qualifications once thought to be 'safe' from the encroachment of new techniques or new pieces of machinery have suddenly become at risk; general management, accountants, clerical staffs, administrators, draughtsmen, and computer staffs themselves are losing their envied secure status and are feeling the cold winds of change.

The cost of retraining such people can be greater than training a young person from scratch, although union pressure may rule out this option. As a result jobs are filled by either young people in their first job or people insecure in their new-found skills, giving those with seniority, long service, or both the psychological advantage over the tyros. Opinions from the senior staff tend to carry an Olympian authority in such circumstances with mere mortals unable to challenge opinions, statements, or decisions through lack of knowledge or self-confidence. This entire trend is reinforced by the fact that if a manager has only vague and unspecified skills, some would cynically say none at all, he or she is obviously less likely to be the subject of skill changes, giving such employees a relative advantage in continuity. Such a state of affairs is likely to be temporary as this type of management will die out when the new systems demand specific skills and managerial production lines take precedence. It must be noted that in Britain at least this will apply only to senior and middle management;

non-executive board members especially will continue to be recruited for reasons more to do with who rather than what they know. An interesting extrapolation of this trend would suggest that as the rate of change speeds up so the control system becomes unstable; there are never enough knowledgeable people at any one place at any one time to form a controlling cadre. Associated with changes in skill requirements has been the phenomenon of employees working themselves and others out of jobs. This too is nothing new. Manual workers on fixed finite jobs, e.g. building a bridge or a road, have always known that the more efficiently they worked the sooner they would be out of a job. It is, however, a relatively new feature of office employment.

Organization and methods staffs with their stopwatches, clipboards, and brown shoes are part of the British shopfloor mythology of management duplicity and they or their management consultancy counterparts have indeed often presaged severe redundancies. These employees are now advertising their talents as essential to increase the efficiency, productivity, or effectiveness of their office colleagues and at the same time reducing the number of jobs available. The new systems based on new computer technologies mean that from time to time the organization and methods department itself is at risk and in turn this means that expertise in systems and efficiency is being discarded, often the only sources actually within an enterprise not to be in the data processing department. The challenge to those controlling the computers is correspondingly reduced yet again because expertise is needed to mount an effective counterargument.

It is for all of these reasons, and I have yet to touch on the consumer aspects of this matter, that there needs to be a greater awareness of the technical sides of computers and electronics. This is not a plea for most employees to be trained to a level of electronic engineers manqué; rather they must be trained to understand the jargon and have a firm grasp of what the computer and its peripheral bits can do. Without a check or control of the type that ordinary workers can provide the full potential of computer technology is unlikely to be reached. Managers will look at the cost minimization and efficiency optimization functions whilst computer staffs and professionals will be concerned with the smooth running of the installation, using the latest technology, their own job security, and in some instances defence against the introduction of a new disseminated system. Control rests between these two parties so that no group is lobbying for a more humane system of production or to make jobs more skilful rather than de-skilling them. Few people are arguing for the use of computers to improve customer or client services in a situation where there is a lot of spare capacity in the computer itself and workers are about to be made redundant. There is immense scope for this form of increased utility but it as yet remains largely untried and untapped. Only if there is wider access to the levers of power and control will this oversight be remedied. Certainly the computer and its technological aura of invincibility is in danger of controlling us rather than us controlling it. Its logic is man-made and there is no inexorable force driving the technology to do certin things or to fulfil only a limited number of ends. In the last analysis we must show that we control the machine rather than the machine controlling us: we decide the ends and the number of them to aim at; the computer merely provides the means.

Chapter 10

Who Benefits?

I N THE NEWSPAPERS, MAGAZINES, AND ON TELEVISION THE
constant message of the 1980s is 'value for money'; the
overriding preoccupation is not to 'be had' or to be on
the right side of a bargain. We as consumers are bombarded
with a media hype unknown and undreamt of in previous
times. We are cajoled to buy things, to use various services,
to wear the fashionable clothes, or if young the fashionable
anti-fashion clothes, and overall to conform to the spirit of
the people that we wish to be identified with. Consumer
magazines and organizations born in the 1970s have reached
maturity in the 1980s, giving tangible effect to the search for
the perfect image, to the new pinnacle in the safest possible
way, and at the best price. What the specialist journals leave
undone the colour supplements take up, telling us that our
lives are incomplete without the proper cane furniture, the
trendy woollies, and the ethnic entree. We are also being told
to complain if not entirely satisfied — a most un-British habit.

If the last quarter of the twentieth century is known for
nothing else it should be considered to be the time when the
enfranchisement of the grumbler came to its full maturity —
when the average person was encouraged to complain,
politically and socially, about the goods and services on offer.
Complaints can be made about everything. Whether it is about
style or durability, conern about the limited range of products
and services available, the policies of a government, a broken
component, or the stock of a supermarket, the principle
remains the same. The consumer associations, the advice
columns, and the ratio and television programmes which all
advise consumers of their rights in addition to the best buys
and deals tell us a great deal about twentieth century
capitalism. People clearly expect businessmen, shops, dealers,
and sundry flotsam to take advantage of them as though this
was one of the inviolable rules of the game. Otherwise, why

would there be such a demand for consumer advice and protection? It is as though the carpetbaggers had won the day and set the standards for probity in commercial transactions.

Given this cynical state of affairs the advent of the computer has offered increased opportunities to those who wish to take advantage of all the free publicity that the consumer advice centres can provide. In many respects this has rebounded firmly in favour of the consumer both in terms of the information available prior to exercising a choice and also in respect of the quality and range of the available products and services. The producer, too, has benefited or at least the producer who can claim to sell products adjudged to be at, or above, the average standard and at a competitive price. What has happened over the past decade is that the consumer has become fussier and is nowadays prepared to shop around in a wider and more sophisticated way than ever before. The back-up for these consumers, the information at their fingertips, is correspondingly greater too, provided they are prepared to seek it out.

In Chapters 5 and 6 the impact of computers on products was discussed and a distinction was drawn between those products that would not exist if it were not for computer technology and those which in one way or another had been amended. The amendments included the ideals of the consumer advice agencies of faster, better, more reliable, more durable, safer, and perhaps cheaper products. That all these advantages have accrued is beyond argument. Housewives, or whoever now does the housework, have a far easier time than their counterparts some ten years ago — or do they? Must we take for granted that the automatic timers, the thermostat controls, and the washing machine cycle mechanisms have all improved the quality of life of those who use them? It is probably true that it was physically far harder to turn a mangle than it is to push the appropriate button on the spin drier, or that using a washboard and soap was much more tiring work than watching a laundrette machine rotate—despite the dead weight of wet washing that has to be carried when the driers are out of action. Have the new gadgets relieved the drudgery and boredom from the house or enabled the housewife to get out and about more often? The answer must come down on the side of 'yes', but only marginally, and then only for those who have been able to afford the most upmarket of equipment and indeed can afford to get out and about.

Taking the argument a little bit further, is the lack of exercise, or indeed less exercise needed to perform household tasks a good thing in itself? The more we understand about our bodies the more the old theories and values appear to be totally wrong. Foods which twenty years ago were supposed to be healthy, like fresh dairy products and eggs, are now thought to be killers by a substantial section of the medical fraternity. In the same way hard physical work is now considered to be good and sedentary work bad in health terms; health clubs, aerobics, squash, jogging, and other forms of hard exercise are now replacing the perspiration of work and the gin and tonic after work. Current theories would suggest that the new technologies in the home are acting as an indirect health hazard.

Housework is only a small example of the possible dichotomy between better and more efficient equipment or systems and the maintenance of a good standard of living or quality of life. Precisely what people want and what the keys are to their motivation are subjects that have puzzled generations of politicians and more recently marketing men, industrial consultants, and psychologists. The subject is frought with difficulties and exceptions to all the rules. Most people would appear to want the newest and latest goods.

These will differ from country to country at the same moment in time as the customs and tastes between countries differ. However, at the same time there will be a number of people who will want goods or want to do things because other people neither do them nor have them; these are the people who like the so-called 'positional goods'. Yet another groups of people take an even more esoteric view and refuse to have the goods or do the things that most of us do or want to do, purely because the others do want them. This is a perverse attitude and one which is demonstrated clearly by the people who proudly boast that they do not have a television set.

Goods and services are not the entire 'be all and end all' of civilized existence, although a visitor from outer space might think this to be the case on a casual inspection or fleeting visit. In the same way the provisions made by governments for defence, pensions, social security payments, and education, not to mention health and the myriad functions that governments need to undertake in a modern society, do not together form a basis for a satisfactory philosophy of life. In some countries religion is undergoing a renaissance, especially the more fundamentalist of its branches, which is mirrored by the growth in the born-again and fundamentalist Christian sects. Clearly in a consumers' paradise more is needed than the cult of bigger, better, and faster. As computers have been partly responsible for the success of this cult in recent times it is only to easy to then blame or attribute the current malaises onto them. In turn this becomes part of an anti-scientific package with the virtues of the simple life exaggerated and promulgated. It is not the computer, nor is it science, that are responsible, because both are in essence neutral. It is the people that design and control the systems and the equipment that must carry any responsibility. There is little doubt that computers can be used in thousands of ways and it is possible for these uses to be tailored more towards the individual human elements than the satisfaction of mass demands, which appears to be the case at present.

Computers have provided us with a method of getting more goods and services to more people in a quicker time and in a fresher, better condition than ever before. Both quantitatively and qualitatively the impact has been enormous. One only has to look at a modern hypermarket and compare it to the corner ship of some twenty years ago to see the difference in he types of goods available and the way that they are bought. The difference is not dissimilar to the difference between stage coach travel and the jet aeroplane on a journey from London to York. All these things must be adjudged to be firmly on the side of the consumer, even though the consumer may not have overtly indicated a preference for the improvement. That consumers will accept the better service is obvious, the choice (given the disappearance of much of the competition) much less so. There are precedents for this anti-market or even anti-democratic approach. In politics and government the early Reform Acts in the nineteenth century were pushed through Parliament with only the minimum of public pressure and demand behind them; more modern decisions are taken on matters such as the abolition of capital punishment when the majority of people appear to be opposed to the decision. In market terms Henry Ford's dictum that they can have any colour that they like so long as it is black sums up the point in question.

Central to the whole discussion as to whether the consumer has benefited overall from the introduction of the computer is the relationship between the producer, supplier, and consumer. In traditional economics the consumer is regarded as sovereign, that is to say that the consumer expresses preferences and the producer then goes away and produces the goods to meet these choices. The market-place is where they meet and the price is the indicator of the demand for the goods. One does not have to be a Nobel prize winning economist to see that this is not the state that exists in the real world. In a classic reversal J. K. Galbraith postulated that the producer was sovereign.

His argument was roughly that it costs a producer so much to plan, design, and mass-produce a consumer durable (a car, washing machine, etc.) that mistakes are just out of the question. Initially, intensive and increasingly sophisticated market research is commissioned and here computers start to make their appearance. Assured that there is a space for the new product the producer then goes full out to create a demand for it before it is on the market. This is the 'hype'. Whether it is a new car or a totally new product like a videodisc, the aim is to appeal to people's sense of the necessary—how have they managed to live for so long without it? In defence of this theory Galbraith points out that it is now almost unknown for a company to produce a total flop, although the De Lorean car may have proved to be an exception to this rule. Products which cost little do not come into this category, nor do services. In such product areas flops are still common, although most will fail at the marketing trial stage, rather than on the wider stage.

Even if the producer is sovereign and the consumer buys or rents what is provided rather than what each person wants then the computer must have had an amazingly beneficial impact on the average consumer. Because it has allowed for the speedier distribution of goods it also allows for fresher goods to reach the shops, and because these goods are now delivered as needed rather than on the next scheduled delivery, which may have meant waiting a week, consumers get fresh goods all day long and year round. The same argument can be mounted on reliability or on the ease of servicing, the durability of goods, the ease with which we can book holidays or seats in a theatre, indeed improved customer service everywhere. Design has improved, transport has become safer, and quality control has, where robotics or computer-controlled testing equipment is used, made a quantum leap in accuracy. In other words the computer and the associated techniques have made life that much easier for the consumer in that old or existing goods and services have changed for the better. As Chapter 6 outlined, there has also been the introduction of consumer-oriented things which could not have existed were it not for the computer. Some of these, like the teletext systems, rely directly on the computer; others use the spare resources released by the use of computers to meet consumer needs, e.g. the retraining of redundant production workers to become service engineers in the Japanese television industry.

It would be simplistic, however, to stop the analysis at this point. There are other questions to be asked and hopefully answered. Do people feel that they have benefited or do they perhaps feel better off? It is almost certain that they do, although high levels of unemployment and thus low real incomes make this a by no means universal answer. It is also highly unlikely that the average person will attribute the changes in their circumstances to any technological reasons. The steadily rising level of expectations has been fulfilled in product terms more frequently and more purposefully than at any other time in modern history, even in the 1950s and 1960s.

It is now that an indefinable concept has to be introduced — that of the quality of life. Has the quality of life risen? If it is measured in consumerist terms the answer must be 'yes' for most people. If it is measured in other terms such as peace of mind, family stability, or personal security, the straws in the wind float in several directions; there is no easy answer. Tranquillizer usage has risen, divorce has risen, suicides have risen, crime is increasing as is vandalism, civil disturbances, alcoholism, drug abuse, and glue sniffing. Is life better because one can now buy carrots all the year round or can afford a videorecorder or is it worse because the old are scared to walk in the streets at night and the young husband or wife has just walked out leaving the other with two young children?

Whilst these are not mutually exclusive questions they are unfair. The increases in the more anti-social behaviour patterns are far more likely to be as an indirect result of the prevailing economic climate and the pressures that this engenders than the advent of the computer. The two things are interconnected, however. If the majority of people are busily acquiring new goods or going off to acquire an expensive suntan then those who are excluded from doing so are affected in a more dramatic and pointed way. If the ability to acquire these 'goodies' is a function of the use of computer technologies, and to a considerable extent this is the case, then the computer is adding to the aggregate of human problems. Inequalities have probably caused and will continue to cause at least as much trouble as either religion or nationalism. These have to be offset against the benefits. In terms of the quality of life there is no way that the debate can be settled, even inconclusively. For every example of computer usage leading to a change in favour of consumers a case can be made for a diametrically opposed example. For every argument suggesting that computers are responsible for a diminution in the quality of living an argument can be mounted citing a different cause.

On a different plane another difficulty intrudes. The proposition is that the quality of life has deteriorated rather than it being bad. This clearly means that there has to be a quality to which it can be compared. But when, and who chooses when, and in any event how do we know that the folk memories of that period are correct? There is always a 'golden age' which had all the virtues; people were friendlier, bacon crispier, cigarettes cheaper, and the trains ran on time. This mythical age acquires its golden hue well after those who lived in it have ceased to occupy any seats of power or hold the reins of influence but reflect on the time when they did. Contemporary writings tend to emphasize the miseries rather than the pleasures, as is the case today, and give the lie to the golden age. The 1980s may well be the golden age of the 2020s, difficult as most of us struggling to find our way through the morass may find it to believe. The point is that there never has been the complete age; there is no time with which today can be compared. A British politician recently commented that she admired the Victorian ideals and wished that they could be emulated in the present day. This presumably did not mean that she admired the workhouse, the double-standard hypocrisy, or the child prostitution, let alone the disease, poverty, and early death rates. Yet Victorians were preoccupied with these matters and the writings of the literati of the time reflect this. We cannot say whether things are better or worse than before because we do not know what it was really like to be living 'before'.

Standardization is one of the major achievements of the last two decades in general, and computers in particular have been one of the major devices to achieve this. This can be both a good and a bad thing from the consumer's standpoint. Standardization of quality or of safety at a high level is an undeniably good thing although not all producers may think the former an unmitigated blessing. In an age when fashions change rapidly and the media exist to disseminate these changes widely, the phenomonon of built-in obsolescence has become accepted. Cars are designed for four years of intensive use and electrical goods for five, and if the motors do not seize up then the steel rusts. Clothes, household goods, and even furniture are being replaced in a way that would have been thought madly extravagent only some twenty years ago. A technology which makes goods last longer or perform in a trouble-free way is at odds with the disposable society and may yet create difficulties. It is not that the manufacturers cannot compensate by making another weak link in the product but that part of the advertising campaigns built on computer and microelectronic technologies concentrates on the better quality and indestructability of the products.

The world car is the classic example of standardization. The giant manufacturers, General Motors and Fords, are both producing a standard car throughout the world. They may not look identical in the different countries nor do they have the same names, but the basic engineering and the major assemblies such as the drive train are almost the same. From the point of view of the manufacturer this gives remarkable advantages in international economies of scale, as well as having an industrial safety margin with plants in different parts of the world. The world car would be only half as effective in efficiency and profit terms if it were not for computers; indeed, without the computer it is unlikely that it would have become a reality. The interchange of parts, components, and assemblies are a vital ingredient in the optimum use of the world car and to track their movements and plan the production internationally needs computers with sophisticated real-time systems using good communications systems. Even the planning of the cars, the market research to unearth the common features, and the design and manufacture of the common components needed the intensive use of computers.

The car is a product where choice has apparently increased

whilst in reality fundamental choices have decreased. This has nothing to do with the fact that the number of manufacturers in the world has decreased; one firm could, in theory, provide a limitless range of vehicles. It is because the market has been so well analysed that the manufacturers compete on the same ranges for the same sorts of people. This leads to similar shapes enclosing similar features, the whole providing similar performances at remarkably similar prices. To step out of line could prove to be a remarkably expensive mistake. To get around the problem companies sell kits of add-in paraphenalia to provide an individual 'personality' to the car and give it a separate character. The immediate post-war days when at least twice as many basic types of car were on sale are gone for ever; the computer does not allow for the luxury of mass producing a drop-head car nowadays, although it does allow for a limited number based upon conventional production.

In passing it has to be admitted that this is in part an example of 'golden age' romanticizing. The 1940s and 1950s were also the years when safety standards were not so rigorous, when exhaust emissions went unchecked, and excessive petrol consumption was an irrelevance. Notwithstanding this, it is clear that the latest wave of standardizations could not have occurred without the assistance of computers. Whether the consumer usage has proved to be an unmixed blessing in this instance is unanswerable; it seems to depend on what a consumer wants and whether this applies to all consumers, the average consumer, or an individual consumer.

The motor manufacturers do benefit, however. They benefit by being able to continue production anywhere in the world where they have a plant making goods or bits of goods which can be used in other countries. In logistical terms it is a great advantage to a company to be able to produce the same goods in country A if there is a strike of workers producing that particular product in country B and being able to export that product into country B. Taking this one step further it is now possible for the company to put far more pressure on the workers in any one country because the ability to do without their services is now well established. In dealing with a militant trade union movement this is of considerable advantage, doubled if one or more of the other plants is in a newly developing country with lax labour laws and low wages. The other great benefits are in the economies of scale, increased possibilities of transfer pricing in international trading, and thus overall lower costs. When combined with the use of robots and other computer-related or organized systems the ability of car manufacturers to make greater returns to capital has been thoroughly enhanced over the last five years.

Possibly because of the cost of tooling up for this breakthrough and also because the depression has hit car manufacturers badly only the Japanese companies appear to have benefited in the manner one would have thought likely. It is probable, however, that the increased returns are merely delayed. Has the consumer benefited? Prices of cars do not seem to be unduly affected; the price of world cars and non-world cars seem to be relatively the same as they were when all companies made individual nationally designed cars. Indeed, the cost-cutting exercises of those European manufacturers which have automated a considerable part of their engine and body shops appear to have made little difference to the relative price of their products other than perhaps to have them not increase by as much as they would otherwise have done. This is not an inducement likely to commend itself to a consumer and moreover is very weak. Consumers have had the benefits of new safety and other less vital additions to their cars based on computer technology. Flashing light systems warning that seat belts are now fastened may be irritating but add to security; computer checks on valve and carburettor temperatures and warnings when they start to get out of line are a great step forward in terms of overall reliability, reducing petrol consumption and breakbones. Cruise at constant speed and speaking computers are examples of less than essential uses but ones which manufacturers believe that the public want in their cars. The benefits are undoubtedly there.

In the medium term the car corporations which have increased their output at lower real unit costs have gained more than the consumer. The driver has a safer and a more economical vehicle to use but at the same price and with all the added disadvantages of more restricted choice. Given that the large manufacturers are trying to appeal to the standard package market the individual motorist is losing out to the fleet proprietor whose influence on design, performance, running costs, and serviceability is now paramount. The computer's ability to store and then analyse facts make it an essential tool in the design of these new cars and the modification of existing ones, and the bulk of the information comes from the car fleets which now buy the overwhelming majority of new cars. Indeed, the fleets themselves, be they for one company or for rental, could not be operated or maintained without a great deal of computer use, or to be more accurate, they could not be run as efficiently and then only by using many more people.

The same applies, to a greater or lesser extent, to many other products and services. Household electrical goods are nowadays more efficient and more reliable in a working sense than they used to be and many of these improvements stem from the use of microelectronics or dedicated computers. Most of the new machines also have extra functions, timers, and automatic working cycle programs for example. Over the past few years the prices of these machines have remained steady in real terms although some of this can be attributed to a desire to get rid of stocks by wholesalers and retailers at a time of depression. The products themselves are simpler to make, as indeed are motor cars. This is due partly to better production and design engineering, both of which are made possible by the use of computers, and partly because there are now fewer components to be assembled, integrated circuitry having replaced the electromechanical components. In turn this means fewer people involved in the production procedures and this process is reinforced by the use of robots and computer-controlled and automated functions. If this was a labour-intensive industry, especially one employing a disproportionate number of relatively low-paid women, conventional economics tell us that other things being equal the price of the goods should fall as the costs fall. They rarely do. Computers can boost profits considerably.

The same argument applies to retail outlets. The use of point of sale computers makes the store or shop more efficient. Because it also makes automatic stock adjustments it makes ordering and buying and general stock control very much more advanced and thus prevents the company tying up its cash in slow moving stock, probably in the wrong places too. Chains of supermarkets thus cut their costs by using the new computer technologies, but the difference in overall prices between those that have installed the new computers and those that have not is very small, certainly far smaller than one would expect if a goodly portion of the savings were being passed onto the consumer. It is true, however, that the profit margins on supermarket goods are low. In this position competition works against the consumers' interests in that the newly equipped company merely has to ensure that it improves its position against its basically less well equipped rivals in a marginal but highly publicized way. If the company drops its prices too much it can suffer a loss in trade as some customers feel that it has moved down-market; other customers may of course be attracted to it. There is an important point of principle in the cases of cars, household goods and supermarkets. If there are cost savings to be made by the use of computers what percentage of them should be passed onto the consumer, the staff, and the shareholders or be invested?

The public is constantly being told that the new computer technologies are vital to their well-being and for their physical interests, yet it does appear, in the United Kingdom at least, that companies are faring better than consumers. A company or indeed any public or private concern that has to account for its costs will sooner or later attempt to minimize these costs by the intelligent use of computers. This is much more likely to be the initial motivation than any notions of consumer benefit; if these come about as a consequence then so much the better appears to be the motto. Business schools and economics teach a variety of logical pricing methods but in the real world few of them are practised. The main UK system is cost plus constrained by what the market will bear. This is partly dictated by the way in which accounts are prepared and published and partly because British management has been amateur in the extreme over many years and the cost plus system is easy to operate. Given this pricing method any cut in costs tends to be absorbed into the system and is not passed on as price cuts.

New products are, however, an exception. These do tend to fall in price over time as the technology improves. Whilst a cheaper component substituted in a car is taken as profit the same cannot be said for the changes in colour television set manufacturing. The price fell by a considerable amount until it reached its present plateau and the same is true of pocket electronic calculators and indeed ball-point pens so many years ago. Videorecorders are not yet a mature product so that one can legitimately look forward to considerable price falls, and this also applies to other newish products like pocket television sets and pocket computers. The older product does not display these pricing plunges, however, and as a result the use of computer technology tends to add to corporate profits rather than disposal incomes. Granted that profits theoretically are supposed to find their way back to consumers, it appears that many of them get lost on the way.

There is one sense in which the corporate use of computers and new technologies is of considerable benefit to consumers and that is in international trade terms. There are two ways of approaching this. The first is that as computers make enterprises more efficient they also make those organizations more competitive. In turn this means that more products are made in the United Kingdom and in turn this means that more jobs are kept in the United Kingdom than would be the case if these goods were imported. The result is that more income is generated domestically and this creates more jobs and more income whilst at the same time protecting the balance of payments. Whilst this virtuous circle is a classical economic oversimplification and applies to each and every industrialized country, it does contain more than a grain of truth. The second benefit comes from one particular form of international trade and that is with the NICs in the field of electronic assembly jobs — a speciality of low paid, easily available female labour workforces. Computers enable the industrialized societies to compete with the low-pay economies and whilst this may not be an advantage to those workers living in South Korea, for example, it is of benefit to the workers in the Northern countries.

An additional point arises out of this phenomenon and

indeed the advent of the world car too. Computers have enabled the giant corporations, the so-called mesoeconomic entities to fragment their production. What Adam Smith envisaged as a division of labour within one factory and has subsequently spread to different plants of the same company now happens on a global scale, literally straddling all five continents. This may benefit the consumer because there may be a better guarantee of supply, but it rarely benefits the workers. Producing components rather than a complete product and often not knowing what happens to these bits and pieces, what they are used for, or where they go is not a satisfactory way of spending one's working life. Regrettably this has always been the case; consumers benefit at the expense of the workers. What is new is that so many workers are also today's consumers — a result of the affluent society. Affluence, however, only applies to those who are in work in the Northern industrialized countries; those who are unemployed or the majority of those who live in the South, the non-industrialized countries, are living far from affluent lives. Most may not be actually starving but that is about all that can be positively maintained, and this truth only holds for the more prosperous of the developing countries.

Life or death, the most important dilemma of them all, has virtually disappeared from the industrial society's pantheon of worries except for the diseases of prosperity like cardiac problems. The human race has an infinite capacity for creating its own problems and one of these is a combination of freedom of choice and the pursuit of status goods. An argument can be mounted to claim that the use of computers has restricted the overall choice of consumers whilst in its place it has guaranteed the regular delivery of a smaller range of goods. Cars are a classic example of this trend but more fundamental changes can be seen in the food markets. The use of computers to determine the stockholdings of individual supermarkets in large chains is tantamount to relieving the local manager of control over the goods available for sale. It also means that goods that only sell in one or two stores are prime candidates for phasing out, as are also those which sell in small quantities and then only slowly.

Put into words of one syllable, only mass sale goods will be sold. This may be efficient, it may be profitable, it may fit the theory of market capitalism, but it does not enhance the standard or the quality of life overall for all. Today there are goods which are no longer available from supermarkets and because supermarkets have made the corner shop uneconomical this means that these goods are not available over whole areas of the country. This applies to certain cuts of meat, to certain vegetables, and to a range of tinned or preserved goods. No doubt a visit to Harrods or Nieman Marcus would ultimately get the order fulfilled, but the high price coupled with the lack of access to either store make such a solution very much the second best or even a nonsense. Meanwhile as the range of foodstuffs available is at best static or falling, in basic terms the number of branded but almost identical processed food products is increasing. The total range of foodstuffs is greater than ever before, but the number of unsatisfied customers is greater too. The same applies to cars, consumer electronics, and services like holidays and even television programmes. Different brands, be they of cars, margarine, cigarettes, soap powder, or the names of situation comedies must not be confused with genuine competition offering the public real choices. The choice of five brands of detergent distinguished only by their advertising is not a good symbol of the impact of computers, but if action is not taken to reverse current trends then this is all we shall have as an example. The sameness of supermarkets, cars, houses, television programmes, and even insurance policies are all examples of the same technique, that of caution prevailing over imagination, of the soft middle ground taking precedence over the harder fringes, of the average superseding the special. The computer excels at this form of analysis and control. It identifies the average much more accurately and quickly and this means that although trends cannot be started they can be leapt upon and perpetuated very swiftly.

Does the consumer benefit from all of this? If one believes that consumers should attempt to maximize their tastes, their choices, or indeed their sensations then the current trends are most counterproductive. If on the other hand one believes that a consumer is happy with what he or she can obtain (or is given) at their local stores then the computer has acted to the advantage of consumers and they have benefited correspondingly. However there are more countries in the world with shortages, with queues, with black-markets, and with allocation difficulties than those where the problem of choice amongst plenty is paramount. Whilst choices may be a real problem to those people who are trying to exercise it, it is wise to put it in a global perspective and see it for what it is — a luxury worry.

It is not merely good enough, in any society, to look at individual uses of the computer, analyse them, and then pronounce whether or not the effects have benefited society, let alone an individual consumer. So many interlocking mechanisms affect complex societies that any one action tends to cause a myriad of subsequent actions — a ripple effect. If, for example, the new cash points in supermarkets cause bigger traffic jams though more customers, then although the consumer using that shop may benefit he or she benefits less overall than they would if there were no traffic jams. What is more, a shopper always using a rival store loses completely because there is no gain as compensation, yet the traffic jam is just as bad for that person. The matter does not end there. Rates may have to be raised to pay for both road damage and traffic control, car mechanics may lose work, trains may get extra passengers, a one-way system by-passing the high street altogether may have to be instituted. These extra factors have to be taken into consideration when considering any cost or benefit accruing from changes, whether they are computer stimulated or not. Such a view must be taken when looking at the impact of computers on work. Not only is there an effect on the quality and quantity of jobs in the enterprise which installs the systems but there are effects on competitor and supplier firms depending on whether the new methods are successful or a failure. In aggregate and if used enough, the new systems will have profound effects on town development, on transport systems, on office design, and on the building industry, local government, education, and even the entertainment and tourist industries.

The effects cannot now be confined to one country or even continent; in Chapter 9 the Swedish government was quoted on the potential hazards to security stemming from the use of communication networks in overseas countries. Security, national or commercial, must at present be a preoccupation to those who have to safeguard these matters, although the changes made possible by the use of computers and satellites may reduce the chances of international sabotage quite dramatically or at the least put it into the realm of James Bond fantasies. International trade patterns have changed over the past ten years and much of this difference can be accounted for by the use of computer and electronic technology in an uneven manner. There has been a transfer of jobs away from the industrialized countries into the developing world, or at least a small number of developing countries. Whole industries such as watch manufacturing transferred from Europe to South East Asia, although there is starting to be a return at the prestige end of the market. Shipbuilding, steel making, electronic assembly, and, slowly, car assembly are following the earliest examples of this drift — that of textile and clothes manufacturing. Computers and the newest technologies may amend this trend. The cost of new capital equipment is falling so much and so quickly that the cheap labour and no strike offers from the NICs are not as seductive as they were once. Some processes, especially in electronics, have already returned to the originating country. Other processes like heavy engineering, especially where assembly is the major task, some chemical processes, and generally the more unpleasant jobs in society, will drift into the developing world through the agency of the large transnational corporations.

The cost of this happening to an industrialized country is an adverse effect on its balance of payments and all that this implies in economic management. The costs of job loss within any one country are on two levels. The first is social — the anger or the demoralization of people who wish to be useful but cannot be so — and the second is the cost in government finance and resource terms of having people doing nothing. Moreover, most people would rather be working and actually contributing to government coffers. It is often stated that the boring, dangerous jobs are those that will disappear; would that this were the case. Because these are the lowest paid jobs in the economy they are the least likely to be replaced, because the savings to the employer are so low potentially. This will be the case unless other factors such as quality control are the overriding reasons for computer use. The higher paid, administrative managerial, skilled, and semi-skilled positions are the more likely to save employers money and are thus at far more risk. If the more unpleasant jobs remain what are the benefits for those who work or wish to work? The answer must be 'not a lot', and herein dwells the fallacy that lies behind the thinking of those who espouse passionately the cause of technology.

The classical economics market economy theory suggests that if each individual, be it a person or a company, does the best for himself, herself, or itself then the best will also happen for society as a whole. In more conventional economics jargon this means that the aggregate of all the individual optimizations will result in one big optimization. As this theory is based on perfect competition which has never existed and perfect information which has never existed, it is not surprising that this Utopian condition has never existed either. If all enterprises took the decision to cut costs at roughly the same time by introducing the computer-based technologies where would the jobs come from? The theory would suggest that the wealth so created (another word for profits) will be used to create new jobs, but this suffers from a number of defects.

It assumes that the profits stay in the country in which they have been made, which in a world dominated by the multinational companies who are so adept at the financial sleight of hand is an assumption that is heroic in the extreme. It assumes that there is an instantaneous readjustment which is very far from the truth, especially in the United Kingdom or the United States. Both countries have their equity capital systems dominated by the large non-bank financial institutions and this slows the reentry of profits into the job-creating primary share markets or the banking sector which can respond far more quickly. As the United States has a well-developed venture capital market this is a problem which affects the United Kingdom more severely but which is never seriously broached by a political party. The time lag may be as long as forty years and not many disgruntled youngsters will peaceably sit by and let this happen. This is also an assumption that jobs will be available in the places where people have become unemployed and still live and which fit the type of skills that the unemployed have. In short, the assumptions make this theory, at least in its unvarnished state, a nonsense and moreover a dangerous nonsense if only because it tries to make us believe that all will be for the best in the best of all possible worlds, which makes it far more difficult for the necessary preemptive actions to be taken. Benefits in terms of the quantity of employment will not come automatically. If working weeks, months, indeed lifetimes were to be amended and shortened; if public sector jobs to meet existing needs and providing person-to-person services when necessary were to be funded; if the local community became the basis and focus for expansion; and if the process were placed in the widest way possible, then people might have a better chance of being the beneficiaries. This is all possible, but at the time of writing is politically highly improbable. It follows that the main group to gain from computers will be employers — not necessarily only in the private sector.

In the public sector people could benefit but this will be dependent upon the reason for using the computers in the first place. If they are implemented to cut costs then the members of the public will benefit by hopefully paying less rates or taxes, although the costs involved in maintaining those displaced public sector workers may outweigh this benefit or at the least make it negligible. If the computers are put in so that the resources released can be used to meet other needs in the public sector than fewer people should be displaced and the benefits actually become available. An example of this form of progress is the use of computers in the health service; there routine administrative tasks can be performed by the computer, but instead of making those who do these jobs at present redundant they should be retrained to become some type of paramedical staff and thus meet the, as yet unmet, needs of patients. This approach could be used across the entire range of public sector services from the police to schools, from coastguards to civil servants, and from town hall clerks to bomb aimers.

In industrialized societies the worker tends to stand less chance of getting a job in the formal economy; the informal economy is a growth sector, but has the added cost of, more often than not, finding that the job has been de-skilled. Boredom is unfortunately not eradicated by computers but is actually on the increase in the workplace. It is not a function of the machine that this should be so; nor do the systems built around the computer have to remove the initiative from employees. If productivity increases are the main reason for having the system introduced then de-skilling is the norm and about 99 per cent. of all new systems are installed for this reason, although with care this can be reversed. That is why the question of control posed in the last chapter is so important. There are possibilities of allowing more control and flexibility to ordinary workers if the design of the system is right, and research on this subject is being carried out in Germany, the United States, France, and to a small extent the United Kingdom. The fact remains, however, that productivity and profitability will remain the key factors in deciding whether or not to bring in a new system. The newer forms of education which are merely imparting knowledge to compliment the functions of the machine or system suggest that this is a widely held view.

Computers offer a very different set of problems to a developing country. Here a more basic question must be asked. Is it an appropriate technology? Whilst each country has its own difficulties and national characteristics the answer, overwhelmingly, is 'no'. In countries where the preoccupations are the basic life and death struggles and starvation or malnutrition are more common than artereosclerosis, where the population growth is a constant worry, where the infrastructure of education and medicine leaves a lot to be desired, and where unemployment is epidemic, computers may make the problems worse. An expensive telecommunications system may please the multinationals but will scarcely help those who cannot afford a telephone. Employment of the wasted resources must be the first priority of developing countries and this should be the criterion in deciding whether computer use is a good thing. If it aids in finding or maintaining water supplies, if it helps to map out the optimum crop rotations, if it helps to run businesses, especially distributive concerns, efficiently, it is very appropriate. If, on the other hand, it is used to replace workers in a factory or office or if it is used in a one-off foreign-owned assembly plant then it appears to be inappropriate. The ideal sort of use is attached to a solar panel system converting that energy into a pump or an electric motor, but the country itself, its government, must decide. The fragmentation of production does damage, or at least has a potential for damage in both the industrialized and developing world.

Health matters are one area where there is little dubiety as to who benefits. People benefit although as the newer techniques tend to be the most expensive they are also the most likely to be found at the top end of the private sector exclusively. Treatments have improved, diagnostics have improved, and the data bases held on computers of tissue typing and the more esoteric of the blood factors have saved lives in transplant surgery. In health and safety at the workplace, too, there has been a big leap forward as the monitoring and sensory equipment improves. The argument about all these things and indeed the possible new aides and appliances for the disabled concerns the fact that there has not been a fast enough introduction and that a great deal of rationing by price takes place, especially in the case of the disabled. There are, however, some encouraging aspects. A home shopping experiment using Prestel run by Tesco supermarkets and the social services department in Gateshead is a useful way of helping the aged and housebound take decisions for themselves and must be encouraged.

The new technologies work in mysterious ways, undreamt of by the innocent consumer. The young woman applying her expensive French perfume in front of the mirror and dreaming of her lover in approved cinema style thinks not at all of the part computers have played in her luxury product. In fact they have assisted in finding the ingredients and the mixing of them so that the perfume remains fresh and retains its smell for longer, and they also manage a speedier and more efficient distribution system which allows a higher percentage of bottles to be delivered in the best possible condition. Mysterious is an apt word in that people have to be instructed in the mysteries of the computer. Education itself is not a clear-cut area like health, where the overwhelming evidence is that computer technology has acted well. The growth of computer learning has upset many teachers and educationalists in that it does the opposite of stimulating the imagination or encouraging the thinking processes. This is, yet again, not an inherent defect in the computer but a rigidity of programming and what is more a function of a program written by a non-educationalist — once more a problem which stems from the 'who controls?' question.

As consumers of goods and services we have some new goods like credit cards or teletext systems, both of which appear as mixed blessings. We do run the risk of becoming massively overinformed and as a result of switching off information *in toto*. The benefit is also less than it might otherwise be because the best interactive system is expensive whilst the non-interactive systems have information that few people actually want. Credit cards upset the financial puritans amongst us. They are a temptation to spend, but as the entire Western society is based on the use of credit this is merely an added apple tree in the entire financial orchard. They have also been criticized as being a risk as so many are stolen and then used fraudulently, but this is like criticizing a plate glass window for being a temptation to brick throwers; by and large they do seem to be a benefit, as do bankers cards.

Whether there are new products or whether goods or services have been amended or otherwise improved, the consumer is confronted by a very different range of things to have or to do and ways of doing them than was the case, say, twenty or even ten years ago. We have better information and better health, we are taller, fitter, and cleverer, but on the dark side we hide behind more alcohol, more drugs, and in the ultimate statement more suicides. In this fast changing world it is difficult to isolate individual causes and effects but the odd general point can usefully be made.

Computers are used to extend the ranges of what we can do and to do these things and others more efficiently and cheaply. In doing so computers should aid in the increase of profits, productivity, and in the appropriate circumstances social returns too. It will also create over the short, medium, and even longer terms a high degree of unemployment. It will unfortunately create two nations: those who have (this includes a job as well as money and goods) and the dispossessed (those who do not have a job and own few goods and use few services except welfare). In a way it is the Marxist analysis come true, with the efficiency that he erroneously attributed to capitalism coming to fruition at least with all the conflicts and contradictions flowing from this new fountain. Who benefits from computer usage then depends on a series of political choices. In an untrammelled market economy the rich will get richer and the poor poorer, but on a greater scale and faster than anything seen since the early nineteenth century. In turn this will lead either to a Marxist style of revolution or a repressive regime run on a combination of bayonet points and 'Rollerball'. As governments intervene in the market system to distribute the fruits of the computer technologies more equitably so the twin dangers (or if you are so inclined promises) recede. The maximum number of people benefiting should be the aim of us all. It may well mean radical alternatives, at present an anathema to all those who have power and control in society today, decentralization with meaning and the widest form of democracy and accountability.

This sort of society, and there is no model in the real world on which it can be based, can actually become more viable with the advent of the new distributed systems and home computers. The turn of the century may see us ushering in the first of the cyberpoliticians.

Chapter 11

Who Adapts— Them or Us?

G EORGE BERNARD SHAW ONCE WROTE: 'THE REASONABLE man adapts himself to the world: the unreasonable one persists in trying to adapt the world to himself. Therefore all progress depends on the unreasonable man.' Shaw would clearly have defined computer people as the most unreasonable of men; their attempts to change the world and the attitudes and responses of the people in it have been good examples of perseverence meeting with no little success. Whether it has all been progress is quite another matter. Whether it has been change for either no good reason or simply laziness on the parts of those who design the systems or those who have had to cope with the consequences is open to argument. Change has been rampant; it has both eased into the corners of our society and confronted us head on in the full glare of publicity.

Change has always had disturbing connotations. Conservation and conservatism, both committed to the preservation of what exists, have a comforting ring to them whilst the proponents of change are more often treated with a degree of suspicion. Those who wish to preserve the existing order tend to agree amongst themselves as the scope for disagreement is so limited, whilst those in favour of change tend to disagree as there are so many ways of amending or changing something. This means that changes come under attack potentially from two sources: from those opposing the changes completely and those who believe that the changes are not quite all that they might be. Given this amalgam of hostility it is surprising that so much change has actually happened so quickly and moreover with so much ease.

The golden age that was described in the last chapter is always the repository of things that are good, unshakeable, and worth while. The loss of these things is often seen as heralding the beginning of the end of that particular state of grace, more often in hindsight than at the time, although there is often a contemporary tendency to overdramatize the impending loss. Thus a new motorway route or a new reservoir through beautiful countryside is too often built up to be the ecological disaster of the century after which the ecology survives virtually intact. This approach which applies to redundancies, plant closures, and almost all planning consent objections does scant justice to the cases in which it is used. The mere fact that the world still spins on its axis and that few of the dire predictions come to pass in a short enough time for people to remember the Cassandra connection gives it a 'crying wolf' reputation. Not all cases, however, allow the public to object or to analyse before the event. It was impossible to object formally to the one pound coin as no objection was allowed, or on a totally different tack it was not possible to object to the Falklands Campaign in that all the decisions were made by a small number of people in secret. It is probably more accurate to state that successful objections were out of the question and objecting for the sake of it is a rather futile exercise. The introduction of computers has come into this latter category.

The 'unreasonable men' who designed, installed, and then operated the new computers and systems have had a relatively trouble-free run from the public. New systems were simply put into place with the minimum of discussion or consultation with either the employees affected, the consumers affected, or the public in general. Who was consulted when the vehicle licensing centre at Swansea, one of the best recorded horror stories in the annals of computers, replaced the smaller establishments in the local areas? Who had a chance to argue when civil service forms, especially in the Department of Health and Social Security, changed from the relatively incomprehensible to the utterly mysterious? Which children or for that matter parents had the chance to object to the new computer-aided teaching methods recently introduced into so many American schools? The answers to these questions and thousands of similar ones is that very few could object. Perhaps no-one would have wished to, although this is a most unlikely state of affairs, but in any event it is irrelevant. Whether or not they would have been totally unopposed or completely overwhelmed by protest is not the issue; the issue is that people are having to adapt to the new circumstances not as a conscious choice but because they had, indeed have, no alternative. In Shaw's terms the reasonable men have had to knuckle under to the unreasonable ones.

Is this state of affairs itself a reasonable one or should a democratic system allow for, or indeed insist on, a wider discussion of these matters? The ethic in the Western world is for all the administrative day-to-day decisions to be left to the specialist, the managers, those who supposedly know best. We leave medical decisions to the doctors and would not dream of interfering with their clinical freedom, at least not many of us would, but why do we extend this right to hospital management and design and the allocation of resources in medical establishments? It is a difficult question to answer without invoking the concept of deference. Despite the fact that the authorities empowered to run hospitals in the United Kingdom have more lay (non-medical) people on them than medical the doctors manage to get their way a disproportionate number of times because their medical knowledge gives them an edge in other fields. In other words, we imbue them with some form of power, and then defer to it.

This is by no means an isolated example although it is an extreme case. After all, in what other profession would the practitioner expect to control the social as well as the business and practical tactics and strategies? Architects not only design buildings but also have a wider role in defining what that small area will be used for and what the people living in that area will do at work or at play. This is aside from the conventional planning processes which have been developed to do just these things. Teachers not only teach but play perhaps an over-important role in deciding which subjects should be taught. Law reform tends to rely far too heavily upon lawyers rather than politicians and the methods by which taxes are levied and collected are determined more by the convenience of the tax inspectorate than of those who are being taxed. Too wide a spread of such decision making has horrendous implications for democracy at all levels, even though efficiency might (and only might) be improved.

Leaving decisions to others generally occurs where there are barriers thrown up by the expertise of a specialist group and reinforced by their impenetrable jargon. In turn this means that the politician can only intervene when either the argument is understood (probably after the interpretation of a friendly expert) or at risk of being made to look silly, and there is nothing worse than this in the politicians' pantheon of horrors. If the result of this neglect is that something has been done — an action taken — which makes life in general a little bit worse or a little more difficult, then the politician has abdicated his or her responsibility. The same argument applies to senior management or administrators in relation to their clients, customers, or staff. The fact is, however, that computer experts rank alongside other professional people and the control mechanisms are sadly lacking. Doctors, lawyers, and systems analysts, amongst others, benefit from the same public self-depreciation which allows experts considerable freedom and power.

We have all had to adapt to changing circumstances. Ageing is an adaptive process whilst moving house, changing jobs, getting married, or retiring are all events which demand the human response of adaptation. Technological change has, over the years, demanded the largest amounts of adaptation of all, both because of the immense number of people who have been affected and because of the depth of the changes which the technology demanded. It now takes a special and creative form of imagination to realize the personal or social changes which the wheel must have trailed behind it, and the same applies to the use of gunpowder, to the magnetic compass, to the crossbow, indeed to the use of the horse. Existing skills became redundant and as a result the hierarchies changed; chiefs and leaders no longer had the talents useful in the earlier circumstances and were overthrown, sometimes violently. Misery and joy must have coexisted then as they do today, and for remarkably similar reasons. However, the changes caused directly by the steam engine and the indirect consequences of its use were massive even by comparison with other fundamental changes.

The end of the agrarian system and the birth of the industrial society gave rise to the towns and cities, created migrations between countries and continents, spawned a new elite, a new politics, a working class, some happiness, and a lot of misery. It created expectations where none had previously existed and enabled a few of them to be met. It changed the pattern of world trade, changed the strategic thinking of the great powers' military forces, changed the pattern of colonial development and thus a subsequent huge chunk of world development, changed the relative strengths and statuses of different nations, changed the religious content of life, and changed the perceptions of one nation about the others. It was, in short, a time when individuals had their accepted notion of the world turned upside down and when the great forces changed tack entirely.

In such periods conventional wisdoms count for naught; indeed they may be positively counterproductive. New situations demand new responses, not a rehash of previous ideas no matter how well they worked in the past, and the more radical the change the less appropriate are yesterday's nostrums. The danger is that a totally new situation is not seen for what it is and that measures to remedy a different state of affairs are put into operation, rather like treating pneumonia with leeches. The industrial revolution, fathered by the steam engine, was one of these times. The conventional politics had to change and the Tory and Whig parties gave way to the Liberal and Conservative parties with the Labour party not far behind in the wake of several political reform acts. Karl Marx wrote his famous works, revolutions abounded in Europe, and anarchism, nihilism, and the more extreme political views replaced the old accepted values. Without the changes the industrial revolution would never have reached its full maturity; the old mechanisms were incapable of working in the new environments. After all a vagrancy act designed to meet the exigencies of a rural existence was of scant use to magistrates dealing with the destitute in the new cities, and the rurally based dioceses had to change rather quickly. The power was leaving the landed gentry and squires and passing to the industrialist, the rather nasty *nouveau riche* northern entrepreneur, who despite the lack of 'breeding' could buy and sell the older generation several times over. This was not exclusively a British phenomenon; on the contrary it was happening all over Europe as industrialization spread. It affected the development of the United States, Canada, and the colonial possessions of the European powers as they changed from being trading stations to accepting the unemployed or others who could not or would not fit into the new patterns of society. The computer is having and will continue to have the same sort of effect as the steam engine, except that whilst the latter replaced physical power the computer is replacing mental processes. In fundamental terms, however, the similarity is marked: both are (or were) ubiquitous technologies as well as being supply side technologies and this conjunction of properties is common *only* to these two technologies over the last two hundred years. Only the public utilities of water, electricity, and gas come anywhere near.

It is not only the fundamental changes which create the need for people to adapt. Limited movements in technology have seen whole towns die and new cities burgeon. The changes in cotton manufacture, in mining techniques, in steel and shipbuilding, even machine tool manufacturing processes are examples of this 'unreasonable' progress. Given the fundamental nature of the computer's impact and the effects that even relatively small changes have had it is probable that the new technologies will demand a degree of commitment and tolerance unmatched since the nineteenth century. It has to be noted that whilst these attributes were needed at that time they were not forthcoming. The far higher level of expectations, political, social, and material, make it a far more urgent proposition that they must be fulfilled in the future.

The changes will create the need to adapt at two levels. The state and its institutions will have to respond on the one hand whilst individuals, families, and separate corporations and enterprises will come under pressure as well. Whether the systems are designed to meet the needs of people or whether people will have to change their behaviour to fit the new system is the key question. Of course, in the real world we would expect there to be a bit of give and take and to find that a compromise solution has been reached and that the question itself cannot be seen in quite such black and white terms. In reality, however, a surprisingly high percentage of the stark choices seem to prevail against all of our notions of common sense.

The decimal coinage introduced into the United Kingdom in 1971 condemned a sizeable number of elderly people to live out the remainder of their lives more or less within the confines of their own homes. They could not cope with the new system and did not wish to be seen in such an undignified position, especially by those younger than themselves. Human beings have a dignity that they do not like losing, especially in public, and also a sense of self-consciousness which comes to the fore on formal occasions. Changes of the magnitude of decimalization tend to provoke the greatest reactions and therefore have the greatest potential for disruption, as do changes which force themselves on people rather than being the result of people exercising choice. It was not possible to opt out of the decimal currency and it will soon not be possible, when the transitional period ends, to measure distances or weights in anything except metric or temperature in anything but Celsius. As with decimalization this will leave groups of the population at a loss as they will not be able intuitively to envisage what the measurement is in terms of everyday experiences.

There is an age differential in these matters. One would expect the more elderly to have the most problems; they have had longer than other people to have their attitudes fixed. This is borne out in practice. Another factor, however, is the seeming inability of a substantial percentage of these older people to learn the new systems at any time, and this suggests that either we sacrifice these old people or we attempt to provide systems which come nearest to the existing ones. The latter choice may mean sacrificing the probable advantages too.

This is not the same as resisting 'progress' or even slowing it down. Progress does not necessarily mean formal change and nor does the fact that there is change mean that progress has been made. The high-rise flats in British urban centres represented change, but only the very brave or the very foolhardy would claim this as progress. The same applies to many of the new towns in Europe, to changes in educational systems and the invention of new exams, and to the scrapping of tramways and electric powered public buses in favour of high running cost diesel ones. Hindsight is a marvellously effective quality; it is such a pity that it is not available at the time of the event. Not making the same or similar mistakes again is probably too much to hope for, but with care and a degree of foresight we might be able to minimize the risks. Regrettably, it is fair to say that this is not being exercised at present. A few examples might be instructive.

Let us first look at the realm of work — something that used to be the common experience for most people in an industrialized country but is sadly less so today. Nevertheless, it is still probably the second most shared experience. When a computer installation is put in or when a computer-based system is installed it is the managers, the analysts, and the consultants who take the decisions. One option would be to make the lives of the workers more interesting and the jobs more palatable. The system, however, is almost certainly supposed to benefit the organization or person who is having it installed, but this should not necessarily be at the expense of the employees. Some two or three years ago it would have been rare indeed to find a system design which had been made with the staff in mind, but fortunately this is becoming a more frequent occurrence although by no means frequent enough. One of the major reasons for this change has been the realization by the employer that the new systems rely upon the skills of those operating them; they are by no means automatic yet and so these skills have to be nurtured and pampered. A science or perhaps art of ergonomics has come to the fore over this period and addresses itself to the physical layout of individual pieces of equipment and how the individual bits interrelate in order to make the employees' lives more comfortable.

Posture in front of a keyboard, the lighting and colour of the screen, the lighting in the room or factory, the noise level and type of noise, the temperature, and the space are all part of this new designing method. Market research is now carried out amongst workers rather than amongst the managers to find out the most agreeable combinations. Through both their health and safety and technology roles the trade unions have an input into this process; the more aware unions initiate it. Flexibility is becoming the watchword. Screens which detach themselves from keyboards, portable keyboards that hide away in drawers, printers that can be tucked into soundproofed areas, word processors that double as computers and vice versa, and work stations, not discrete offices but places where anyone passing by can lay down their biro and work, are all in the current fashion. All of this represents a step forward but only a small one in solving one quarter of the work problem. Systems or bits of equipment that fall short of their full potential because the employees can neither understand nor operate them fully is another most important and costly problem. A system that is understood and does appeal is called in the jargon 'user friendly', which for computer jargon is unusually self-explanatory. Correspondingly, an unfriendly or hostile system is one which patently does not appeal.

The concept of a user friendly system for the employees is as relatively new as ergonomics but should not be confused with it. The main point of a machine or a system is that it is designed to be used by the operator or operators; a system which is only capable of being used half of the time or to only half of its potential or capacity is obviously twice as expensive as it should be. A computer which invites an operator's interest by having an operating program which is easily understood and leads the operator from stage one to the end with an easy inevitability is user friendly. If the operator is at ease with the program or system then he or she is more likely to use it efficiently so that the interest of the user and the owner (if they are different people) correspond exactly. It pays both sides of the industrial relations equation to have well-developed, well-thought-out software. Managers are more likely to be computer illiterate and thus computer-phobic than any other group of people in the workplace. From their point of view a user friendly system is as near to everyday communications and life as is possible and a system rather like the 'mouse' is highly desirable. User friendly means adapting parts of the system to the operator rather than the operator having to adjust and probably not managing to do so efficiently; that is why it is such a desirable quality to build in, a quality moreover which generally only needs to provide patience, commonsense, and a sense of humanity.

Different skill levels and the retraining required by the use of a new computer system can lead to many stresses and strains as the changes were not sought by the people affected. New systems often require employees to acquire new skills, and new and strange demands are made on their time and their concentration — all of which adds a dimension of self-doubt to the general uncertainty engendered by the new techniques. Adaptation in these circumstances can be painful, not to say traumatic, with the bulk of the trauma being borne by the older employees and those who have the most invested in their own success or failure. Retraining can be very much a gamble for the insecure and a high level of industrial tenderness has to be shown to those struggling with new concepts and languages, especially if they doubt their ability to master the new system. Many staff members will have to resign themselves to the unpalatable fact that they will no longer be getting the promotion that they thought was theirs by right and will also have to adapt to the even more difficult circumstance of younger subordinates being promoted in their stead. The skills appropriate to the company change and the odds are on the younger employees or school-leavers being the people most capable of acquiring them.

However skill levels can also change in a downward direction, especially for the skilled manual workers. Machine minding rather than operating became a feature of the change into numerically controlled equipment and the progression into computer control has only widened and deepened this trend. More types of lathes, machine tools, welding rigs, and riveting machines are now linked to each other through computers so that skilled men sit by waiting for breakdowns or watch computer screens. Printing is another very skilled craft area where amazingly sophisticated machinery has affected the types of jobs done. Key stroking direct input may be the well-publicized effect but colour printing itself is now highly computerized. The types of jobs have changed and the types of people who can do them have changed too. As Chris Clancy of Adplates has pointed out, 'The people who design the systems are totally different from those who used to do the work—now they are the same sort of person.' He pointed out: 'People who do things physically may not be the same sort of people who envisage things mentally.' This applies as much to the Washington Metro or a computer-controlled machine as it does to 'print monsters'. De-skilling is also a feature of the new office technology, of printing, and of the semi-skilled robotic work performed on production lines. Thousands of quasi-jobs are being created in this way; in Japan they have become one of the largest categories of employment, and the ability to cope with the unutterable boredom is one of the most valuable skills for such jobs.

The final quarter of the unitary work impact is the effect that computers have had, and will increasingly have, on the aggregate amount of work available in an economy. The initial effect was favourable as the lack of experience and the type of machines and programs available led to inefficiencies in both the operations and the running of the installations. In recent years, however, the efficiency has improved dramatically whilst the machines themselves have become easier to handle, cheaper, and very much more powerful, with the overall effect of increasing the productivity of the capital outlay as well as the productivity per person. A steady and relatively undramatic loss of jobs has resulted from the change, across the width of employment. The public and private sectors, the manufacturing and engineering sectors, clerical work, managerial tasks, and professional jobs—few groups have been immune. From the point of view of a society as a whole the adjustment problem is potentially immense. The likelihood that there will be a permanent lack of jobs, or at the least a period of anything up to twenty-five years with relatively high unemployment cannot be treated with equanimity by any democratic government. From its point of view the work ethic will have to be amended and new forms of working patterns such as flexi-time and flexi-years, three-day weekends, work sharing, study leaves, retraining years, early and flexible retirement will have to be considered seriously rather than dismissed as outlandish leftist notions.

The other possible adjustment process is on the side of computer usage. They need not be used as intensively, i.e.

beneath their potential, thus relieving the pressure on jobs. This state of affairs can be brought about by unions refusing to work the new systems or by employers, probably with the encouragement, indeed coercion, of governments, refusing to implement the new technologies. The potential pressures are considerable and will require the greatest level of political adjustment since the Second World War. Politicians of both the Right and the Left will have to alter their rhetoric and the assumption of fixed social classes and the resulting instinctive attitudes will be increasingly irrelevant as the class of the unemployed or not really employed grows in numbers. If politicians refuse to adapt, and there is evidence to suggest that in both the United Kingdom and the United States this defensive conservative view is being maintained amongst all the parties, then the potential for radical political action from either wing will continue to grow. Central government is thus faced with what will probably be recognized as its most fundamental peace-time task this century other than the debates and choices on weapon systems. Local government too will have its own problems and responsibilities.

Not only will there be fewer people working but they will, in all probability, be working in different places. At present most people go to work rather than the work going to them. This involves travelling to an office or a factory or shop, a park or a museum. Most of us have to use some form of transport to get to and from work and overwhelmingly this is either the private car or public transport, bus, underground, tram, or train. Office workers in the large cities are very heavy users of the public rather than private system and often choose to live close to the commuting services for their own convenience. Computer-based technologies will have a major impact on office employment, partly because there will be fewer people needed to do the tricks but also because the technology will, as I have described, make it possible for people to work from home or from their neighbourhood workstation. It is difficult to think of a set of circumstances which would have more of an impact on public transport than this.

Fewer commuters on all of the methods of transport will mean that the services themselves will be endangered as there are threshhold levels of usage below which the very existence of the services is called into question. In turn this will threaten the infrastructure of the city as those people who use it for entertainment or for their shopping find it inconvenient to travel in or out. Shops, offices, threatres, restaurants, and clubs, all of which make up an essential part of a thriving city, will come under pressure and perhaps be forced to close. This reinforces the vicious circle of decline in that fewer people, especially those from the outlying areas or indeed foreign tourists, will be attracted. Cities were, apart from the artificial capitals like Canberra, Brazilia, or New Dehli, organic systems; they have grown and continue to grow or decline in response to the commercial or industrial stimuli that created them in the first instance, although of course the type of industrial or indeed commercial stimulus is nowadays a very different one. If the prime stimuli are no longer relevant no amount of inducements or penalties will alter that fact, and either one has to recognize that the city is unlikely to reclaim its former glories and leave it to its own devices or one has to come to terms with the problem and invent a net set of stimuli. Local authority officials, mayors and councils, and community councils will have to face a set of serious decisions on these matters in the near future.

Will they be able to adapt? This is no idle question for local government is known as a most conservative branch of administration. It is a decision compounded by two other factors. The first is that the size of offices needed will be smaller as both the equipment and the number of people operating it diminish in size and the type of person and family wishing to live in and around the city centres changes too. Whilst I shall explore these factors in more detail in Chapter 14 they do pose a problem in terms of who adapts. Clearly these side effects are not severe or high-profile enough to stop or reverse the trend to computerization; many only occur well after the computers have been installed and in any event are the result of cumulative actions. There will thus be no real pressure building up against computer installations from any of the representative bodies which are concerned in these affairs. As adaptation will only come about as the result of pressure or of special pleading and moral persuasion the odds are stacked very heavily against changes on the computer users' side. In turn this reinforces the need for local government and local politicians to change and adapt. They will have to be more imaginative and flexible in their approach than ever before and conduct a dialogue with their electorate on a far deeper and genuine level than has previously been the rule.

Whilst the large town and city centres change and the planners and architects adapt to the concept that the successful company shows off by building a small head office, the suburbs will change too. From being mere dormitories they will become centres of small workstations and shops, and the planning laws will come under considerable strain as people work from residentialy zoned homes. Many of the suburbs were not developed to sustain a large day-time population and have neither the civic nor the private amenities necessary to sustain or entertain a large permanent population. Yet again the local dignitaries and institutions will have to adapt and forge themselves into genuine communities. The concept of centre and suburbia may indeed be a thing of the past as the computer levels out the distinctions between where we work, play, and live.

User friendly systems apply just as readily to the consumers of computer services as they do to the workers involved in the processes. Transport and commuting are cases in point. The tendency over the past decade was to make automated systems as highly visible as possible and to use them as examples of efficiency and progress. This trait is all very well, providing that the system that the public has to use is easily understood and mastered. This, regrettably, has not always been the case. The Washington Metro is a highly automated system as far as passengers are concerned. The ticket machines, the add-fare machines for those whose tickets contain less than the required fare, and even the entrances and exits are machine controlled. The only human beings other than police and cleaners are the people sitting in their boxes for a no-doubt important but utterly mysterious purpose, who tend to brush off queries with an imperious gesture towards one of the waiting machines. It is an efficient way of doing things and whether it is coincidental or not it is a relatively cheap system to travel on. However, some people, especially out-of-town tourists and the old, cannot cope with its intricasics. All year round one can stand and watch people looking at the machines in total bewilderment, unable to work out what money goes into what machine for their journey. As this depends on the time of day, how many other journeys one expects to make, and what change one has this can be a complicated transaction. It is also possible to watch people giving up and presumably using a bus or a taxi. Surveys have shown that older people are frightened by the system, rather as they were by decimalization in the United Kingdom; some have been upset enough to curtail their social life.

Young people, however, revel in these new techniques and as they represent the future it is possible to ignore the plight of the old or worried and dismiss their complaint as a temporary aberration and one which will die out sooner rather than later. It is a rather inhuman argument. It is condeming thousands, perhaps hundreds of thousands, of people to substandard lives and if the new system is supposed to improve our lives it has to be adjudged a failure if so many people are discomforted to such an extent — despite the fact that they are in a minority. Democratic political systems are characterized by a willingness to take account of the views of minorities and not ride roughshod over them. This form of intolerance is more often found in totalitarian or fascist regimes. There is a danger that the designers of public computer systems are not taking a sufficiently democratic approach; it may also be a case for more adequate public supervision. That there is a form of technological fascism is not often postulated or denied; in short it is not a very widely canvassed subject except amongst committed scientists and technologists themselves. This relative indifference should not be taken as representing approval for unfeeling policies; it is far more a reflection of the awe of computers in which so many people stand and their consequent inability to come to terms with the specialized forms of protest and lobbying that they feel is needed. This feeling is almost certainly wrong; plain lobbying and ordinary, even inarticulate, protest have been rewarded with some degree of success in subjects as complex as nuclear power. Without a change in attitudes about computers on the part of the public and on the part of the professionals we shall be condemning a minority of the population, generally the aged and those who find difficulty in coping on their own, to a second-class existence. Adaptation is a relatively sensible request by the planners and designers to the public at large, but only if it is possible for people to adapt. Where it is not possible there must be a responsibility placed upon the computer people to adapt their systems to include otherwise excluded sections of the community.

The Washington Metro takes us back into the realms of the quality of life, as indeed do many of the questions posed under the umbrella of 'who adapts?'. It is not reasonable to expect that technological changes can be introduced without there being social and other major changes in the way that society works. The car changed society radically, bringing with it a sense of freedom and wider horizons to ordinary people. Yet it has also caused hundreds of thousands of deaths and mutilations world-wide, it trails lethal exhaust fumes, and its motorways destroy beautiful and valuable land. Despite all these disadvantages it is difficult to argue anything other than the car being of overall benefit to society. However, had the initial attempts to make the car and its drivers react and adapt to the existing mores of society when a man with a red flag had to precede the vehicle at walking pace it is doubtful whether it would have had any impact at all. Horizons would either have remained limited or been approached very slowly indeed. In the event, whilst people and entire societies adapted to the car, Los Angeles appears to be designed for it. There has been an important element of the car having to adapt too. Speed restrictions, the rules of the road backed by the law, and more latterly the safety standards and the emission control laws have forced both the motorist and the car manufacturer to adapt to society. There has had to be a considerable give and take. The same should be the case in respect of computer technology usage, no matter where it takes place.

If a back-up system for the aged, or perhaps a simpler system for everyone, had been provided in Washington the same dictum would apply to a whole host of other uses where some, if not all, people find it difficult to adjust and as a consequence live a lower quality of life. Form filling is one example of this, being an unwelcome and widespread occupation. The difficulties are twofold. Too many form designers fall into the computer trap, which consists of asking for apparently irrelevant information, and masses of it, purely because there is a capability of processing this information. This involves most people in wasted time completing forms that are there for the convenience of the researchers or, if a more sinister connotation is put upon the practice, to satisfy the snoopers. This sort of form is exemplified by a large number of license application forms, many job application forms, bank, credit, and other financial application forms, and almost any form associated with a local authority—from skip permits to rate rebates.

Form filling has never been easy. Filling in the normal income tax return, a form as yet unsullied by computer requirements, has always been a task on a par with solving *The Daily Telegraph* crossword—difficult but not quite as difficult as it looks. Computers have added an extra dimension, however. The squares in which you have to put the letters of your name and address, and there are rarely enough of them, leave the form filler in a quandry as to how to complete the address, if at all. The jargon in which the forms are now written is even more abstruse than in the days when an anonymous form compiler sadistically and remotely benefited from the filler's dicomforture. Questions are sometimes not answerable with a simple 'yes' or 'no' and filling in the form becomes like being the victim of a brilliant cross-examining lawyer who restricts you to three answers when you desperately need to qualify the answer. The end result is similar, too: the letter of the law may be observed but the truth has not really emerged. In the same way these forms elicit broad categories of data without anyone knowing whether they are the correct categories. Many people, indeed a growing number, are finding it difficult to adjust to the new forms and cannot fill them in correctly. This is not only annoying for the form-filler but time-wasting and costly for the recipient who has to return it. Worse than this, it may not be spotted as an error and the wrong data are recorded; even worse, the wrong decision may be reached based on the incorrect information. It is thus in everyone's interest to have easily intelligible forms designed and laid out so that an individual both knows what he or she is doing and can fill the appropriate bits in correctly whilst ignoring the inappropriate sections. Anyone unlucky enough to complete an insurance form recently will know exactly what is meant here. Given that it is a relatively easy task to redesign the offending form, this is one area where the onus must be on the computer experts to adapt.

Other areas come more into the compromise positions. Consumers have had to bear the brunt of errors perpetrated within computer systems and have found it difficult to persuade the powers that be that they are right and it is the computer that is wrong. Earlier in the book there were examples of people losing their jobs or facing financial ruin because of computer-based errors. The trouble caused by this form of mistake is far greater than a similar mistake made by a person, although the odds are that the computer error was in fact a human error too. The legitimization of facts, including erroneous facts, remains one of the greatest dangers of computer usage. There needs to be a proper investigative and appeal system to cover these kinds of eventualities, a system we shall discuss in Chapter 13. This is, however, a compromise adaption. It recognizes that mistakes will be made, something computer professionals prefer not to admit publicly although will readily admit privately, and tries to remedy the situation.

There was a time when the use of the switchboard of an organization was a pleasant experience, reaquainting oneself with the friendly operators. At times the call was lost in mid-word or it took five minutes to get a line; therefore, in the name of efficiency new, computerized exchanges and switchboards were developed. Instead of achieving a greater success rate, more calls than ever before are lost. This is not the fault of the new equipment but of the people operating it; it is in a sense too sophisticated for the average manager, if not secretary. It is a clever but flawed system, depending on ordinary clerical, administrative, and managerial staff to adapt their habits to the new technology, using the automatic transfers and the coded dialling patterns rather than using the operator. No doubt people will adapt over time. Office juniors are now entering employment where it is the only system that they have ever known. In the meantime, however, we shall just have to put up with voices getting lost in the system and with unannounced and unwelcome calls being put straight through and turning out to be the tax inspector.

Who adapts—doctors, nurses, patients, or the new medical techniques—or perhaps no adaptation is needed? Far too many of the new, highly sophisticated techniques are soulless, machine intensive, and intrinsically lonely. The intensive care monitoring systems obviously enable a patient, indeed many patients at once, to have their vital functions kept under constant surveillance. The problem is that the patient is wired into all kinds of gadgets and as a result can feel frightened and dehumanized. The same occurs in childbirth with mothers and the unborn baby tethered to machines and oscilloscopes, and has resulted in a vociferous demand to move back towards more natural and personal delivery methods. A desperately sick patient is in a totally different position in that recovery may depend almost as much on human contact and the imparting of a will to live as it does on the machinery. A compromise position will have to be found with personal contact and nursing running alongside the sophistication; it is certainly not sensible to ask the patient to adapt in such circumstances. Some computer techniques have drawn an excellent response from patients. Computers interviewing patients in initial case and history taking have been successfully experimented with. They proved especially good at the more embarrassing type of case history; indeed it has been suggested that they are better than doctors in these circumstances. Other companies involve doctors taking patients through a computer diagnosis system — a system which in theory embodies the wisdom and knowledge of the best medical brains. The doctor is there to humanize the system.

Whilst people may prefer non-human company in embarrassing circumstances they do appear to prefer human service or at least a presence to that of computers. This may affect how far and how fast the automation of, for example, the retail business will go. A supermarket with robot shelf-stackers, laser scanning, and credit card cash desks controlled and monitored by television cameras may not be frantically welcomed by its customers. Such a supermarket may indeed lose custom to its less *avant garde* competitors, even if it has lower prices. Quite where efficient systems will have to be traded off against customer satisfaction or preferences has yet to be seen, but it is probable that there is a limit to the amount of adaptation customers will be prepared to accept, especially if there are alternatives available.

Teachers are having to adapt to teaching machines, as are older children; the younger ones will grow up with them. Parents are having to change too. Down the centuries parents have had formal and informal effects on their children's education and this has depended upon an understanding of what their children were doing. Teaching machines and other computer-based teaching methods are a new departure in that they revert to a technically presented form of rote teaching and learning. As the programs are not available at home, whilst the old course book could have been, the parent is effectively cut off from the educational process. Home tapes and teaching programs may help to fill this gap, but whether they do nor not technology in the classroom is having an important effect on the relationship between parents and children, with the teachers bearing the brunt of the resulting bewildered anger in the middle.

Education, health, and other state responsibilities are being transformed by computer technology. Politically, the controlling mechanisms of these services are having to adapt as well. Members of Parliament can now research their questions or their speeches using new computer data bases in the House of Commons library, a minor step to the outside world but a major one in the 'House'. Even in the elections leading up to a new government, technology is changing long-established habits. Opinion polls are now appearing to lead the politicians rather than the politicians leading the polls, and the very real possibility of tactical voting is made that much more viable by regular public poll information. In the 1983 United Kingdom general election the television station Granada, operating on Channel 4, produced its regular election Granada 500, except that an additional 600 people were given home terminals and after each programme in the series were asked to vote on a proposition or series of questions. This immediate response pattern from people sitting at home rather than in unfamiliar and somewhat intimidating halls or studios is something that politicians and political journalists alike will have to adapt to. Changes in policy may be more readily made whilst as a corollary the party activists will be dismayed more than ever. Whether such changes can be usefully called democratic is a proposition that will be debated fiercely in the coming years.

The process of adaptation has been highly visible on the consmers' side in recent years. In the home we have bought and adapted to new electronic devices like calculators or microwave ovens or remote control television sets. Our habits have changed with the advent of videorecorders, much to the annoyance of the advertising agencies who cannot accurately measure the television audience any longer, and home film watching. Credit cards, teletext systems, money dispensers, adverts for word processors on peak time television, and the sales explosion of microcomputers themselves show a remarkable degree of the acceptance of change. Nothing stands absolutely still but the past decade has been remarkable for the speed with which changes have arrived. Whilst there have been changes on the part of the computer professionals not enough have been in terms of adapting to customers or clients. Most have happened as the result of experiences which resulted in the loss of custom or of goodwill. Individuals and groups of people are having to adapt themselves far more often. In Chapter 13 we shall look at what mechanisms are, or will be, needed to cope with this trend amongst others, especially in the light of the fact that the computer revolution is only just starting — 'we ain't seen nothing yet'.

Will we adapt to have shopping and banking using teletext systems? Will we feel comfortable using videotelephones? Could customer resistance develop and those new delights join such inventions as the electric mousetrap in oblivion? In the course of this chapter there have been specific examples which were intended to demonstrate the principles of adaptation rather than their importance. To attempt to list all the areas where we have or where we might have to adapt our attitudes or lifestyles would have been a boring not to mention foolhardy exercise, if only because the moment it was written it would it would have been out of date.

Human progress can be as much in terms of spiritual matters — as much concerned with values — as it is with the physical betterment of human beings. Society may benefit from more goods if employees now work five shift systems, but those workers will not find the new patterns easy to adapt to and nor will their families. The fact that such a system is a product of the computer age is vital as it exemplifies the dual nature of this particular technology. It is highly probable that individuals, groups, and entire nations will have to change their ways and habits at the behest of the computer systems designers because they will be arranged in such a way as to make this inevitable if the systems are to work. For much of the time this may be no bad thing; the old ways of doing things have had little to recommend them except familiarity. There are too many times, however, when the changes required are unreasonable, could have been avoided, or impinge unfairly on a minority of the population. Such cases stand as a warning to us all not to allow the engineers and designers the entire discretion in what are as much social as technical matters. When it comes to who adapts it has to be both them and us, the difference being that there are more of us and fewer of them who have to adapt; in the last analysis that should make a considerable difference.

Chapter 12

Force for Good or Force for Evil

RATIONAL PEOPLE HAVE TO BELIEVE THAT TECHNOLOGY itself is neutral because to believe that it is inherently good or bad is tantamount to believing in spirits residing in inanimate objects. Whilst the less than competent programmer may well believe that the computer that is being worked upon has a life and will of its own, it is in fact the tool *par excellence*, the perfect example of a machine that does precisely what it is told to do. This explains the attitude of the poor programmer; he or she has not got the instructions right and the computer is totally unable to respond in a satisfactory manner. This human control over the machine applies as much in the uses to which we put the computer as it does to the way that we make it work. The fifth-generation computers are intended to be neuristic and our definitions may have to be changed subsequently. In the last chapter the expression 'user friendly' was floated to describe a system which was easy to use and was accepted or liked by the user or consumer; it is possible to use the same concept for classifying the uses to which computers can be put.

From the earliest historic times the dual nature of mankind has been prominent — the good and the bad, Cain and Abel, the saint and sinner, or man's inherent goodness against the original sin. Literature has worked on this theme and produced memorable works, the most famous of this genre being Dr Jeckyll and Mr Hyde. Man is clearly capable of both good and bad actions with the same person displaying both traits at very nearly the same time. Even the truly bad people have their apologists to pick out their virtues and publicly display them; for example Hitler was supposed to have been fond of animals and this characteristic tended to mitigate his bad reputation. Good and bad are often intertwined in a mysterious way, with the result that the black and the white are never quite where they should be.

331

Most people would agree with the suggestion that religion is broadly a good thing whilst as many people would agree that war is a bad thing. Yet by far the majority of European wars, as well as massacres and tortures, have had their origins in religion; indeed, one religious denomination or another actually started many of these wars. Even in those started by other people the armies of both sides needed blessings by their respective churches. Good and bad thus meet and overlap. The concepts of the holy war in Islam or the righteous war in Christianity are paradoxes if one believes that both religions argue a combination of the sanctity of life and the brotherhood of man. The inquisition was the first embryonic totalitarian regime yet it was built upon religion. Religion, of course, only accounts for a minority of the good or the bad happenings in the world. Individuals, or groups of people motivated by politics, by nationalism, by greed, or by altruism, are capable of performing very wicked and very good deeds.

There has been a lot of scope in the world for such actions. The great powers, the United States and the Soviet Union, glower at each other with their acolyte countries tending them like fussy seconds at a duel. At times of detente the posture becomes softer and the language of the cold war is concerned more with sporting jargon than with megadeaths, but these periods have a feeling of impermanence about them. The Third World, or developing countries, may be client states of one of the power game participants or they may be non-aligned. Whichever is the case it is highly probable that there is malnutrition, unemployment, a chronic balance of payments problem, industrial and agricultural stagnation, and a worried, perhaps frightened government. Relationships between countries are too often governed by mutual suspicions and dislikes and in such circumstances information obtained through the normal diplomatic channels is supplemented by more irregularly gathered material. This applies as much to contacts with supposed allies as it does to relations with hostile governments.

The gap between the rich (northern) and poor (southern) countries is huge and growing year by year with the resulting inevitable jealousies and frictions which sour the relationships between even supposed allies. In turn this deepens the levels of mistrust. Most countries now maintain a high level of men and women under arms and a sophisticated weaponry system. Some of the less-developed countries obtain advantageous trade terms for the purchase of weapons, some client states even receiving them for next to nothing along with 'advisors' and technicians to service them. This contrasts most unfavourably with the parsimonious offerings of food, medicines, and industrial equipment. None of this is calculated to reduce the tension between states and the advent of international terrorism and highjackings has given the paranoia an extra twist. For this to be raised to almost disaster levels needs only one false move or perhaps a false interpretation of a move. Computers would seem to be almost irrelevant in such circumstances, especially when nuclear capabilities are added to the equation, except for the fact that computers are now vital components in the monitoring tasks and indeed in the control of the communication systems and the nuclear hardware itself.

The quality of life within many industrialized and developing countries is showing signs of distress too. Unemployment in the 1980s is pandemic and is affecting the youth of almost all countries. Terrorism is an ever-present threat in many countries and the measures taken to prevent it destroying democratic institutions border on the undemocratic themselves, if not actually crossing the border into dictatorial powers.

The world is thus a very disturbed place. This is not to say that the people in it are incapable of enjoying themselves or indeed are spending an inordinate amount of their time worrying about *the crisis* (any crisis) or the human condition. Most of the uncertainties, most of the mistrusts, most of the insults, and most of the half-truths come from governments and politicians; people left to their own devices are not overbothered about this facet of global conflict.

People are not neutral; at least the people who have pretensions to power and control are not neutral. They are biased, have prejudices, and will use all the means at their disposal to achieve their ends. The possibility of conflict, terminal conflict, has never been greater and as a result the use of computers has never been so terrifyingly important. Conversely, the physical needs of a substantial fraction of the world's population have never been greater and in this respect the use of the computer takes on a life and death aspect, but in a diametrically opposite way. In global terms literally billions of lives rest upon the use to which computers are put and who is using them.

The key to their crucial role is efficiency. The weapon systems could work without computers but at a far lower level of reliability and accuracy, whilst the coordination of relief systems and planning would be that much slower and inaccurate if computers were not in use. In any potentially good or evil situation a machine that can muster the virtues of being faster, cheaper, and more accurate is one which can accentuate the result and make the outcome (whichever it is) more likely initially and more certain latterly. This efficiency can be directed towards communication systems or signalling methods, aiding either preparaion of a war or the safe passage of a train, the most effective business communication system or the most well-equipped spy ring. These differences demonstrate the dichotomy of the computer. In this respect it is no different from any other piece of equipment; even simple motor cars can be used for peaceful or warlike purposes. The difference comes in the scale and depth of its penetration and the utter dependence of many of the newer weapons, businesses, and communication networks on some form of computer. It is no exaggeration to claim that without the computer not only would many of the products and systems not work but that they would not actually exist. In short and bluntly, computers are now in a position to enhance life or destroy it. Fortunately most of the choices that have to be made, even those under this dramatic chapter title, are not as fundamental to the human race although all are important in their way. Good becomes even better whilst evil can take on a new higher dimension of nasty when computers are used.

The most dramatic of all the examples of the use of computers is in the defence industry, where electronics have become as important as was the horse in mediaeval times. When used for defence purposes are computers a force for good or a force for evil? Many people will argue that the peace has been more assured since microelectronics improved the guidance and communication systems of weapons. As one expert in defence systems with a remarkably high kill probability are now standard equipment. The argument depends for its validity on the premise that the better the weapon the greater the deterrent and in turn this depends on the assumption that weapons are a deterrent to war when roughly evenly matched on either side. If these articles of faith are true then the use of electronics in weaponry is a good thing in that it becomes more deadly and thus more likely to prevent the other side from using their weapons. Because there has not yet been a nuclear war or even nuclear weapons used in a limited way since the atomic bomb was dropped on

Nagasaki, there is a tendency to believe that the deterrent theory must be true.

Many people believe the exact opposite. The more the sophistication, the more the 'kill probability', the greater the chances of a gigantic disaster is the other viewpoint. There are no longer two sides for there to be an even balance of terror — too many countries have their finger on the trigger. The increasing complexity of weapons is giving rise to new sets of problems. On a purely diplomatic and strategic front the difficulty in operating and servicing these new systems is so great that many of the recipients of them in developing countries have to have technicians from the manufacturing country to install and operate them. This leads to international risks if the weapon systems are being used in a proper war situation; it only needs one technician or adviser to be captured for an international hullabaloo to break out or one to be killed or wounded for a series of government lies to have to be put into operation. Vietnam, Afghanistan, Nicuragua, El Salvador, Hungary is a roll call of countries outside of the Middle East where technicians have been caught up in real conflicts. Nowadays Africa with Cuban, Soviet, Israeli, South African, French, and American technicians thick on the ground along with Lebanon, Syria, and Iraq are the flashpoints of the world. The computer control of weapon systems, be they anti-tank or aircraft missiles or anti-personnel devices or indeed of the aircraft or warships themselves, is so complex that even if the local troops are trained to fire or operate them their servicing needs to be done by employees from the manufacturers. The new sophisticated systems thus carry with them the possibility of the escalation of conflicts to the industrialized countries — a most unwelcome development. Electronics have the ability to act as a carrier of the plague if one carries through the mediaeval analogy.

This is not the only reason, however, why the argument against the new deadly weapon systems has captured a surprising amount of public attention all around the world. In recent years there have been rumours concerning the spread of nuclear weapons to countries who do not play the military/ diplomatic game according to the rules as laid down by the great powers. Israel, Pakistan and India, and Iraq and Libya ·are but some of these and are moreover countries which are in a constant state of tension with their neighbours. It does not matter whether these rumours are true or false because the mere fact that such rumours abound signifies a deep-seated worry and adds overall to strategic instability. In turn this raises the chances of war both because there are more fingers on many triggers and also because there is less chance of being able to predict responses with accuracy and 'second guess' all the other states. The lack of trained personnel in these countries is an additionally worrying factor in that the chances of an accidental or erroneous firing or launching is enhanced if no foreign technicians are in attendance; whether they are or they are not, danger lurks around the corner.

The new weapons are so frightening because of their capacity to kill so many innocent men, women, and children. They would be frightening in another sense too if the public realized the circumstances. Computers and electronics have virtually taken over the delivery systems of nuclear devices and the early warning or detection systems. The sophisticated equipment can go wrong, as we have seen in recent years with the sporadic 'red alerts' caused, we are told, by flocks of birds. How many other malfunctions have there been that we have not been told about? How near have we been to pushing the nuclear button? This question is compounded by two other new factors, both of which have a direct dependence on computing.

Tactical or field nuclear weapons depend on computer electronics to give them the accuracy which makes them so viable. The commanders in the field are now suggesting that they need to have control over these weapons rather than the Chief of Staff because of their need to deploy them quickly. This would take the decision to use nuclear weapons out of the hands of elected (or otherwise) civilian politicians and put it firmly in the hands of the military. Some experts are now arguing that this is the case in reality anyway and moreover that it applies at least as much to the big strategic nuclear rockets as it does to tactical weapons. The new electronic surveillance systems, be they on a satellite or hydrophones under the sea, still give a country only up to fifteen minutes to prepare their responses in the event of an attack. Because of the difficulty in establishing contact with the political wing and the time that it takes to prepare negotiations with the enemy the military effectively has the last, perhaps the only, word in these matters. As the arguments in favour of using nuclear weapons depend on the sanity and judgement of the politicians controlling them (this has always seemed to be a counterargument to me), the public might not be too happy if this version of the facts is indeed true. The greater the electronic and computer impact on weapons the more the military must have overall control of them.

ADA is a new computer language designed to the specifications of the US Department of defence and destined to be used in systems which have a high degree of interaction with the external environment. An example of this would be the guidance system of a cruise missile which works on an integral map of the terrain which it is passing over — or supposed to be passing over. It is a high-level language, very complex and relatively easy to make mistakes with — so much so that experts have been sounding the alarm bells about where it should be used. Indeed, the recipient of the Turing Award given by the US Association of Computing Machinery said at the award ceremony in 1981:

> I appeal to you, representatives of the programming profession in the United States, and citizens concerned with the welfare and safety of your own country and that of mankind: do not allow this language in its present state to be used in applications where reliability is crucial, that is nuclear power stations, cruise missiles, early warning systems, anti-ballistic missile defence systems. The next rocket to go astray as a result of a programming language error may not be an exploratory space rocket on a harmless trip to Venus; it may be a nuclear warhead exploding over one of our cities. An unreliable programming language generating unreliable programs constitutes a far greater risk to our environment and our society than unsafe cars, toxic pesticides or accidents at nuclear power stations. Be vigilant to reduce that risk not increase it.

Tony Hoare of Oxford University is by no means the only academic, journalist, or computer practitioner to believe this to be a language fraught with dangers and in need of much further development.

By using a computer language that has shown itself to be unreliable and difficult to use in combination with the military control of the systems the impact of computers seems to be a force of evil, if only because the likelihood of global destruction is increased albeit probably accidently. The demands that are being made of computer scientists by the weapons designers are starting to outstrip the ingenuity of even this brilliant group of people. ADA is a good example of this happening in practice, but is only a small example. As the guidance systems have to become ever more sophisticated and react with not only fixed external points, a map for example, but also with moving external phenomena, enemy rockets, jamming, radiation, or even re-entry from space, the need for very high-level languages grows. This and the development of other software may prove to be the drag factor which slows down the apparently inexorable headlong rush of computer use.

Almost everyone will agree that war is an evil thing. If computers make wars more likely let alone more deadly, then they become a force for evil; if the converse is true then they become a force for good. I believe that the former must be the case with the increased probability of a conflict outweighing the balance of power or terror thesis. It may be that the odds are now firmly upon an accidental or careless war rather than a premeditated one, but this circumstance is very much a feature of extensive computer involvement and will be of scant consolation to those killed, wounded, or mourning. Yet again the neutrality of the technology is unchallenged although the nature of the technology used in defence leads inexorably into the fallibility of humans, and with weapons of death on this scale the prospect can be frightening in the extreme. Some people argue that computers are as neutral as is the gun and that it is not true that people alone are responsible for their misuse. Whilst I accept that the properties of a computer can direct people to evil-doing I also reject the analogy and the basic conclusion.

Some people believe that government is evil. Fortunately these tendencies are a minority view and are confined to the extremes of both Left and Right, the anarchists and nihilists. Far more people believe that too much government is a bad thing, especially those on the more conservative wing of politics in Europe and the United States; it is a respectable, indeed necessary, position to hold in places like Texas if one wants to be successful in politics. Thus there is a view that computers, by making government more efficient, are acting as a force for evil. There is also a more traditional point of view that by acting as a pivot around which increasing centralization of government revolves, it acts against the basic interests of the people.

Computers certainly have been the stimulus for and provided the means to run the very large departments of state. Without computers there could not be value added tax, could not be the comprehensive social security on a national scale, could not be government planning of the economy and trade, and could not be the plethora of government statistics that appear each week of the year. Computers are thus responsible for the government's ability to take on extra functions as well as the increase in size and remoteness of individual departments. Whilst the fact that government takes on extra duties and impinges increasingly on the individual may not be, in itself, a bad thing, let alone evil, political judgement will decide, and the remoteness of government or of its constituent parts must be a cause for concern.

Democracies rely on regular elections to make the system of accountable representation work. It is now, however, enough to rely on this alone. Problems can and do arise mid-way between elections for individuals or small groups of people, and there should be mechanisms to satisfy their potential grievances. Whilst many countries have now taken up the Scandanavian innovation of an Ombudsman, the departments of state or ministries still need to be sufficiently small to respond to the complaints of an individual — and better still avoid taking arbitrary decisions in the first place. The larger the department the greater the chance of maladministration, and thus the more likely it is that government itself attracts a bad press and reputation. Whilst corrective mechanisms can be set up, better press and complaints departments for example, preventative measures cannot be taken as the sheer size of the organizations make this impossible without a drastic reorganization.

It is possible to reorganize on much more decentralized lines, and this does not mean the shifting of a suboffice away from the capital city. As computers have been used as an agent of centralization and growth, so the new generation of computers and terminals alongside the newest telecommunication systems can be used as the means of devolving government powers geographically and heirarchically. Put simply, decision making and problem solving can now be made at the point where the difficulty arises; this is faster as well as being far more humane. Large and indifferent bureaucracies (and these are not merely governmental) are not evil but are certainly avoidable, and if avoided would enhance everyone's quality of life. The use of terminals in local sites linked to a central processor and operated by local people, e.g. placed in a local post office or library and self-operated, could be applied to benefit questions, unemployment queries, housing problems, and pension rights, and would be a cheap and practical service.

Centralized government uses computers in other ways too. Many countries have a preoccupation with security, especially internal security, and given the high level of terrorism this is not always surprising. The security forces use all means at their disposal to collect and collate information on suspects, and clearly the computer plays an important role in these procedures; indeed, it is tailor-made for such a function. Several fundamental questions are raised by these uses, however. The most fundamental is what freedoms can be jeopardized, and for which people, in defence of freedom overall? Can one run a state committed to liberty whilst curtailing the liberty of some of the people or even all of the people? When, if a state moves along this path, does it cease to be a truly democratic state and start to drift into totalitarianism or dictatorship?

George Orwell envisaged a dreadful world in his *1984*, which must be based on computer-driven technologies. Surveillance, thought manipulation, torture, nationalism — none of these elements are absent around the world today and are justified by the regimes practising them in the most practical of ways. Yet in Orwell's novel there was little pretence of the state allowing freedoms; the state even controlled the language. In the real world surveillance is increasing; personal data bases are enlarging in an almost completely covert manner. Disturbing examples of this occasionally break surface and are picked up by the media. Whilst they come from around the world West Germany appears to be the most accident prone. Germany has, of course, suffered considerably from urban terrorism and as a result the government has taken countermeasures. These involve the use of computers in logging incidents which have the most tenuous of connections with suspected terrorists or with leftwing political activists — a sensitive area with East Germany alongside.

If you are innocently travelling on a train or a bus to visit a friend or on a business trip it is unlikely that you will take much notice of your fellow passengers. It is even more unlikely that you will notice the cars in a street in which you have parked or the patients in the dentist's waiting room. All of these cases have ended up on the computer of the security services because a fellow passenger or a patient or another driver was a suspected person. In each case the people in the same compartment or bus or waiting room were checked as thoroughly as possible, put onto the computer files, and so became suspects. The fact that they were innocent was not conclusive — they were only not guilty this time and they remain actively on the computer files. All cars are also checked, which requires access to another computer and again their owners (or drivers in the case of a hire car) are put into the memory. If you are unlucky enough to be travelling unwittingly with another suspected person on another occasion your file will probably be transferred into another part of the memory along with people with far less innocent reasons for being there.

If there is a law which prevents certain people holding or being appointed to civil service jobs on political and security grounds and you are applying for one of these posts your chances in these circumstances of getting it would be near to zero. This sequence of events can and does happen in West Germany — not often, but it happens. It can be argued most plausibly that the fact that it happens at all is a bad thing and that sacrifices of this nature, and a sacrifice it is, are not compatible with a free society. The opposite view is that this is merely the cost of freedom and is therefore worth paying.

The same sort of cost is paid in most countries nowadays. West Germany is only prominent in this respect because their system is that much bigger and more sophisticated than most others and does not seem to be capable of discriminating between the accidental and the premeditated. Every government has a duty to protect its nationals against violence, whether externally or internally sourced, and must do its uttermost to protect property too. However, each democratic government must also guard against the arbitrary use of power, especially by the government itself, and must safeguard the freedoms that it is attempting to protect. If there has to be a service which keeps individuals under surveillance then it should be as overt as possible and be open to public scrutiny. When computers are used in this system information is not only retrievable far faster and analysed more readily but information from other computers can be obtained through discrete terminals. In such circumstances there must be dangers that the state will be holding information on people that is wrong and perhaps maliciously inspired, and consequently produce serious injustices. 'Police state' is an evocative term, and one redolent of all the worst aspects of life, yet computers make it possible for this condition to creep up upon us all without overmuch fuss or publicity.

Computers can do far more than this in the legislative and governmental spheres. Totalitarian states demand a totality of obedience, but then so do dictatorships; the difference is that in a totalitarian society everything is within the purview of the state—religion, art, music, sport, recreation, childbearing, in short the way people live. A totalitarian government not only demands absolute obedience but also absolute belief. There were totalitarian states before the twentieth century, the Inquisition in Spain and its South American colonies of that time for example, but they are now that much easier to administer and run. Communication media like the radio, telephone, and television allow for both the dissemination of the standard messages and propaganda as well as a means of control. Computers add another weapon to the arsenal of the dictator. Records are more easily kept and information is more readily available. The surveillance of the population, what it does, and where it does it becomes much more complete. Clearly this, in the West at least, is a force for evil. Great care has to be taken that the democratic systems are not perverted in the same way by the use of similar techniques. The fact that they are democracies gives governments a responsibility to ensure that this does not happen, but also means that it is necessary to get meaningful opposition mobilized on the matter. The subject is so esoteric and so diffuse, however, that the chances of it influencing the votes of many people is minimal and thus the traditional democratic safeguard is absent. We only know about the mistakes and injustices which must obviously be the tip of an iceberg of surveillance and record keeping. In the following chapter I shall return to this subject.

If state security is really spying on one's own side then spying for the enemy, both at home and abroad, is another area where the computer has proved to be beneficial to the practitioners. Whether this is believed to be a force for good or for evil will probably depend upon which spies are more successful — theirs or ours. Treating it more seriously, spies are by definition covert. Anything which is carried on in the twilight because it cannot stand the light of day and which consequently attracts no public scrutiny and no accountability must carry with it the suspicion of us all. This applies as much to other government operations as it does to internal and external security. Computers confer power on governments as we have seen, and it becomes ever more necessary for them to respond in a totally open way and not hide their existence, their uses, and the contents of their installations.

Democracy is a word which in public relations terms is called a 'halo word', or a word that none dares to disagree with. Freedom, choice, beautiful, good, and neighbour come into the same category. Each nation finds it necessary to describe themselves as a democratic state, the Soviet Union included, and in truth there are many forms of democracy. Computer technology can have a very considerable impact on the way we run and regard our political systems and politicians, in that it allows for the possibility of instant referenda whilst sitting comfortably at home. Whilst I shall look at this sort of system in more detail in Chapter 14 it is worth noting that in California, lecture theatres at the universities are being equipped with machines which allow students to feed in the answers to questions posed by the lecturer. This type of machine response which depends on instant or very fast responses may be adequate to deal with matters of fact but carries with it many dangers when used in matters of judgement or opinion. Democracy is too delicate a matter to be the subject of trendy, populist techniques, and moreover ones that lend themselves to manipulation and corruption, e.g. the notion of instant decision making. Government must be representative, not a frenetic scramble to air, and put into effect the first or most popular prejudice of the day — a kind of legislative lynch law. There will be no absolute imperative to use such techniques but in the last analysis people, regrettably some with an eye to their own short-term advantage, will be the deciding factor as to whether they are used or not.

Computers are a marvellous tool for the collection and dissemination of all sorts of data and, as I have discussed, this can be used by governments in an attempt to control political opposition and monitor the behaviour of the population. The police also use these methods to keep records of criminals and suspects. The problems that can arise here are twofold. Suspected persons are not in anything approaching the same category as convicted criminals and to maintain records on them, often consisting of uncorroborated hearsay at the best and downright malicious lies at the worst, is conducive to neither peace of mind nor justice. Compounding these matters is the fact that in the overwhelming number of cases the person in question has no idea that the files are being maintained, let alone the contents of them. In most states the security services have access on demand to police files (though not vice versa) and this makes the accuracy of the contents even more of a vital issue. However, this category is not confined to agencies of law and order; the private sector are adept at it too.

The maintenance of 'black lists' and 'fair lists' is as old as the work and commercial and trade processes themselves. There have always been people whose prime motive has been to 'do down' other people and organizations which have taken a similar attitude. Black lists are most often associated with the relationship between employers and workers, in particular the hiring (or not hiring) and firing of workers. Strange as it may seem, this has rarely been used to protect the consumer against shoddy work and any other form of incompetence; rather black lists have been used to protect the employer against politically motivated or militant workers. In industries where there has been a tradition of casual working and short-term engagements — in shipping, construction, theatre, cinema, and music — black lists have been a fact of life; in others they have grown over the past twenty years or so.

Computers make the maintenance and updating of black lists much more efficient; they also provide the opportunity for third parties to interpose themselves in the black listing processes. There are now organizations which offer to provide prospective employers with information concerning applications for jobs. The information is held on computers and passed to the central organization by 'affiliates' — other companies which use the service. These black lists do not officially exist but enterprising journalists have called the organizations posing as employers whilst using the proper recognition code and have obtained information on various workers they suspected were on the 'non-existant' black list. By and large this information is concerned with the trade union activities and record of the person as well as political affiliations. Given that both the employers and the third party organizations are politically active too, the information is not as closely scrutinized or as accurate as it might be. The computer itself adds legitimacy to the information, as it usually does, and the upshot is that several 'harmless' people have been unable to find jobs in their trades or industries and often do not know why. Even when they are rightly on the list it seems bizarre that countries which boast of their political freedoms allow systems which deny jobs to some people who exercise these rights.

The third parties offering their services are of two distinct types. Those which service affiliates tend to be either industry based or politically motivated (obviously right wing) or both; those which sell their services tend to be the sort of agency which also sells its services in debt collecting and private detection jobs. This latter agency will offer information on a far broader basis — criminal records, if any, debts and credit worthiness, sex life, married life, health, friends, and acquaintances. At least some of this information is obtained from other computer systems before going on the agency's own computer, whilst some of the other information has been obtained without a proper concern for the morality in obtaining it or its provenance. This form of black list handling is more common in the United States than in other industrialized countries as yet, but the United Kingdom especially is catching up quickly.

Black lists, however, are used in other ways. Commercial black lists, e.g. a list of companies which trade with Israel and which then circulate in the Arab world in order to stop Arab governments or firms trading with them, are commonplace. Band credit lists, both of individuals and companies, government black lists of companies trading with, say, Afghanistan or Rhodesia (as was) in defiance of policy, black lists of goods that can be sold to various countries, arms to the Soviet Union or plutonium almost anywhere, sportsmen who have played in South Africa — all these are now held on central computers and can be whistled up locally at the touch of a button. Even one United Kingdom union is said to have used their computers to tag individual members as politically acceptable or hostile. Those acceptable tend to get on delegations more easily and those hostile tend to have the notices of important meetings mysteriously delayed or mislaid, appropriate by the use of the same computer.

The private and public sectors can and do collide in such matters. Governments are strangely lax in the way in which they allow relatively important personal information to be distributed to the private sector. Conversely, in West Germany the national law prohibiting the employment of government employees if they have certain political predilictions has to rely upon information gleamed in the private sector. These alliances are worrying. Leaving aside any legalistic arguments about possible restraints of trade, the morality of depriving a person of their livelihood because of their political learnings is dubious in the extreme. It is an example of self-defence drifting into totalitarian behaviour and this cannot be condoned in a democracy. It is not the case that black lists could not exist without computers; it is the case, however, that they have become far blacker!

Games are fun. Children learn through their games. Professional games players give hours of amusement to the public as well as themselves and in particular computer games have rekindled the interest of adults in games. Yet some games are not quite as innocent as the games we play as children, yet like them they are intended to teach and to accustom us to 'truths' we may not accept in other circumstances. The nuclear survival games played by local bureaucrats are designed to reassure the public that there will be survivors and that someone will be available to care for them. The training of the local people is almost irrelevant. The police, especially senior policemen, play games at refresher courses in their colleges where civil insurrection and riots are simulated or predicted and the appropriate actions have to be taken and the proper forces deployed. War games are played by most armed forces around the world and as with the police the computer proves the board, the dice, the rules, and responds to moves like an opponent.

It is preferable by far to have a war fought on a computer where the only casualties have been the odd stray electron and the only holding manoeuvres those over farm land. It is more civilized to have a riot in the confines of a cathode ray tube than to have broken windows and bones. Indeed, it is often said that war games always end up with both sides losing, and this knowledge actually forestalls conflict. It would be even more preferable if these games did not assume that the violence and the cataclysmic events were inevitable and a part of life. They are not, yet if we continue to believe that they will be and then train ourselves accordingly the chances of them happening is increased — they become self-fulfilling prophecies. These sort of modern, realistic games were not really possible before the computer — war games were literally as they sound. If not a definite force for evil, computer uses in war can only be described as a force for good by a relatively small number of people, for after all killing is evil. Even many of those who believe in the principles of the 'balance of terror' and 'law and order' (these two seem to travel together) do not generally welcome violence or death. In that sense they would prefer to see a world with no weapons, small armies and airforces, and fewer police. A technological shift like intensive computerization makes this less likely to happen.

The two groups of people who stand to lose by a reduction in the armed forces, police, and all their equipment are the professionals in the forces themselves and those who supply them their equipment. Computers place the control of these systems more firmly in the hands of the expert and moves the comprehension as to what weapon is needed and how many people are required to operate it even further away from ordinary people. In turn this means that more and more people understand less and less about defence matters. We are told, and without evidence to the contrary are almost obliged to believe what we are told, about the other sides, the 'enemy's' weapon systems. This chain of circumstances will result in more weapons, more people involved with them, and more risk of an accident. Computers are very much a force for evil in such circumstances in that they result in control being passed to the two groups with the most to lose should there be a move to diminish the escalation of military hardware provision. What makes this a black proposition is that as the sophistication of these new weapons grows so the tendency for the professionals to have sole control of them grows too. Computers in this instance can only exacerbate existing problems.

Computers can also be put to uses which can be described as unalloyed good although it is possible to postulate counter-arguments, even in the most open and shut of cases. For example if computers are used (and they are) to monitor and control the environment of a prematurely born baby in its incubator and this saves its life most of us would hail this as being an example of a computer being used in a good way. Yet some people would claim that the birth rate is too high anyway and with limited and finite world resources the computer could have been put to better uses by doing something else. However this is on a par with approving of death and destruction — a minority taste and probably such a minority that it can be safely disregarded in both cases.

Computers being used to save life or alleviate suffering, whether directly as in an intensive care unit or indirectly in the invention and testing of new drugs, will always be described as being good. This can be extended to services to the aged, to the disabled, to the mentally handicapped, and to the very poor and disadvantaged, whether these are in industrial or in developing societies. In short, the current views of what is a good use of the computer are those which would be put into the category of 'apple pie and motherhood' — the universal good things. The majority of places where and reasons why computers are used fall into categories which are not as clearly defined.

This does not mean that people are ambivalent about computers — far from it. It is more the situation where some people think that computers are being used well and towards a good purpose whilst an almost equal number would believe the opposite; this of course is ignoring not only ᵹ considerable number of 'don't knows' but probably even more 'don't cares'. Computer games are an example. Many people believe that the advent of the 'game on a chip' has been the greatest advance since manned flight, giving hours of innocent amusement to all and sundry, especially the young people who others wish to keep quiet and out of sight. Others believe that the games are turning us into a country of electronic zombies and morons, that the noise of the games is likely to precipitate violence, or that the games are making parental control of the young even more difficult. Yet other people believe that the computer games' preoccupation with violence is leading young people into a more callous and unfeeling position and one where they are becoming less capable of distinguishing between right and wrong. Given any fact human beings have an apparently limitless ability to pronounce upon it whilst reaching completely different conclusions.

Are we becoming overinformed? Are the new teletext systems and the new data bases actually helping us to make decisions and to regulate and run our lives and our societies better than before? On the other hand, are they giving us the shadow of information, rather than the substance, the illusion of knowledge rather than its meat? Whilst most people would not describe the new data base systems as evil few would describe them as good—potentially they can be either, depending upon which information is selected to be shown and for what reasons. It is as easy to edit facts as it is to provide opinion. Some matters may be given undue prominence, others ignored completely; the selection of data is an onerous task and one which should be exercised with restraint and sensitivity. Teletext and other data base systems do tend to give information a cachet, a significance, and a legitimacy which it would not have if it were to appear in a paper or a journal. Whilst there is no suggestion at present that such 'tampering' takes place, whether for political or other reasons, there can be no doubt that it is a strong temptation, especially for highly motivated people. Used in this way the whole system of information provision could be subverted towards partisan ends; this, it must be stated quite firmly, is not wrong provided that the people using the information system know that this is the case. We all live with the press doing precisely this, and most of us know it and discount it accordingly.

This precept must apply to many of the computer's uses— the people must know that they are being used and when their effects are so significant as to impinge upon the general public, or part of it. Not to do so is suggestive of manipulation and of a second-rate fraud, not to mention the potential for a massive loss of public confidence amongst the population at large if and when they find out that they have been 'conned'.

The computer may enable some of us to work from home rather than have to be tied to the office and indeed this is being done with some success in both the United States and

Britain—but is it a move in the direction of good? It may give the opportunity for some people to work who otherwise may not be able to and that is good. People looking after young children and disabled people are two examples. Increasingly, however, we go to work to meet people and to talk, discuss, and argue. Work is the main place for interacting with other people; shops, leisure facilities, or other service places come a poor second, third, and fourth. What happens when this socialization is withdraw and we are thrown even deeper into isolation? This is not an idle academic conjecture, even today.

Leisure time and the entertainment which fills it is being spent increasingly within the home. Television, videos, films, games, home computers, and hi-fi on the electronic side have combined with 'do-it-yourself', home brewing, off-premises alcohol sales, and the growth of take-away cooked food chains. New forms of shopping like hypermarkets have replaced the small chatty shopkeeper and cars carrying one person have siphoned off many public transport users—not that a crowded metro carriage is ideal for long conversations. Modern living is becoming more fragmented with individuals indeed family units becoming more isolated, whilst the concept of the family in its traditional sense is breaking down as divorce and living together surplant marriage; and single parent families increase. Working from home adds a large new dimension to this tendency and although it will remain a minority activity it will grow sufficiently to be a significant problem.

Is this a force for evil? Will marriages survive the strain of partners not only being at home together and one or both attempting to work there, but also having to talk to and be nice to each other over long periods. Will suburbia, where there is little community life, change to become a rounded place in which to live rather than a dormitory. Working from home sharpens the need for answers to these questions; it also reinforces the need for social changes and new social forms and attitudes. Without these changes the stresses and strains caused to domestic life and community balance will overwhelm the existing state of affairs.

Change, although often upsetting, need not be too traumatic. If changes are made slowly and willingly rather than as a result of *force majeure* the amount of dislocation and personal suffering will be far less. There is a tendency, however, to characterize all change as bad, even evil, and this has resulted in the defence of some of the more reprehensible practices throughout history, a defence which has often been mounted by the victims of the practices themselves. From the disenfranchized arguing against universal suffrage to women arguing in favour of female circumcision the syndrome of 'turkeys voting for Christmas' has long been a quirk of human behaviour. The defence of the *status quo* and the appeal to tradition, often inexplicable in rational terms, is one of the strongest of human reactions and this will necessarily colour the approaches to a change as fundamental as those of working from home. It may well be that in ten years time we shall regard the rush hours, the large office blocks, the suburban blandness, and even the institution of life-long marriage as products of reaction and wonder why we defended them so vehemently and for so long.

Decision making is a universal chore shared alike by the present farmers, the captains of industry, housewives, and those who have retired. Computers are supposed to aid decision makers by providing them with more and indeed more relevant information and providing that we approve of the decision makers themselves this must be a good thing. There do appear to be indications, however, that this theory is far from the reality of practice. Many authorities now believe that the average decision maker is overinformed and far from being able to make faster and justifiable decisions is mesmerized by the sheer volume of data, and like a chicken staring at a chalk line directly in front of its beak is incapable of movement or work. This has to be a force for evil. There are a very small number of people whose decisions regulate the ways in which the rest of us live our lives; politicians, government employees, industrialists, religious leaders, and trade union leaders are examples. If computers make it more difficult for them to come to the right conclusions, at the right time, then life for the rest of us becomes that much more problematical and uncertain. It is also a step along the path to anarchy. If we lose faith in such a wide spectrum of our establishment organizations we are left with few pillars of wisdom to which we can cling. Extremes in politics feed upon situations such as this.

The good and evil dichotomy lives on in human beings. Computers are just one way, albeit in high profile and wide ranging, in which it can manifest itself. Decisions will be taken by a small number of people which will affect the use of computers but which will have profound impacts on millions of other people around the world. In military terms it may be the choices between war and peace, in medical terms between life and death, and in social terms between freedom and slavery, and lastly and perhaps least in political terms between democracy and dictatorship. There is the overriding danger that we shall lose control of these machines and that, for example, because they can make weapons that much more deadly that this is the logical, perhaps only, way to go.

There are choices; there are no inevitabilities. Mankind must learn not to be mesmerized like the chicken: it is only a prelude to having its head chopped of.

Chapter 13

Defensive Mechanisms

THE FEELING OF BEING FOLLOWED, OVERHEARD, AND SPIED upon is not exclusive to those who are paranoid; such things do happen. Those who believe in the conspiracy theory of history tend to suggest that these are regular occurrences; others intimate that they occur in the rarest of instances. Whenever a series of articles appears in the press on the theme of 'people have nothing to fear if they have nothing to hide' it is a sure sign that a scandal proving the exact opposite either has happened recently or is about to break. As they are little known and mysteriously placed behind locked doors whilst controlled by people who speak a different language, computers are prime suspects as agents in snooping or spying. The fact that they can be used for such purposes was established by the early breaking of the Enigma code and the subsequent flood of fiction linking computers with state security and espionage. Books like *1984* have reinforced the view that computers can be used for sinister purposes — and indeed they can.

If computers can be used as the major tool in the surveillance of a population then their use in controlling that population may not be far behind. Any democratic society will have to set up defence mechanisms against such uses if it intends to remain democratic.

The privacy of individuals, their right to withhold information about themselves, and the possibility of unauthorized use of this type of information is another area where society will have to be on its guard. There are many areas where computer data bases hold information on individuals and where the information has leaked out to people or organizations who used that information in a manner calculated to damage these individuals. The security of such information and the collection of this category of information in the first instance is now viewed as a matter of concern in all industrialized countries. This is so much the case that the Council of Europe prepared a Convention on Data Protection which was finalized in 1981, entitled *The Convention for the Protection of Individuals with Regard to the Automatic Processing of Personal Data*. The OECD also prepared guidelines on the same subject in 1981. Many states in both Europe and North America have legislation along the lines set out in the Convention: West Germany, France, Holland, the Scandinavian countries, Austria and Switzerland, the United States, Canada, and Australia are amongst these countries. Notable by its absence is the United Kingdom, which in all fairness tried to enact protective legislation but this came to nothing when the general election of 1983 was called. Although this legislation will be presented again to Parliament, it has attracted opposition and critism from bodies normally as far apart as the civil liberty organizations, the British Medical Association, and the organization representing the data processing managers. By now the Bill should have become law and it will be interesting to see whether the government took any note of such disparately sourced objections.

The reasons that the UK government gave for the need for this Bill were unusually honest in that they did not correspond to the normal political claims of 100 per cent. altruism. The first reason, as given in the 1981 White Paper *Data Protection*, was that the growth in the use of computers posed a threat to privacy. However, it then went on to state: 'There have been few reported instances in this country of information held on computers being misused so as to threaten the personal privacy of individuals.' Why then is the government bothering one may legitimately enquire? The reason is given in the next few sentences. The Council of Europe Convention when ratified will allow countries with data protection legislation to refuse to allow personal information to be sent to countries without the protective law. 'This could threaten firms with international interests operating in this country and the activities of British computer bureaux which increasingly process data for customers in many different countries.'

The reason why the United Kingdom is to pass legislation protecting the individual thus has little to do with the welfare of individuals; after all there is virtually no problem claims the government. It is all to do with the protection of companies, and large companies to boot. No wonder so many groups are opposed to the substance of the Bill although certainly not to the idea of a law. They are opposed to the present Bill because it is designed to get away with the minimum possible to satisfy the new Convention and indeed the new OECD guidelines.

Another question that may well spring to mind is why such a body devoted to trade and commerce should take such an interest in human rights against all of its historic precedences? The answer lies in the power that is vested in information. A sure sign that this is the industry of the future lies in the purchase of companies specializing in information technology by the large transnational oil corporations, organizations which can sense power at a mile distance even when it is behind barred windows.

In essence there are two areas of concern with data manipulation and storage: individual privacy and individual and national security. The problems do not stem from the computer itself; rather they come from the holding of files or data about people on a named or identifiable basis or conversely the holding of secret files. It has to be assumed that if some information is classified as secret then always there will be people who will go to extreme lengths to discover what it is. Otherwise why make it secret at all if it has no intrinsic value? Computers can both improve and worsen the problem. Ever more impenetrable codes can be produced on the one hand, whilst electronic security can be lax on the other. There have been many recorded cases of schoolboys using the national or international telecommunication systems to break into the computer data banks of organizations and withdrawing information. Whilst these pranks have been harmless in terms of damage to the system concerned the fact that schoolboys can manage such a sophisticated feat does not bode well for the security of systems against determined professionals. The film *War Games* brought this subject to everyone's attention.

This book is about computers and their impact on society but it must be mentioned that insecurities in data systems are not the sole, indeed are not the major, cause for concern. Most data commissioners from countries with data protection laws testify that the overwhelming number of complaints that they receive concern manual data storage systems. This may underestimate the effect of computers in that it is difficult to trace or even know if there has been a leak of information from an electronic system unless an error has been made. Reinforcing this is the practice, pointed out in Chapter 12, of obtaining information, if not illegally, then immorally. If national or industrial security has been put at risk it is hardly likely that the perpetrators will volunteer the information about the breach of the system. If it is personal confidential information that has been disclosed the perpetrator, who presumably wants to make more cash and thus do it again, will not volunteer his or her responsibility either. It is thus almost certain that the extent of computer leakages is severely underestimated.

At one time people appeared to believe that computers and the lack of privacy were synonymous; these people talked in terms of computers versus privacy as if it were some social wrestling match. Whilst a part of this tendency lingers on the debate has now shifted ground. Having recognized that computers are with us on a permanent basis people are seeking to mitigate the worst of their effects and this involves the use of friendly systems as much as it does the protection of data. Within the United Kingdom the subject has been live for many years. As far back as 1970 the Younger Committee on Privacy was set up. It reported in 1972 and set out guidelines for the private sector. Little happened after this until 1975 when in one and a half White Papers the government announced its intention to legislate and as a consequence set up the Lindop Committee to advise on the legislation. Eight years later these efforts are just coming to fruition — a very long gestation period. Before setting out the principles underpinning data protection legislation it is a worthwhile exercise to attempt to analyse the problem in fundamental terms.

It is not so much the holding of individual bits of information on the computer but the possibility of putting these bits of information together in a damaging or misleading manner that worries people. As Paul Sieghart, speaking at a symposium in London, pointed out, the definitions in this area are fraught with difficulties. He pointed out that the storage of a name is neutral but a name stored under the heading 'persons suspected of subversive homosexual fascist activities' is a somewhat different kettle of fish: yet only the name is stored. Then again a name might be linked with the name of a hotel and someone else's wife; the linkage or concatenation or processing is all-important, the data itself less so. The first of Sieghart's 'golden keys' is thus the regulation of applications rather than of computers, of people, or of data.

The Lindop Committee found only fifty or so different categories of tasks to which computers are put and most of these they found to be harmless in themselves in relation to privacy; they are what Sieghart calls 'subject friendly'. Sieghart goes further in that he suggests that the users of the data have a common interest with the subjects in making their systems leakproof, although many believe this to be a somewhat naive approach. Whilst those managing the vast DHSS installations might share a common interest with the subjects on their files, those of delivering the right benefits to the right people at the right time, other government departments might wish to concatenate that set of information with their own. Not only may this information be put together in a wholly inappropriate way but the possibility of separate bodies also concatenating in an equally less than appropriate manner is quite high; indeed, within the security services such manoeuvres are a standard procedure. In essence it is the case of a collective response being the problem; the individuals acting separately are beyond reproach. Subject friendly thus is a relatively good thing rather than being an absolute; several 'subject friendlys' can get together and form one subject hostile.

Subject friendly systems can fail on two counts. Firstly, there is the possibility that the system is leaky, that unauthorized people can gain access to the information held in it. Alternatively, the people in charge of the system may be mendacious enough to sell the information to a third party. The leaky system can usually be rectified with the use of applications of money or of expertise; the second problem can only be stopped if and when such actions are made illegal and subsequent infringements detected and prosecuted with sufficient regularity and vigour.

Subject hostile systems pose a completely different dimension of threat to the public. These are systems where the interests of the users are in complete conflict with the interests of the subjects about whom the information is being collected and held. Security services and black list information come into this category. It is almost impossible to reconcile the interests of both parties in such cases; conflicts of motive as well as tactics arise. The cooperation of the data user will not be forthcoming so there must be a separate protection mechanism if the inviolability of data is to be taken seriously. Most of the instances where data processing is used, however, could be monitored with the cooperation of the data users. Third party interference is a possibility, even in the most benign of subject friendly systems, and this must be protected against too. If the second of Sieghart's gold keys, 'openness', stems from the subject friendly systems and can, indeed must, be applied to subject hostile cases, then the third of the golden keys, 'independence', is both a logical extension and a necessary addition to these arguments. Openness applies equally to the problems of access to the data held on a subject by that subject himself or herself, as much as to the framing of the rules by which the regulations of data and access to it will be controlled. Independence refers to the policing system which has to administer the rules and which not only has to be fair but has to be seen to be fair. These three golden keys are those which are used to safeguard the individual in the countries with data protection legislation and which form the basis for the supranational codes of practice.

Are there in fact problems or is this a hype by the liberal elements in society to point out the dangers of a Big Brother state? The mere fact that the United States, West Germany, and France, not to mention the OECD, have legislation or its equivalent gives the lie to it being some form of left wing plot, whilst specific examples show that there is indeed a cause for concern. The National Council for Civil Liberties (NCCL) not unnaturally is extremely interested in the matter and has delineated three problem areas: the fact that the subject may not know that information is being held about him or her (secrecy), the fact that the information being held may be wrong for a variety of reasons, and the fact that although the subject may not be able to see it, indeed is not allowed to know what information is held, other people often can (a lack of proper confidentiality). One well-publicized case demonstrates all three areas.

Jan Martin applied for a job with an independent film company run by an eminently respectable ex-BBC journalist/producer to make industrial films. Having given her the job the producer was telephoned by one of his clients, a large company, telling him that if Jan Martin came anywhere near their establishments she would not be allowed in. The reason for this unexpected move was that she had a connection with terrorists; furthermore, the information was genuine as it came straight from Scotland Yard. However Jan's father was a recently retired detective from Scotland Yard and as the producer had, to his eternal credit, told Jan the whole story he used the old comrade's network to discover how the computer had labelled Jan a terrorist. The reason, indeed the entire story, is so outlandish that it could be in the plot of a James Bond film or perhaps 'Alice' — the worry is that this was real.

Jan and her husband had been on holiday on the Continent and had stopped at a cafe in Holland just before getting the ferry home. The cafe owner thought that Jan's husband looked like a Bader Meinhof terrorist whose picture had been on the television the previous evening and phoned the police to tell them. The police did nothing about it as they had already detained the man in question but they noted the sighting and the identification. Somehow, perhaps through Interpol, the information reached Scotland Yard and then perhaps through Special Branch or perhaps through a friend (paid or otherwise) the information reached the company. It is of no use to claim that this case proves that the system in Britain cannot be all bad as the story has a happy ending, because how many of us have a father who has been working at Scotland Yard? Whilst I would be loth to suggest that such errors happen all the time it is almost certainly not the only one and the areas of potential damage include personal finances, job applications, and security. Only a data protection law and moreover one that is rigorously policed and enforced can ensure that such errors happen less frequently in the future, but even then this outcome is not certain.

The Council of Europe Convention lays down basic principles for data protection which, if implmented, would stop further Jan Martin cases, but only if computers were being used to store or transmit the data. Article 5 deals with the quality of data on a person which is undergoing 'automatic processing'. Such data shall be obtained and processed fairly and lawfully, stored for specified and legitimate purposes, and not used in a way incompatible with these purposes. The data shall not be excessive for the purposes and should be adequate and relevant as well as accurate and up-to-date. Finally, the data shall not be identifiable to individuals far longer than is absolutely necessary. Unless domestic law provides appropriate safeguards personal data which reveal racial origin, political opinions, religious and other beliefs, health, or sexual life may not be processed automatically. Article 6 goes on to extend this to personal data relating to criminal offences. The enormous loophole here, of course, is that this only applies to computer-based records; any government or other body wishing to circumvent these restrictions could easily do so by using a manual or mechanical system.

The security of data is of prime importance and not only in respect of unauthorized access. It is only too easy for the installation to suffer flood or fire damage, especially as so many machines are sited in basements, and a determined saboteur, politically motivated or otherwise, would be very difficult to stop. Other than having the best of environmental conditions as well as all the latest fire prevention appliances and siting the machinery above the potential high water mark, only duplicate or back-up systems will do. These of course must be situated physically well away from the main installation; indeed they are often in other countries. It is a foolhardly organization which does not hold its data in duplicate or even triplicate. Security, however, can also be breached because the internal codes have been broken or the telecommunication circuits have been penetrated.

Pepsi-Cola are the latest of the companies to feel the bite of the young, imaginative mind misusing the computer. A group of schoolboys recently broke the internal codes by using a simple home computer and then got on-line to all the installations. Amongst the least harmful of the results was the appearance of lorries laden with unwanted crates of the drink all over Canada and lorries full of empty crates sent to the most inappropriate of places. Whilst no sensitive personnel data was involved it could have been, and certainly highly confidential commercial information was at very grave risk. The same procedure has now been performed in the United States on nuclear research establishments. Because of these elements and because of more sinister unauthorized access instances the Convention has an article dealing with such matters as well as unauthorized alteration and dissemination of the information.

Individual data subjects are then given further rights. A person must be allowed to establish the existence of an automated personal data file, its main purpose, and the identity and the place of business of the controller of the information. A data subject shall have the right to get confirmation that a file exists on him or her and to obtain the data in an intelligible form. This right can be exercised at reasonable intervals and must be without excessive delay or expense. A person must be able to correct or indeed erase data which has been processed contrary to the articles of the Convention and there must be a remedy at law in the event of such requests not being complied with.

The Convention is a big step forward, especially for a dreadfully conservative country like the United Kingdom. There are two major loopholes, however, for any government which wishes to exploit them. The first has already been mentioned and refers to the fact that the Convention only affects data which have been 'automatically processed', thus leaving all manual data bases inviolate. The second loophole is that the Convention exempts any data which might protect state security, public safety, the monetary interests of the state, or hinder the suppression of criminal offences. Some governments insist on appointing their data protection committees, and the data protection ombudsman or officer is not only responsible to this committee but is serviced by government department staff. In such circumstances the impartiality of the officer called upon to determine whether a matter is, as the government claims, something not covered by the Convention must be suspect. A second portion of this loophole is that an unscrupulous or congenitally secretive government could extend and elaborate upon the license which it has been given. Certainly governments which mean to legislate at the minimum level have great opportunities to exploit in these respects.

The article in the Convention which forced the issue in the United Kingdom was the one which gave exemptions to the rule of free movement of data across national borders — a sort of information *laissez faire*. There are two instances where a signatory to the Convention will be able to prevent data leaving the country: the first is for particular types of sensitive data and where the country to which the information is going has no regulations protecting the information; the second is where information is only routed through a country to get to a non-signatory country. These safeguards are most important. It is as easy to store data and retrieve it across half the world as it is to store it in the same neighbourhood of the same town. Data are a truly international commodity but unlike physical goods can literally transcend frontiers. Without the existence of the international dimension in the Convention there would not so much be a loophole as a yawning chasm into which most of the national legislations would fall and disappear without trace.

Countries that have no data protection or control legislation are becoming known as 'data havens', the analogy being to the tax havens that some companies, rich individuals, and dubious banks use as their nominal home base. The problem is not as simple as it appears on the surface. It has been estimated that 80 per cent. of the world's data processing is done by US-owned companies and much of this has been done in Europe. As data protection laws spread around Europe so the American companies are moving their operational bases to more accommodating countries. International magazine mailing lists are one example of this genre. The interesting cases will arise when the Convention proposals are in full force and the data commissioner in one (or several) of the signatory countries is asked to ban such information being used. The same sort of case could arise with a transnational corporation information system based in a country with its own laws and where the data base conflicts with these laws.

The very nature of transnational companies make them

vulnerable to the cross-border provisions of the new Convention. They tend to divide their operations between countries so that central and peripheral data bases are needed whilst personnel from the companies are often moving from country to country and thus their records are mobile too. Whilst one can sympathize with the administrators of these companies in that their methods of working will have to change marginally, there should be no doubt as to which is the more important objective — individual privacy or corporate convenience. Some businessmen have been mouthing angry words about the new legislation and arguing that the European countries will never become the centre, of information processing with their new and irritating restrictions. They argue that information will be the major source of power in the next century, taking over from energy, and that it is vital for there to be free flows of it across national borders. From the point of view of the large computer and telecommunication manufacturers and provides there lurks the prospect of markets lost and more importantly strategies to be abandoned. New markets for smaller and discrete networks will undoubtedly arise as the new laws arise, so that lost markets will be partially offset. Nevertheless, some of the more grandiose plans involving satellite transmissions and communications will only be practical if the data transmitted is carefully tailored to the requirements of the new laws or the laws are disregarded. Given the immense amounts of money and prestige that are at stake it would come as no surprise to find the second of the options used more frequently than the first.

Almost all of the nations which have data protection legislation use the mechanisms of a register of data system users and a registrar to oversee the register and to receive and process complaints and questions. The United States is somewhat different in that the law only effects the federal sector and each department is charged with giving effect to the Act where it affects its own data bases. This legislation applies to all records not merely those that are electronically processed. Another major difference between the US and the proposed UK legislation is in the area of exemptions, and this clearly marks out the difference between a nation which believes in protecting the citizen against arbitrary government and one which believes that the art of government is best carried out away from the public gaze.

Exemptions in the United States are few, indeed the mere fact that the law applies to government and not to the private sector is a good indication of the prevailing ethos, one which treats government with grave suspicion but looks upon private enterprise as benign. In complete contrast the UK government has no qualms about the use of legislation to constrain the activities of the private sector, or if it has it has disguised them well. The government, however, is attempting to lengthen and expand the areas which will be exempt from the law and has been attracting some severe opposition as a result. Not only is the notion of national security being expanded all of the time to curtail access to apparently innocent government installations, but the areas of law enforcement and medical records are particularly worrying to those concerned with them professionally.

It has been suggested that police files should be exempt on the grounds that law and order might otherwise be prejudiced. Whilst there might be certain sensitive pieces of information most of it is routine. Why should a person not know what the police know about them? The information may be wrong, out of date, or interpreted wrongly, and any individual should have the right to correct it if necessary. The British Medical Association are upset because most medical records are still held manually so the Act will have little impact on medical disclosure. However, one section would appear to allow the passing of medical information from a hospital to the police without this transaction being registered, that is to say without the patient ever being able to find out. Not only could this seriously hamper the doctor/patient relationship but it would also lead to an escalating condition of mistrust between medical staff and hospital administrators.

Most data protection laws allow for access to individuals and lay down standards of collection, use, and dissemination, have codes of practice to guide users, and subjects have an appeals mechanism and legal constraints and penalties either in the criminal or civil codes. The intention, for no good reason, in the United Kingdom is to not have codes of practice. There will also be the added disadvantage of users not having to keep a log of all entries into their systems. This can leave the way clear to illegal and unauthorized dissemination of data and moreover makes it far more difficult to determine who has been responsible if this has actually taken place. The signs are that the UK government do not want a strong law, merely one that will satisfy the new Convention and the OECD guidelines, but only time will tell whether this somewhat cynical interpretation is correct.

It is strange but wheeas a holder of a manual filing system holding sensitive personal, commercial, or even defence-oriented information will use all the relevant and up-to-date security systems and the same people treat computer security with a cavalier attitude. It is possible to code all of the information into and out of a computer which although not unbreakable would make life difficult enough to discourage nearly all of the possible entryists; yet such codes are rarely used. Most systems have an entry code for the users but these are proving to be ridiculously easy to break, as the recent exploits of schoolboys and presumably criminals and probably spies have shown. People are allowed to enter physically many large installations without any real security checks, and it is only too easy to gain access by means of either a remote terminal or by a combination of telephone, a home computer, and a modem. The film *War Games* suggested that this could be done to the real-life defence systems of any country and it must be admitted that such a penetration is more likely today than ever before and the possibility is entirely due to the high dependence upon computers.

There needs to be far more awareness amongst the users of computers that the machines and the systems that they use are vulnerable. This is especially true of the small user whose security is almost non-existent.

New laws will almost certainly spawn net methods of circumvention. Whether these will take the form of clever legal methods or the setting up of illegal data bases or merely ignoring the laws, or indeed combinations of the three, is as yet a matter for speculation. The formation of small data bases in manual form based on the distillation of computer information must be one of the favourite ploys of the future. It will be rather like the days of US prohibition with bootleg information coming from speakeasy installations. Overall, whilst the new data protection laws around the world will prove to be a step forward, it would be foolish in the extreme to expect too much of them. Exploitation of information will still be a lucrative business so that the incentive to break the new laws will be as great as ever. Governments will still be anxious to keep a watchful eye on those who it deems to be the threat to its own existence or perhaps on its political opponents, which yet again provides an incentive to widen the exemptions from the law and thus weakens the protective elements in the entire package.

Democracies are fragile things and depend as much upon

a high level of individual self-awareness and control as they do on political mechanisms for their continued existence. A state based upon the coercion of the subjects through fear engendered by the large and centrally controlled computer-based personal information system is not democratic, despite its electoral system which may well fulfil the mechanistic definition. A state which uses this information to suppress or to discredit the opposition political parties is even further down the road to dictatorship. The temptation to use such methods is ever present and is growing as the technological ability to do it successfully and cheaply gets ever more refined. Both governments and large corporations have the wherewithall to undertake such monitoring tasks and it is in everyone's long-term interests to see that the possibility does not become a regular reality. Only truly effective data protection laws coupled with the most open of government and corporate systems will achieve this end.

There are worrying straws in the wind that the battle for the open uses of data and, more particularly, computer files is already being lost. The spread of the increasingly powerful mini- and microcomputers has meant that data can be stored in virtual secrecy, whilst only one or two people are needed to maintain the data bases. It was at one time possible to trace an installation through the employment of expert computer personnel but these days have now passed. Small computers or intelligent terminals or even the spare computing capacity of a text processer can be operated by single non-computer skilled staff who, with the minimum of training, can wield as much computer powr as some dozen operators and programmers not five years ago. Not only is this trend continuing but it is accelerating at a Lamborghini type of rate. It is probable that in less than five years time there will be no need for anyone other than analysts and the occasional programmer to run the large installations, always of course accepting the need for service engineering. The ability of government to run surveillance systems and corporations to maintain 'illegal data bases' is thus being enhanced on a day-to-day basis. This technological trend is reinforced on a social basis, especially in the United Kingdom.

Managers, especially middle management, although senior management is afflicted too, suffer from a collective inferiority complex. At least this is the only charitable explanation for the defensive positions taken up by individual managers or their representative organizations when confronted by the trade unions or the media or anyone else who is even vaguely denoted as 'the enemy' or hostile. Information is one area in which managers have a virtual monopoly and is the one which they are most loth to relinquish. Attempts by workers in the United Kingdom to find out what is actually happening in an enterprise are met by stonewalling attempts of an epic nature or by cries of 'managerial prerogative or we have the right to manage'. Information is seen as the last vestige of power by much of UK management. This bodes ill for attempting to find out what information is actually being held on a workforce and what installations hold it, let alone what outside agenies a company may be affiliated to in order to find out about its workforce or its applicants for jobs. Unless UK management changes its character it will not cooperate with the new Act in spirit, although it will certainly fulfil its obligations on the surface.

For its part government is little better. There are many small computer installations not on the government's own directory and this number is bound to increase. A combination of smaller and 'unofficial' computers and wider exemptions from the Act could make it a mere cipher as far as the government is concerned. Taken together these trends do not auger well for the safeguarding of the individual.

Not that the problem is always as clear-cut as it may seem. For example, personnel records may contain estimates of future job prospects, promotions, or possible moves, none of which are part of the formal assessment programme; indeed, there may be good reasons for the subject positively not seeing them — reasons of morale, of motivation, or of peace of mind. As a result it is likely that such records and subjective judgements will be held on manual registers to avoid the new legislation, such individual assessments being noted on the computer register as existing — and that alone.

As long as it is still possible for computers to aid and abet organizations or individuals to gain and then collate or concatenate information about people without their knowledge, let alone consent, there must be a cause for great concern. Individual and collective liberties are at risk invoking nothing less than potential political, commercial, or personal blackmail. Monitoring mechanisms must be seen to be independent, especially in respect of complaints against the government itself, and the person in charge will have to have enough resources and enough 'clout' to ensure that the job is done properly.

The concerns are not exclusively British; people in countries with some legislative protection feel threatened too, be they in Europe or North America. In Germany and France there have been well-publicized misgivings about the state collection and holding of information on people and organizations, some of it wrong, on computers. In the United States reports of people's movements traced by their credit card records and of massive interstate police computer information contacts, even down to the car computer acting as a 'spy', have alerted the civil liberty and other movements to the onward march of computerization. They are also alerting people as to the extent of their vulnerability — now the time is approaching for these people to do something about it.

The civil liberty organizations around the world must be conscious of the latent threat that computers pose not merely to privacy but in the least analysis to freedoms in general. Politicians and parties, trade unionists, employers, and organizations using data should all be on their guard against abuses of computer power, wittingly or otherwise. Being so powerful computers demand powerful defence mechanisms. We must not be put off by the inevitable government pleas of too expensive nor the other users who claim that precautionary measures are administratively difficult. Neither money values nor values in terms of time or effort can be used to measure freedom and democracy. Computers can threaten both of these, indeed are threatening both. They must not be allowed to succeed if we truly value both of them.

Chapter 14

'The Future'

ALL TOTALITARIAN AND DICTATORIAL POLITICAL PARTIES run well-regimented, aggressive youth movements. The theme of 'tomorrow' is both potent and headily optimistic. Every political party, all philosophers, and all governments try to claim the patents for the future, the rights for the next generation. Parents, teachers, and the elders in all societies worry about the future and want, if not the best, considerably better for their children. As we have seen this goes hand in hand with a yearning to return to a mythical 'golden age' when life was better, laws were obeyed, and the young were not quite so threatening. Until recently, however, most generations have believed that they had reached some form of ultimate standard with the technology that they used. Even in Victorian England, where a middle class were committed to the idea that mankind was the master of the environment and that money combined with ingenuity could solve almost everything, some people believed that the electric bell represented the highest peak to which consumer engineering could raise us.

No-one believes in any form of limit, a view which is as recent as the advent of microelectronics. Television programmes which devote themselves to scientific advances and prototype products are partly responsible whilst space travel, men on the moon, heart transplant surgery, and clever products like videodiscs have also played their part. We now expect to be surprised. Indeed, in industrialized societies we now believe in the impossible because it has already happened! Little wonder or, indeed, consternation is shown when contemporary fiction depicts the future as a computer-driven nightmare—we have become immune to such threats and predictions. Whether this is really a display of amazing faith in the inherent goodness and responsibility of mankind or whether it is a manifestation of utter defeat and resignation

383

remains to be seen. In the meantime the passive responses have encouraged the proselytes for technology to widen their horizons and to redouble their efforts.

The computer revolution is only in its infancy. Despite the rapid advances which have seen an amazing increase in power combined with an equally astonishing decrease in price and size, in the words of Al Jolson 'You ain't heard nothing yet folks'. The current state of the art is leading to major changes and innovations in computer use almost every day. The current state is transitory in the extreme; evolution of computer technology is very rapid, so much so that even the experts, the designers, and the foremost academics cannot keep up with it. This leads us into a half-world of business managers learning about the existence of a new technique and attempting to order it only to find that by the time the machinery is being manufactured the idea is eighteen months old and has been superceded twice. How can businessmen survive in such circumstances? How can the traditional notion of capital investment withstand such rapid changes and in turn capitalism adapt itself to the consequential permanently increased number of bankruptcies and failures?

If we are behind in exploiting the current technological states, that is there are commercial and social uses which remain unexplored, how much more complicated this will become when a further dynamic is added. Such a development is, if research proves to be positive, just around the corner and is called the fifth generation: the first-generation 'sci-fi' computers.

There are two important streams in this step forward. The fifth-generation systems are intended to be far more 'user friendly' than at present. The inputs to the computer will be voice, graphics, or handwriting and the computer will recognize people, their voices, and their general characteristics:

the fifth-generation is the start of the twenty-first century computers. Naturally this applies to robotics too, reinforcing the science fiction image. Sensors, or rather the lack of them, which has held back the development of computers, robotics, cybernetics, and other equipment for many years now have a top priority rating, especially in Japan where the massive research effort is at its strongest. The second strand is actually more fundamental—it is an attempt to break away from what is known as the 'von Neumann architecture'.

When people think, as they do all of their waking hours, they are juggling with several different inputs and sensations simultaneously. Some thoughts remain submerged, whilst some slide peripherally to the surface and form a background to whatever we have chosen to be the dominant thought patterns. A new or different input, sensation, or a change of emphasis in the background may also force a change in our response and the way that we approach that particular moment. At present computers do not operate like this. They do not have sufficiently good senses to detect everything about the environment, let alone changes to it, but more importantly computers are programmed to work in an entirely different way.

Computers take one task and finish it before moving onto the next one. They perform these tasks or calculations exceptionally quickly and there may have to be hundreds of thousands of them in a single calculation but all are done on this linear serial or consecutive basis. The ability to reason, to deduce, to display, and have 'intelligence' is very much a function of multiple processes stemming from multiple inputs. This is precisely the target the highly ambitious fifth-generation project is leading to. The fifth generation will have simultaneous rather than serial working. This allows for prioritizing, reasoning, and thinking; indeed, they are rather disturbing computers. Artificial intelligence which is capable of reasoning and learning is the objective at the end of the MITI sponsored research. If money guaranteed success then there would be little doubt that before this decade is through the '2001' and 'Star Wars' computers, robots, and equipment would be in use outside the laboratory. However, neither money nor resources guarantee such rewards and although the project is theoretically a winner, whether it develops and, if so, who does it, is still very much an open question. It would be a brave person who would bet against these or similar changes happening over the next decade and a person foolhardy in the extreme who believed that computers had reached a point where further development was impossible.

New uses, new computers stimulating new uses, and new techniques amending existing uses are certain in the future, providing faster changes, more changes, indeed unthought of changes. The development of computing is also a leap into the unknown and by definition this will mean that products and services not envisaged today will be standard in the decade of the 1990s — rather like mass credit cards were in the 1960s or computer dating was in the 1950s. The most surprising thing that could possibly happen is that we shall not be surprised.

The more everything changes the more it stays the same is a well-known but perhaps somewhat optimistic (or pessimistic, depending on how you are looking at it) view of the world. It sums up history to the point where technology has replaced, or acted as an adjunct to, physical labour, but no more than this. Once the thought processes are involved in technologically based systems the change takes on an added dimension; the way we approach matters and indeed our own thought processes come under external pressure. Things are no longer the same in any respect. Attitudes to work, money, goods, information and other people have all changed, and continue to do so, even faster today. As computer systems develop so these differences will grow until ultimately we have a very different form of society and different relationships with it. This is the stuff of science fiction, of futurology, and increasingly though not inevitably, of nightmares.

The use of computer technology has had an appreciable, if not overwhelming, impact on the way that people interact with each other. Many of the side effects of computer technology have been to split up groups, to isolate individuals and families, and to promote solitary and domestically based work and leisure activities. The trend of watching television at home (or even in the office) rather than going out to the cinema or theatre has been reinforced by the use of videocassettes of feature films to play on home recorders. Cable television, with an ability to deliver a choice of twenty such films each evening, on sport, pornography, or any popular mass programme for what will ultimately be a relatively low cost, will add further to the home entertainment trend. This is only the tip of what will be a rapidly forming iceberg. Other factors are ensuring that people will spend more of their time in the home rather than at work or outside for other reasons. In turn this will have major repercussions on family life and the composition of the family, on transport provision, on home and office building, and on the development of cities, suburbs, and rural areas.

The amount of leisure time available will increase or perhaps it is more accurate to suggest that there will be more time spent not working. Most people will either be working fewer hours per day, days per week, weeks per month, months per year, or indeed years in a lifetime, or many will not be working at all. The amendments to the working lifetime, whether they are earlier retirement or later entry into the labour force, longer holidays, or year-long study leaves, will inevitably lead to more time being spent within the home, as will complete unemployment. Predictions or prophecies are most unreliable in such matters but one can dimly discern shadows of future developments.

Many forecasters believe that unemployment will be with us through to the twenty-first century and will be oriented towards the young and more especially those young people with the poorest record of educational attainments. More women will be at home without paid employment. There will be more job sharing, perhaps even permits to work, a school leaving age of at least eighteen (paid for the last two years), less night shift production work but more night-time maintenance work, and twenty-five hours paid employment per week with little or no overtime will not be unusually low. The likelihood is that these hours will be spread over three days rather than five so that the new leisure time will be taken in large blocks. Retirement will be part-time, then full-time, and will be taken between 50 and 65. Computers will have some degree of responsibility for these changes as they will for the changes within the home. As the cabling of homes goes ahead so the computer potential of each home increases too. There has been a significant drift towards working from home for typists using word processors, for programmers using home terminals, and for managers. Home working that an unenviable reputation in most countries as a method of paying exceptionally low wages for not very skilled jobs, but this is now changing to a marked degree. Another form of homework will be by the self-employed, especially in creative programming and analysis. Most of these prophecies have been discussed by economists, philosophers, sociologists, futurologists, scientists, and ordinary people; it is both sad and instructive that politicians have not joined in.

As an entertainment centre, shopping and banking centre using Prestel (or its equivalent), work station, and centre of social life, the home appears destined to take on new functions. Problems resulting from such changes stare back at an observer from all angles. Nowadays we get most of our social contacts from the workplace. If we spend more time at home how will we meet people, where will friends come from, and will we develop electronic friends, use picture telephones as a substitute for meeting people, or play video telephone bridge as a substitute for kicking one's partner under the table? How will permanent relationships, marriages for example, stand up to the extra strains of partners being in close proximity to each other when one suspects that the reason for their survival has been the relative lack of contact and togetherness. When the diminution of personal stimulation in the new forms of shopping or when using public transport are taken into account too, loneliness or a marked lack of variety in social contacts will become major sources of concern.

At the same time it will be easier, perhaps nicer, to live at home. Domestic robots and control and systems computers will do both the menial tasks and plan the cheapest uses of energy or food or even travel. Appliances like washing machines, bathroom scales, cookers, do it yourself equipment, or even light switches will all become more sophisticated and more reliable — even 'intelligent'. Whilst many factors will be increasing the hours that people spend within the home so the need to be there diminishes. Free time will emerge, time which could be used for educational or socially aware purposes or, on a less high-minded Victorian vein, to enjoy oneself, to travel the world, and to do and see new things. Whether we do them or indeed run a society which gives people the chance to do them will depend upon a series of political choices. Income and wealth distribution are crucial here as is the educational system and the welfare benefit schemes that are in operation. People need to know of the existence of various leisure activities as well as have the money to be able to partake of them, and in Britain at least this implies a very class conscious response.

The end of the twentieth century will see many other changes. New foods, genetically engineering or of protein derivatives, will parallel new developments in health care, new drugs, and new surgical techniques. Our method of transport will be different in that hydrogen, electricity, and nuclear fuel bases will replace petroleum products and magnetic forces and gyroscopy will be the two most promising fields of scientific research into energy conservation and motive power. None of these broad brush categories nor many of the changes which we cannot foresee so easily will be researched or produced without computer inputs somewhere along the line. If theatre and cinemas survive they will be using computers at the box office, in seat allocation, within the performance itself, and in the auditoria. Holography will be an 'old-hat' entertainment medium and will be incorporated into television receivers and videophones. Existence will be much more controlled, more predictable, and much longer, but perhaps as a result a touch more boring—but perhaps not, so much depends on the uses to which computers are put. This overall view of technologically driven societies is very much the view of non-discriminating science fiction writers. It is unlikely to be true in that all areas of potential conflict have been omitted. The income and wealth distribution point that has just been made is probably the most fundamental of these.

A society needs to have all of its citizens believing that they have a fair stake in what goes on. If a substantial minority of people are cut off from this they will not acquiesce, at least readily, in the success of those who have that stake, who can afford the latest gimmicks and gismos and who have jobs. If these people are young, if no attempt is made to find jobs or quasi-jobs for them, and if no attempt is made to provide a reasonably independent standard of living for them, then control measures may well have to be instituted. Bayonet points, metaphorical or real, do not stimulate the creation of a harmonious society or one which would settle into relaxed indolence—indolence with tension is quite another matter and a distinctly possible one. However, if there must be some form of equalization of incomes and wealth within one country it is at least as important to diminish the manifest inequalities between countries.

It is more than possible that computers will be used in a way that will widen the existing gap between the rich industrialized countries and the poor less developed countries (LDCs). Transnational corporations have an enhanced ability to work out their optimum strategy and so avoid cash traps where there are restrictive exchange controls and to automate jobs in those countries. How long these growing inequalities can survive and how long the governments and the people of the have-not nations will tolerate their status is an open question. The more the gap widens the less stable the world becomes; trade suffers overall, arms are stockpiled, and more militant or more repressive regimes take over these countries, so heightening the global tensions. These stresses now take on a far more sinister aspect because of the increased efficiency of weaponry, most often caused by computers.

One reason for having to rewrite a technologically based scenario *in toto* is that it runs the risk of having blown itself out of existence. They industrialized world has always earned itself a great amount of money by selling arms to the non-industrialized countries and this habit seems to have hardened rather than diminished as the sophistication and prices have grown. In the past wars, skirmishes, battles, or insurrections in and between these countries were seen as a combination of sales proving grounds, an exercise in the rebuilding of demand, and a music hall joke. Certainly the Falklands Campaign gave a massive boost to French technology and to Exocet sales. Nowadays the fear is that these local wars will spread, will not be contained so easily or readily, and that the enhanced ability to kill people will be unleashed against those who produced the weapons. The North–South divide, so well documented in the Brandt Report, is a classic example of the type of circumstance which could lead, if not to Armaggedon, to a global Paschendale. Simple truths of computers and technology do not exist. Uncertainties and particularly political choices will determine whether all of us, some of us, or none of us enjoy the potentially luscious fruits in the electronic orchard, and indeed whether the fruits themselves are nectarines or crab-apples.

Computer technology asks all sorts of fundamental questions and poses very difficult problems, and none more so than in the arts of government and politics. Marxism now commends itself to both China and the Soviet Union, to Asian, Central America, and African countries as well as to East European states and millions of individuals in capitalists countries. It can scarcely be called a minority taste if measured by the number of people being governed under its precepts, yet not one capitalist country has had a revolution in the way that Marx not only described but asserts is an historical inevitability. There are three effects that computer technology is having but more importantly will continue to have on Marxist thought. It has an effect on class, it has an effect on efficiency, and it has an effect on the cost of capital.

Marx described and delineated the class system basing it on what he observed in Germany and industrial Britain in the nineteenth century. Much has changed since then but it is only in the past two decades that the working class itself has changed. Computers have not only replaced many of the semi-skilled manual jobs but old working class identified industries — coal, rail, docks, cotton, steel — have all shed labour massively; either computer techniques or developing countries have taken the jobs. In their stead have come a combination of new jobs and the jobless. The new jobs are those in factories where the operatives are technicians, where dirt does not go hand in hand with work, or in offices where the computer is dictating the terms under which men and women work. These new workers, indeed, the unemployed, do not identify with steel workers, car workers, or miners; they see and feel that their problems are different, their status is felt to be higher, and their identity with management is stronger. In short the new working class does not feel itself to be working class, and thus will not respond to the cliches and rhetoric which commended itself so strongly to millions of workers only twenty years ago. Property ownership, other forms of ownership, and a different feel to their status have altered the complexion of UK, indeed European, politics. The rightward leaning political parties have capitalized upon this whilst the leftward looking parties have mainly had to struggle. Trade unions are affected too as their membership, starting to reflect the new ethos and aspirations, becomes less prone to take industrial action and generally lose much of their cohesiveness in a social and political sense. One of the latter-day Marxist engines for change will no longer be firing on all its cylinders.

When Marx wrote he made a quite warranted assumption that capitalism was efficient and that companies maximized their profits. It is only with the benefit of hindsight that we can see that both assumptions were in error. If capitalism were efficient and profit maximizing it would never have conceded paid holidays, sick pay, short working weeks, or recognized unions. It was certainly in a position to hold out against such demands. Equally there is little doubt that the very large enterprises, the megacorporations, do not maximize their profits (ITT's efforts in Chile are a case in point), and overall these companies are certainly not efficient in a production and sales sense. This may be one of the major reasons why the promised revolutions have not yet materialized; the contradictions and the schisms have been neither sharp nor deep enough. Now along comes a technology which makes capitalism more efficient. Productivity is increased, output rises, profits rise, whilst people become unemployed. Suddenly the contradictions are sharp; the injustices and the inequalities are growing and are highly visible. Whilst the revolution may not be around the next corner, computer technology implemented within the basis of conventional conservative government which allows markets to allocate resources could be a matter for grave concern. Whether this happens in Japan or Britain, the United States or Denmark, the social and political stresses will strain the fabrics of society — it could be a difficult few decades if not a pre-revolutionary (not necessarily Marxist) era.

This has to be offset against the changes in the class structure and indeed those who Gorz described as non-class, the unemployed — an academic but important point in Marxist theology. The labour theory of value can only work if one accepts the notion of embodied value, that is the value of the labour that has gone into the making of the capital equipment that is used in the productive process. To be realistic this must mean that the cost of such equipment rises over time. Microelectronics plus computers have reversed this trend violently. The cost of capital investments is falling, computers and control systems get cheaper daily, and the theory of embodied value becomes less realistic alongside it. The future on unchanged politics or theories is unlikely to be stable in either capitalist or communist states. Both could be rocked to their foundations by the new computer developments; both may prove to be irrelevant to a nation's needs. The future may well see new theories to fit new facts, new politics to appeal to new workers, and new forms of government to control new technologies.

Many of today's familiar certainties will no longer exist. Money, that is the physical coins and notes, will become less significant as credit and electronic cash transfers become more prevalent and computer terminals at home provide a 24 hour banking service. Fares on public transport or bills in shops will be met by credit cards in the future almost certainly using holographed pictures and fingerprints to prevent fraud and theft. There should be far better equipment for the disabled, new equipment at work, at schools, and in places of entertainment, new goods in the shops, and new services available. Outer space will be used as a medium for defence and offence, for some industrial purposes like metal purification, drug manufacturing, or even building computers themselves, and for telecommunication purposes. In the 1990s space will be the equivalent of the 'wild west'.

There will be choices and they will be extremely important choices, but as they will never be put in stark fundamental terms at the time decisions are made they will not seem to be so important. Whether we decentralize is an example of this. It is unlikely in the extreme that an election will be held on this matter or that legislation will be introduced compelling overtly decentralized government. We might find, however, that some local authorities break down their services to a community level and allow decision making to be made at this level. Central government may enact legislation increasing regional or local powers one year and adding to local governments' responsibilities five years later. Federal states could proceed in the same direction with each constituent part getting more power. The opposite could be just as likely, however. Central government may decide to attract more powers to itself and denude the periphery of its duties and responsibilities. Whichever way it goes it will be the result of a political decision hopefully taken democratically. Computers themselves could be used in either direction, reinforcing decentralization or imposing central control; they are perfect tools for either. People will decide.

Choices within the workplace will be made in the same way, on a piecemeal basis. Negotiations between unions and managements will amend the working lifetime as well as allow for some form of orderly introduction of the technology, although there will be disputes and misunderstandings from time to time. Governments will almost certainly attempt to set the environment or criteria in which the changes will take place by using their own powers as employers or by some legislative actions. The changes are of course immense and mirror those in the non-work world or perhaps even drive them. Types of work and the amounts of work will change and almost permanent retraining will be rule. Older people will probably not be able to cope and younger people will probably receive inadequate schooling. It is not a peaceful prospect and nor is it one where happy endings can be foreseen easily; the light at the far end of the tunnel will more often than not be that of an oncoming express than the brightness of amicable solutions.

Power relationships will change too. The employer–union confrontation changes its character as a small number of people have very strong leverage; computer people will have far more industrial power than miners and only slightly less than electricity workers. They will not wish to use this power regularly, if at all (their strength is also their greatest weakness), and the result may be frustration amongst certain computer and non-computer personnel. Sabotage is not an elegant notion yet it is one that present-day trade unionists are starting to talk about. This is not the axe through the cable variety or fires, explosions, floods, or jam smeared in the works. It is a sophisticated idea with skilled programmers and analysts destroying or amending the system from the inside — a change in program or interception and substitution of messages. Before the decade of the 1990s is over there will have been several such industrial actions, ot one of which will have received any publicity; indeed the actions may be several weeks old before the employer notices it.

The shift is bargaining power will also effect the trade union hierarchies themselves. The traditional aristocrats in the large metal working and mining industries will have to defer to the more middle class based white collar unions. The influence and power will pass to the occasionally militant moderates and the political role of the trade union movement will be diluted considerably all around the world.

It is possible that the power of the politician or government will diminish too, especially with respect to members of the public. The new computer system will, when cable and teletext systems are in place, make it as easy to run national or local referenda as it will be to choose the shopping. If this method is chosen then the functions of politicians, indeed full-time government employees, change dramatically. The notion that a wise person is elected to exercise their judgement is lost and on a party basis manifestos or programmes will be guides rather than mandates. If the public, having voted for the policies of Party A and elected it, insist on a public referendum on the implementation of one of these policies, even if it is within six months of the election, there is clearly a new notion of representative democracy at large. Parties and group policies will count for far less than they do today; indeed, it is very difficult to determine on which basis people should choose a government party. Instant referenda are only an option, not a compulsory part, of computers and telecommunications. They will be offered by cable and television franchise companies initially as a gimmick to enliven political programmes or local commercials, but once started there will be an immense pressure to keep and convert them to more serious uses. Populism of this sort is unsurprisingly popular and will not be easy to withdraw (except by referendum) once it has been put in place.

What sort of life is it that computers are getting us into — peopleless shops, personless factories, automated transport, more global tensions, less work, better products, new products, more reliable products, a home-based culture, better weapons, an information glut, and a longer life? But will it be a happier life? Once again, and for the final time, computer technology has little direct influence on this — people have. People elect politicians, politicians serve the people; companies produce goods and services and people can, for the most part, choose whether or not to buy or rent them. In theory people control what computers will be used, where they will be used, who will use them, and for what purposes.

1984 is too close to some human experiences to shrug it aside as only a clever novel (which it is). It is also one form of blueprint for a computer-based 'high tech' society, but neither a pretty one nor one which would command much public approval. Yet how easy it might be to slip into this or a similar form of regime. War legitimizes censorship and the 'manipulation of news' and allows a government to treat the national interest as sacrosanct and opponents of it as traitors. Censorship is encouraged, as is hate, hostility, suspicion, and fear. Referenda can sanctify the secret police, telephone tapping, two-way television, and the use of propaganda-stimulated hysteria. Free speech is abolished — never to return. Opposition is treason and the wealth of computer technology is turned against the population in general. Information storage is used to determine and recognize deviancy and information dissemination is used to manipulate and subdue, not inform and widen. Communications are for spying and snooping, not exchanging news and views. Some of the less reputable British press fostered a form of hysteria during the Falklands Campaign and showed how easy it is for opposition in these circumstances to be characterized as anti-country and pro-enemy. We must not slip into this path.

There have been several fictional models of the nightmare state but all have depended upon two factors: the existence of a technologically oriented means of subduing the population and the formation of a dominant elite controlling the numerically stronger masses. Strangely there is no common view of the ends, except power for its own sake. Computers figure prominently in the control systems, as do telecom-munications (computer based, of course) and drugs (computer developed, of course). The need that some people seem to have to control others does not appear to have diminished as civilization has progressed and whilst that need remains there is always the danger that facism, dictatorships, or totalitarian states can arise.

Computers not only make such states easier to start but they make them far easier to control. Roman governments based on bread and circuses took a remarkably long time to destroy themselves, a worrying thought in that they provide a model of society which is likely to occur if one of the nastier alternatives wins the day. From the point of view of those controlling affairs its basic advantage is that whilst controlling one is also providing 'the masses' with what they want, or think they want. Acquiescence of this type using video and cable entertainments could easily be elicited whilst also fragmenting society and thus making it more difficult to organize resistance. You cannot eat democracy, wear it, keep dry with it, and cure yourself with it — it is not the be all and end all of life. For a starving person in the Sahel it is of no consequence whatsoever — he or she would rather eat under a dictatorship. It is easy to overstate the benefits of a democratic system. It does, for example, imply that the basic human needs are being met so that arguments can proceed around and about the fringes. The advent of a dictatorship abolishing freedom is something to be deplored but freedom to starve is not a good advertisement for democracy and if that dictatorship brings bread where there was none the argument becomes gray rather than the comforting black and white.

Human beings may respond to the prospect of a future by rebelling either before acquiescence has drifted in or been imposed, or at any stage along this route. Obviously the latter point is the more likely to be effective; human dignity will still be intact. If such a discussion appears to be taking an excessively gloomy view of the future this is not quite the case. Every reasonable hypothesis must be explored, at least in outline, and this scenario is one which has been blessed by many a scientist, social and real. The nature of the democratic process is such that it can do little to halt the process once it has started and if there are people who are determined to push the model ahead.

The checks and balances on scientists, let alone politicians, are not sufficient for there to be confidence in being able to monitor and then perhaps constrain or contain their work. The introduction of computers and then the methods by which they work are such diffuse processes that a political system cannot come to grips with them. Challenges in politics have to be addressed to the larger abuses or problems and to be successful have to be understood by many people so that concern can be demonstrated. Computer installation and use fails on both counts.

Computers will be installed and used in government and also across the length and breadth of the private sector and other bits of the public sector. Another place to challenge what the computer will be used for is at the workplace and the challenge has to be mounted by employees and their unions. To date nearly all the dialogues that have taken place in this area have been about the impacts of computers on the workers themselves, on health and safety, or productivity, on training, and on manning levels. Only the Lucas Aerospace shop stewards (and more recently Lucas Electrical) have questioned the very existence and basis of the computers and the products that they help to make. Whilst it was a great success in public relations terms it has also been a failure in that Lucas have taken no notice and real limitations have been very slow to emerge. This does not seem to be a promising route for the control of computers either, although it may have other promising aspects.

Yet it is not all as black as it seems. Granted that whilst it is relatively easy to spot an evil person it is much more difficult if that person is sheltering behind a technological system. However, sometime or another he or she must emerge, be recognized, and can then be stopped in precisely the same way as most potential dictators have been over the years. In addition the pressures building up to a dictatorship can be relieved. Vast inequalities with no hope of redress can be alleviated, the haves can be made to share with the have-nots, and opportunities can be opened for all rather than just some people. If the political imperatives leaning towards internal revolt are not there then the chances of either a left wing revolution or a right wing coup become almost negligible. In other words, a democratic system can, indeed must, provide the social and economic basis for its own survival. This will not happen on its own however — it requires active and positive policies and thoughts.

Future governments will thus have a responsibility to maintain democracy by managing both the computer technologies and the economy so that the majority of people benefit from them rather than a few at the expense of the many. For this to happen governments must be backed up at different times and in turn this demands responsive government and what is more responsive political institutions. Wider knowledge of what computers can do and are doing would be an advantage amongst ordinary people (if such people exist) and both politicians and government employees. The obfuscation of governments on the employment and unemployment creating effects of computers must end and more truthful and credible projections emerge. A better informed, better equipped nation will handle computers in a far more sensible way than one which leaves all of its technical decisions to experts with no let or hindrance to their own scientific bent.

Even such a well-informed, educated, and trained set of people is only a start. Laws on privacy, on data protection in general, on open government, and on information that must be made available are needed too. Without information on the information systems even the most knowledgeable of people cannot hope to monitor what is happening. If representative democratic systems are to survive in this fast moving environment then they will have to become more responsive to change. Referenda are one method of achieving this but have all the populist disadvantages. More frequent elections or perhaps elections every year for a percentage of the representatives might be feasible ways of making those in government responsive to changing circumstances and to the public's misgivings about the consequences of the changes. In the first industrial revolution the political system in the United Kingdom changed fundamentally with five Reform Acts, two of which were revolutionary in that they led to far wider male suffrage. The changes in the second industrial revolution, led by the computer instead of the steam engine, will be no less dramatic and will need similar imaginative responses.

Computers and computer derivatives will be part of our everyday lives by the end of the twentieth century, much as electricity is today. The wonder of the machines will have passed as young people who grew up with them take them for granted. As physical entities they will be less imposing than at present, they will be cheap enough to be used as promotional giveaways, and all but the elderly will know how to make them work, if not how they work. They will be used in the home and at work, in transport and in leisure pursuits, in love, in health, and in education, in shops, banks, and travel agents. They will be in products, they will be a part of a house or flat, they will design buildings and machines, and they will play games. They will listen, talk, move, think, reason, and perhaps argue. It will be a true cradle to grave technology. Only the most determined drop-outs in industrialized societies will be able to avoid them completely; paradoxically most of the world's population living in the less developed countries will not know of their existence, even by the end of this century.

Who will have benefited from them will depend upon who controlled them and who had to adapt to them. Will all the potential for doing good and worthwhile things come to the surface along with governments committed to the democratic ideal? Will they be used to bolster the ambitions of those whose need to control others and lead them down the darker political byways? In short, will computers liberate or control us?

Not since the steam engine has any single technology had the capacity to create such wide-ranging change. Mankind will eventually be challenged intellectually by its own creation; many experts believe that computers will soon beat anyone at chess all the time. The mental superiority which humans have paraded over the rest of the animal kingdom and which they continually boast about is going to be attacked. Will we have to look up to the computer which diagnoses our illness in the same way that we afford status to a doctor? Will we have hierarchies of robots and give an extra polish to the clever ones? The mores of people as well on the trappings of society will be there to be challenged.

Optimisim has to prevail and suggest that despite the firepower we will not blow ourselves up and that despite the opportunities for evil most people, most countries, and most governments will use computers to enhance life. Optimism, however, must not be blind. To achieve even reasonable goals will require more vigilance, more patience, and more hard work than has ever been needed before. Young and old, men and women alike will share the responsibility for this; technological skill will have to be tempered by wisdom and political expediency by statesmanship. In democracies the entire establishment is geared to optimism and this must be seized upon and used. Computers are such powerful tools that we owe ourselves and future generations nothing less.